CONQUEST
OF THE USELESS

CONQUEST
OF THE USELESS

REFLECTIONS from the
MAKING of *FITZCARRALDO*

WERNER HERZOG

Translated *from the* German
by Krishna Winston

ecco
An Imprint of HarperCollinsPublishers

HarperCollins books may be purchased for educational, business, or sales promotional use. For information, please write: Special Markets Department, HarperCollins Publishers, 10 East 53rd Street, New York, NY 10022.

FIRST EDITION

Originally published in Germany as *Der Eroberung des Nutzlosen* by Carl Hanser Verlag in 2004.

Designed by Mary Austin Speaker
Frontispiece photograph © Kramer O'Neill

Library of Congress Cataloging-in-Publication Data is available upon request.

ISBN: 978-0-06-157553-2

09 10 11 12 13 OV/RRD 10 9 8 7 6 5 4 3

FITZCARRALDO:

To your dogs' chef! To Verdi! To Rossini! To Caruso!

DON ARAUJO:

To Fitzcarraldo, the conquistador of the useless!

FITZCARRALDO:

*As truly as I stand here before you, someday I shall
bring Grand Opera to the jungle! I will outnumber you!
I will outbillion you! I am the grand spectacle in the forest!
I am the inventor of rubber! Only through me will rubber
become a word!*

—Dialogue from the film *Fitzcarraldo*

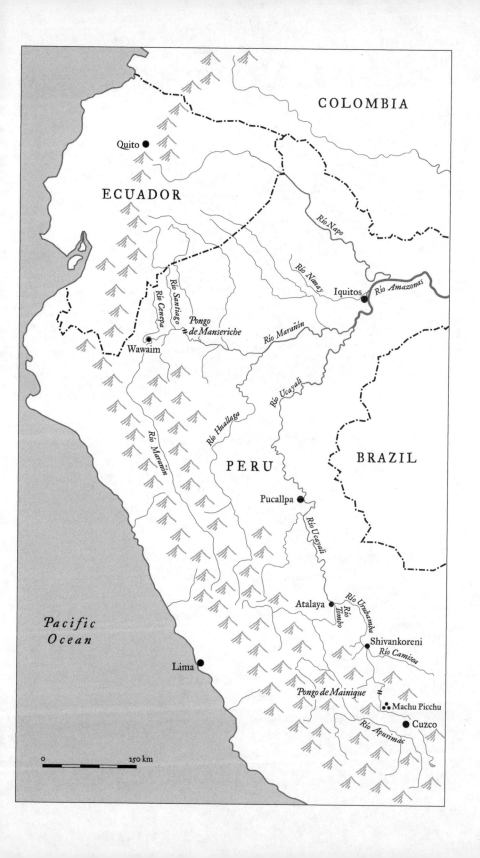

COLOMBIA

Quito ●

ECUADOR

Río Napo

Río Nanay

Iquitos ●

Río Amazonas

Río Santiago

Río Cenepa

Pongo de Manseriche

Río Marañón

Wawaim

Río Marañón

Río Huallaga

Río Ucayali

PERU

Pucallpa ●

Río Ucayali

BRAZIL

Pacific Ocean

Atalaya ●

Río Urubamba

Río Tambo

Shivankoreni

Río Camisea

Lima ●

Pongo de Mainique

Machu Picchu

Cuzco ●

Río Apurímac

0   250 km

PREFACE

For reasons that escape me, I simply could not make myself go back
and read the journals I kept during the filming of *Fitzcarraldo*. Then,
twenty-four years later, my resistance suddenly crumbled, though I
had trouble deciphering my own handwriting, which I had miniatur-
ized at the time to microscopic size.

These texts are not reports on the actual filming–of which
little is said. Nor are they journals, except in a very general sense.
They might be described instead as inner landscapes, born of the
delirium of the jungle. But even that may not be entirely accurate–
I am not sure.

W. H.

January 2004

CONQUEST

OF THE USELESS

PROLOGUE

A vision had seized hold of me, like the demented fury of a hound that has sunk its teeth into the leg of a deer carcass and is shaking and tugging at the downed game so frantically that the hunter gives up trying to calm him. It was the vision of a large steamship scaling a hill under its own steam, working its way up a steep slope in the jungle, while above this natural landscape, which shatters the weak and the strong with equal ferocity, soars the voice of Caruso, silencing all the pain and all the voices of the primeval forest and drowning out all birdsong. To be more precise: bird cries, for in this setting, left unfinished and abandoned by God in wrath, the birds do not sing; they shriek in pain, and confused trees tangle with one another like battling Titans, from horizon to horizon, in a steaming creation still being formed. Fog-panting and exhausted they stand in this unreal world, in unreal misery—and I, like a stanza in a poem written in an unknown foreign tongue, am shaken to the core.

San Francisco, 16 June 1979

In Coppola's house on Broadway. Outside the wind is howling, whipping the laurel bushes. The sailboats in the bay are lying almost flat, the waves sharp-contoured and restless. The Alcatraz Light is flashing signals, in broad daylight. None of my friends is here. It is hard to buckle down to work, to shoulder this heavy burden of dreams. Only books provide some measure of comfort.

The little tower at one corner of the house, foolishly designed for meditation, is flooded with such glaring light that whenever I venture into it, I stay for only a minute before being driven out again. I have pushed the small table against the one available unbroken stretch of wall, all the rest being taken up by windows that are filled with this demented light, and on the wall I have used a sharp pencil and a ruler to draw a mathematically precise reticle. That is all I see: set of crosshairs. Working on the script, driven by fury and urgency. I have only a little over a week left of staring mindlessly at that one spot.

The air is cool, almost chilly. The wind rattles the windows so hard that I lose sight of the point and turn around, facing directly into the light, so clear and piercing that it hurts the eyes. On the Golden Gate Bridge those moving dots are cars. Even the post office at the foot of the hill offers no shelter. As I toil up the steep slope, blown leaves on the ground catch up with me. It is the tail end of spring, but the foliage is yellow and dark red. The wind whips the leaves ahead of me across the rocky hillside, and by the time I reach the top, the fist of the void has swept them away. Once more, despite all my attempts at fending it off, a shuddering sense creeps into me of being trapped in the stanza of a strange poem, and it shakes me so violently that I glance around surreptitiously to see whether anyone is watching me. The hill becomes transformed into a mysterious concrete monument, which makes even the hill take fright.

San Francisco, 17 June 1979
Coppola's father plays me a tape of his opera. As he listens, his face takes on an entirely uncharacteristic expression, chiseled, stern, and intelligent.

San Francisco, 18 June 1979
Telegram from Walter Saxer in Iquitos. Apparently things are looking very good, except that the whole situation might collapse from one moment to the next. We are like workmen, appearing solemn and confident as we build a bridge over an abyss, without any supports. Today, quite by chance, I had a rather long conversation with

Coppola's production man. Over a hamburger and a milk shake he tried to convince me that he would take the project's fate in hand. I thanked him. He asked whether that meant thank you, yes or thank you, no. I said thank you, no. Coppola is not completely back on his feet after a hernia operation. He is displaying a strange combination of self-pity, neediness, professional work ethic, and sentimentality. The office on the seventh floor was trying feverishly to get a hospital bed delivered and set up in the mixing studio, and another one in some other location. Coppola did not like the pillows and complained all afternoon about the various kinds that were rushed to the spot; he rejected every one.

Los Angeles, 19–20 June 1979
Executive floor of 20th Century-Fox. It turns out that no proper contract has been signed between Gaumont, the French, and Fox. The unquestioned assumption is that a plastic model ship will be pulled over a ridge in a studio, or possibly in a botanical garden that is apparently not far from here—or why not in San Diego, where there are hothouses with *good* tropical settings. So what are bad tropical settings, I asked, and I told them the unquestioned assumption had to be a real steamship being hauled over a real mountain, though not for the sake of realism but for the stylization characteristic of grand opera. The pleasantries we exchanged from then on wore a thin coating of frost.

In the evening off to the cinema, where Les Blank cooked for the audience watching his films; he calls these performances *smell-around*. For the first time I saw the tattoo on his upper arm, two masks on strings: death laughing and death weeping. I could not stay for the end of the last film because my flight was leaving at midnight, a wretched affair with stops in Phoenix, Tucson, San Antonio, Houston, and Miami; the stewardesses, who had to put up all night with an impossible first-class passenger, call this flight a *milk run*.

Caracas, 21 June 1979

No one came to meet me. My passport was confiscated immediately because I had no visa; allegedly they will return it to me when I leave. Several men who looked German were standing around expectantly, scrutinizing the incoming passengers, but I did not have the nerve to approach them.

Caracas, 22 June 1979

Caracas, Hotel Ávila. Slept a long time, woke up quite confused. I must have had horrible dreams, but do not remember what they were. There is no running water; I had wanted to take a long shower. I am keeping Janoud's money with me; I have a feeling things get stolen in this hotel.

The morning meeting with filmmakers was lively. I saw a bad feature film and lowered my expectations to a flicker. Caracas caught up in a frenzy of development. Nasty little mosquitoes are biting my feet. It rained heavily in the morning, and the lush mountains were shrouded in billows of mist, which made me feel good. The taxi drivers here are not to be trusted. I have not eaten all day. *Signs of Life* is playing; the guards at the entrance are bored. There is a melancholy peeping in the trees; I thought it was birds, nocturnal ones, but no, I was told, they were little tree frogs.

A young man from Caracas who wants to make a film about the mad poet Rafael Ávila, known as Titan, told me about him and gave me one of his poems. Titan lived in a village near Maracaibo, sang in bars, and went mad. There is a plaster bust of him in the cemetery, with a large mustache, a contorted face, and unkempt hair. Someone has painted his hair and beard in bright colors. His gravestone carries the inscription

Las vanidades del mundo
Las grandezas del imperio
Se encierran en el profundo
Silencio del cementerio

Caracas, 24 June 1979
Five hours at the airport, with some passengers hysterical because the flight to Lima had been canceled without explanation; the next flight does not leave until four days from now. That gave me time to inquire about my passport. It was not there, and only after a series of coincidences did it turn up. It is a mystery to me how I managed to get on the overbooked Aeroperu flight. On the plane a stunningly beautiful Peruvian woman was seated next to me, clearly a member of the country's wealthy oligarchy. First she said it was too hot, a short while later too cold. As we were changing planes in Bogotá, she called after me that it was very hot, and on the plane she said it was very cold in Lima at this time of year, and I should have a warmer jacket. She said this not so much in a spirit of helpfulness in the stifling, grimy, overcrowded plane; rather, she spoke to me in the tone she would have used to reprimand her gardener or her house servants.

Lima, 25 June 1979
A sleepy country at which God's wrath has cooled. At first they did not want to show me the article in *Spiegel* because it was utterly

shameless, but they would not tell me what it said, either. Then we were off to the stadium. The entire segment of the playing field in the eastern curve, where our goal was located, was raised about ten meters by means of a hydraulic system. For warming up, the goalie had spread out several rubber mats, scattered far apart, which allowed him to throw himself here or there. When the game got under way, the goal was actually lowered to be level with the rest of the ground, but the net had sagged so low that it looked like a tunnel. The opposing team, which was probably the Spanish national team, had on utterly confusing jerseys, with the result that they merged with our players into a single undifferentiated riot of color. After the first wrong pass, made by me in the honest belief that the ball was being passed to someone on our own side, I ran up to the linesman and asked for a time-out, then ran after the referee, because there was already great confusion around our goal as to who was who, and the Spanish players were also not that happy. But the referee claimed there was nothing he could do, and I yelled at him that all we needed was thirty seconds and we would take the field in white. But the guy remained stupidly obstinate, as if he was in cahoots with the opponent. I knew the only hope of winning the game would be if I did it all by myself; then no wrong pass to the indistinguishable opponents would be possible, so I would have to take on the entire field myself, including my own team, because they might confuse me with the opposing team, too. But that was not the end of the torment.

Lima, at Joe Koechlin's new house. Lotus garden, blossoming trellises, cactus garden. His mother was using a shard of glass to scrape oil paint off an old rocking chair. Walter, Andreas, Janoud. Photos. Patagonia came to an end yesterday, and since a little while ago the dogs are all out: all of them have come to an end.

Lima, 26 June 1979

Vargas Llosa would like to be involved in some way, but he is tied up till the end of September. By then it is possible that everything here will have collapsed. Gold is the sweat of the sun, and silver are the tears of the moon. From here on only fragments. Uli and Gustavo at the airport, but as if in black-and-white photos. All night long arguments over how we should do the work.

Iquitos, 28 June 1979

Gloomy mood this morning. Call it quits? After so many months of work? A mild case of the flu, my nose constantly running. Fitzcarraldo's ship in the jungle by Puerto Maldonado. The lookout point at Tres Cruces. Casting propellers. The business with the dolphins. Striking teachers locked themselves into the church ten days ago and are ringing the bells. At the market I ate a piece of a grilled monkey–it looked like a naked child.

Iquitos, 29 June 1979

When you shoot an elephant, it stays on its feet for ten days before it falls over. When I got back on the ice after two minutes in the penalty box, a puck struck hard from a short distance away smashed into my head. There was a pulsing flash of light before my eyes, and I became weightless. On the boat to Belén: roast alligator was served. Women delousing children, children carrying much too heavy burdens held by forehead straps. Boats passing, everything in slow motion. A large pile of empty tortoise shells. Chickens tied by the legs, swinging in an empty-looking radius. At night the cooking fires glow. Enormous fish at the market, fruit juices surrounded by swarms of flies, filth.

Children playing marbles between the houses' stilts. Vultures that spread their wings like Christ on the Cross and remain in that statuelike position, presumably to cool off or to drive away itching mites. In early times it was interpreted as the posture for prayer, and because of the mites the eagle became the favorite heraldic bird for coats of arms. Cattle heads, skinned and bloody, on a hand cart. The women crouch in the brownish water, doing their laundry. In a bar a man was lying on the floor unconscious, dead drunk. By fifteen most of the girls already have one or two children. This city seems to be inhabited exclusively by children. Today is a holiday. In the evening up the Río Momón by boat.

Iquitos, 30 June 1979

The house en route to the Río Nanay is slowly getting organized. An ailing chicken is supposed to have its neck wrung if it does not get better today. The Indian who does chores here has instructions to that effect. Discussion with the carpenters, but every tone, every gesture is so transparently and ineptly acted that you can see they are lying. A discussion about the basic question of having women in the house. The decision: all right to have local girlfriends, but they should not stay in the house when their men of our crew are away for a while. It is not right to have female friends from the village become a permanent majority. They should all rather live in their own houses here, as the men of our team, just because some of us are almost always away in the jungle. Yesterday on the Río Momón an American tourist with whitish folds of belly fat paddled toward me. He was in a fake canoe made of plastic, and said hi. At the lodge he will be out of circulation for a few days at any rate.

In the evening to the movies, an Italian horror film, so extraordinarily bad that even the locals noticed. Guests arriving at a lonely castle are all murdered. It turns out that the countess is mad, and the count shoots her as well, because she kissed the blond, vigorous hunk of a poet. He does not have long to live, either. In the end all that is left are the dogs, howling and snarling their teeth; earlier they tore one of the guests limb from limb as he was trying to get away, for the lord of the castle shot himself in his chamber, unable to bear the truth any longer.

Afterward I went to Belén to have a brandy in one of the dives. The cardplayers were so loaded that they were playing in slow motion. When they had to pee, they did not even leave their stools but just swiveled around and pissed against the board walls. In the one where we were drinking, which was as small as a newspaper stand, the tavern keeper's wife and child were sleeping on the floor, without a mattress, blanket, or pillow. A scruffy, drunk old Chinese man showed us open scabs on his forearm. He approached us several times, wanting us to take a good look.

In the house a calculator has been stolen. Our watchman checks the same drawers thirty times to see whether it is still missing. To find a spot for oneself in the house is not easy, because the two rooms are too small and crammed with stuff, and the table in the entryway serves as the workplace for everyone, including the strangers who come and go and drink beer.

Steep steps by the slaughterhouse on the river where murder takes place; what I saw there bore no resemblance to proper slaughtering. A cow escaped into the river and swam away. Two men jumped in after her. In the slaughterhouse one of the Indian butchers cut his own toe by mistake and was bleeding heavily, but because he was wading up to his ankles in slimy blood and guts he did not really notice at first and had to hunt around to figure out where his blood was coming from. He sat down on the stomach of the cow that had just been killed and was still thrashing around and examined his foot. Next to him was a pig that had been pierced in the heart; after a while it got up and walked away.

The butchers knock the pigs to the ground, grab a foreleg and pull it up, bracing one foot on the pig, and then they stab their knife with calm accuracy into the heart. Because the pigs scream so hard, a pink piece of lung is often extruded from the wound.

Foundry: a crucible in the ground like an iron volcano with a scalloped rim. Corrugated tin on poles forms a roof over the whole thing. Pails on yokes for carrying, pigs grunting, chickens, ducks. In the midst of all this a pig is slaughtered, children are nursed. A dwarfish, crippled woman is sewing on a sewing machine; she can hardly reach the pedal. In the background palm trees, between them a decomposing pile of garbage in which hens peck around. Scrap iron, molds, a bench vise, a bellows. The whole thing resembles a Bronze Age midden heap in which blacksmithing and pouring goes on. This is where we will have to work.

In the discotheque into which someone pushed me it is so dark that the waiter collects the bill with a flashlight. The eyes of the girls you meet here are black on black, where the darkness is most intense. Shirt collars stand out as the most glaring ultra-white, and the writing on the most glaring pieces of paper is impossible to see. At the next table someone smashed his glass on purpose. The waiter brought me a beer and wanted to know whether we also wanted señoritas.

At the Indians' request, we bring chain saws, machetes, and shotguns to the Río Cenepa, as well as a large canister of poison for arrow tips. They no longer know how to make it themselves. Vivanco says they will pay for a spoonful with a gold nugget.

Río Marañón, 1 July 1979

Nauta. The entire afternoon spent going upstream on the Río Marañón; I never fully woke up, having not slept much, and because the
speedboat is overloaded there was no place to stretch out except on
the roof. The children along the banks speak Spanish with a strange
rhythm. The canoes are tied up along the bank with ropes made from
liana bark, which is very tough. People spend their days here watching
the river. An archaic calm and composure in the mothers' gestures as
they pick over their children's heads, searching for lice. They bite the
lice in two with their front teeth. In the marketplace people are lying
on the tables, sleeping. Life stands still. Only the river is in motion,
flowing sluggishly. In the tavern the half-naked tavern keeper did
not bring us anything, because an old man with ragged clothes and a
squashed ear was massaging his neck. Women and children in white
garments passed by outside; they belong to a sect.

Evening, before sunset. Stopping in a village beyond the mouth
of the Río Tigre. A silent wall of children was waiting for us. We
hung the hammocks, which are all too small, under an unoccupied
roof. Not a sound from the river, not the slightest; it flows in complete silence. I cannot hear it even though it is just a few steps away.
We all have the flu. In the light of the moon, which is not even half
full, your own body casts a clear shadow, which obediently shrinks
when you tell it to heel. Faces seated around a flickering lantern.
Growing restless, I had gone outside to see whether the river was
still there. At night the rivers have a fever. Yet onions are lying on the
table. Outside in the dark all that can be made out of the Indians are
their fingers, with which they are holding on to the porch railing. For
a long time I stared in the direction of the faces in the pitch dark, till
the fingers gingerly let go of the railing and plunged into the night.

Río Marañón, 2 July 1979

A rest stop in the village of Saramuro, from where Huerequeque set out just ten minutes before we got there. We will catch up with him in the evening, because our boat is more powerful. All morning I dozed on the roof of the speedboat, next to me Walter, who was drunk as a skunk and was sleeping it off. Only when the boat hit big waves now and then did I wake up for a moment and see the jungle and isolated huts passing. Today the river is not carrying as much dangerous drift-wood as the day before. In Saramuro Vivanco bought meat, half of a wild boar. It is heavily salted to prevent spoilage. When I spat into the water, a fish snapped up the floating spit, but let it drift up to the surface again a few meters downstream.

Río Marañón, 3 July 1979

Leaden, labyrinths of weariness with no escape. Lying on the roof again. Stopping in a village before the confluence with the Río Pastaza. In the evening sun I saw the mountains off in the distance as delicate, unreal pink strips. The village boys were having their evening soccer game, and the teacher, hardly more than a child himself, was playing with them. We asked him whether we could sleep in the school. And there we spent the night, with a blanket on the floor and a mosquito net over us. The teacher is walleyed, and while talking with him I try to focus on one of his eyes. In a hut next door they cooked a chicken for us. The school itself is a hut on stilts, with a thatched roof and a raised, bouncy floor made of tough liana bark, split lengthwise. Under the hut grunting pigs, a few chickens, ducks, and dogs, the last almost naked from mange. On the platform a slightly raised fireplace made of clay, with two stones positioned parallel to one another to support a rack, actually two iron bars. The fire never goes out; it glows all night long. The children stare at us silently with their dark eyes. Garbage is tossed right down to the pigs, and dishwater is simply poured through the floor. Swarms of parrots fly screeching toward the evening sun as if they had urgent business of which we are unaware.

A local man had hollowed out a tree trunk and filled it with a hundred pounds of cocaine, which he set adrift. He followed the floating tree trunk for weeks in a dugout, until he reached Leticia, over the border in Colombia. There the trail of the drifting tree and its escort was lost.

When I went into the forest to take a shit, a pig followed me, snuffling and waiting with shameless greed for my shit. Even when I threw sticks at it, the animal took only a few symbolic steps backward.

During our trip on the river heavy rain had begun to fall. We looked in vain for the village of Delfus, which seems to have disappeared, either because the river swept it away or because the river has changed course, leaving Delfus far inland in the jungle. While searching for our gasoline drums in Saramiriza we learned that they were being stored farther downstream, and we found the boat *Huerequeque* and the drums on land. A good twenty people live by the hut there, almost all children. The ducks stand out in the rain, silent and motionless, thinking intently about nothing at all. In the kitchen hut there are two fireplaces, the earth very nicely raised on beams, so that the fires burn on a clay hearth. Hanging above it smoked meat, several slaughtered tortoises, on a rack the flat head of a huge fish.

Río Marañón, 4 July 1979
The hut was so thick with mosquitoes that I took my coffee outside, flailing my arm. At night the boat is full of them, too. Only

when we move at top speed, creating a stiff breeze, do the mosquitoes hold still, hiding in corners from the wind. Huerequeque arrived last night, and we loaded the wooden boat with nine drums of gasoline. I doubt the boat will make it through the Pongo de Manseriche rapids. I bought a few grams of gold dust in a little medicine bottle with a cork stopper. In Saramiriza the entire riverbank had been washed away, and soon the village will be swept away, too. An attempt was made to reinforce the oil depot with iron braces, but now the supports are standing in water, with the shore completely gone.

A small green parrot with a yellow breast and black crest landed on my finger and preened. Its feet, gripping my finger, are very warm. A yellow-spotted kitten was lying outside in the dirt, dying. I could tell immediately from the way it was lying on its stomach, its hind paws stretched out. Bubbles of foam were bursting around its mouth, and it was racked by convulsions. When I moved away, the mother cat came and licked the kitten for a while, but then wandered off. Chickens came and began to eat the kitten, which was still alive, but soon let it be. A duckling came over, peeping, but at that point the kitten had almost stopped moving. On the large, smooth leaves of a banana plant droplets form; they are the color of silver balls. Wood and gold are the kitchen words. A fragment of speech floated to me on a rain shower; the Italians had apparently found gold in the Pongo. Next to me a parrot screeched and giggled like a human being. It kept calling in Spanish, "Run, Aureliano," and would not stop. It was like the soundtrack of a Woody Woodpecker film. "Birds are smart, but they cannot speak," Fitzcarraldo would teach his parrot to say in the film. The dead drag the living down with them.

In the godforsaken garrison of Borja, below the rapids, an Indian soldier was reading Clausewitz in a Spanish translation. In the Pongo, our engine died twice because the waves buffeted the boat so hard that the gas tank was ripped off. The first time it happened, the boat rammed into the cliffs, because without the engine it could not be steered. The water level in the Pongo is rising, and it is hard to imagine that the large wooden boat with the gasoline drums can make it through. Still completely numbed from the immense power and fury of the rapids, when we reached the Pinglo garrison, I finally washed my hair; in the last few days it had become all matted.

In the Río Santiago the body of a soldier who had been shot came floating along, on his back, swollen, the legs bent at the knees and the arms bent likewise; he looked as if he were raising his hands. Birds had already hacked out his eyes and eaten away part of the face. The *comandante* here advised letting him float by—so as to avoid any trouble; they would have to deal with him farther downstream. He gave the swimmer a gentle nudge with his boot, and the corpse spun around once before the current took hold of him.

In the evening we reached Santa Maria de Nieva as the last light was fading. On the way the boat ran aground and the propeller broke. While we were tied up on the bank replacing it, Indians watched us through the branches from their nearby hut, remaining silent and motionless, and they remained motionless as we set out again, going upstream. In Nieva, Jaime de Aguilar showed us gold dust, which he had folded neatly into a piece of stationery. The *comandante* in Pinglo makes hundreds of his Indian recruits pan for gold in the Río Santiago, and he already owns sixty-five beer bottles filled with gold dust. I saw youthful soldiers working on a sandbank.

For the first time I saw cacao, freshly harvested. I peeled the kernel, which looks like a large, misshapen bean, and was disappointed by the bitter taste, for what is inside looks like chocolate. Our canister with twenty-six kilos of pure curare, for poisoning arrow tips, made a great impression. For a spoonful of this black, sticky mass, you can get yourself a woman to marry, I was told in a respectful whisper by a boatman, as he cleaned his toes with a screwdriver. Here all the proportions are off; the fishhooks in the little general store are as big as my palm, and bigger. The Indians paint their faces black, which makes them invisible.

Santa Maria de Nieva–Río Cenepa, 5 July 1979
Santa Maria de Nieva. W. dreamed he had received a whole zoo as a gift, and when all the animals escaped soon afterward, he had seen Vivanco rowing in a canoe with one of the escaped animals, but on a road, without water, rather than a river. The animals, once rounded up, were all slaughtered. During the night there was such a loud rushing sound that I thought it was raining, but it was the rushing of the Marañón. In the rafters above my bed cats were fighting furiously, with deafening howls; it went on for hours. Indians leaned on the windowsills and looked in at us impassively as we got up and had breakfast. A boy of about five joined our men's circle at the table, quite matter-of-factly, as if he had belonged for a long time, and now and then chimed in with questions. Overnight, to judge by the crowing crescendo that swelled to a terrible roar, the roosters became giants. Up in the church a small cluster of Aguarunas, all members of a sect, were reciting their morning prayers, their arms crossed over their chests. To the left a Peruvian flag hung above them.

Sailing up the Marañón. Before the confluence with the Cenepa there is a very beautiful Pongo through the last mountain chain. As we arrived in Orellana, the young men were playing soccer, among them the teacher. Today the village is known once more by its Indian name, Wawaim. Apparently rumors are swirling around to the effect that we are planning to dig a canal from the Río Cenepa to the Río

Marañón, and that that will dry up the fields. A fairly young, intelligent-looking man with long hair asked me whether filming or being filmed could do harm, whether it could destroy a person. In my heart the answer was yes, but I said no. A child had been bitten by a snake; I heard the mother wailing; she was crying, people told me, but it was a song of lament. Relatives arrived and an older woman joined in the singing. The child was lying on the floor in a hut, very quiet and solemn. Vivanco came running with medicine and tried to find out what kind of snake it had been, so he could administer the right serum.

We ate at the house of the teacher, who has a table, whereas the women and children crouch on the floor. The salt was a flat brick, hard as a rock, from which we tried to scrape a bit, but we were given to understand that we should dunk the whole slab in the soup. The chicken was so tough that it was practically impossible to bite off a piece. Walter said it was a Formula–1 chicken. Aside from papayas there is almost no fruit here, no beer, which you find everywhere else, no coffee, no general store, but they do have yucca, corn, bananas, some chickens, no pigs, not much fish. The people's gestures are unfamiliar, gentle and lovely; they move their hands like orchestral conductors in time with a soft, shy melody that emanates cautiously from the depths of the forest, like wild creatures that emerge from the sheltering leaves now and then to go down to the rivers.

A spot on the bank of the Río Cenepa glowed in yellow and orange, and upon approaching I saw that it was a huge swarm of butterflies. We had to turn back because of a storm. Something entirely different is brewing on the nearby border with Ecuador; the Cordillera del Condor, visible from here in the misty, steaming forest, forms a natural barrier. There is a strong military presence, and a mortally afraid Indian soldier, not more than seventeen, fired a shot at our boat on the Cenepa; it struck the water near us. All those in the boat froze. I was about to slip into the water, but was then embarrassed and decided not to, because the young man seemed much more shocked at having shot at us than we in the boat were, his target. Here you have to show identification everywhere, even the Indian natives. The white people, the teacher told me, have always come to plunder, never for any other reason. A few months ago a lieutenant in the Peruvian army went berserk at a remote outpost on the Río Santiago. He declared war on Ecuador and attacked with twenty-four soldiers. He advanced over thirty kilometers into enemy territory along the river's upper reaches, and apparently it cost a great deal of effort to go after him and bring him back.

Wawaim, 6 July 1979

For the night I had fixed myself a bed by laying flexible sugarcanes on a half-collapsed frame. In the part of the school that serves as a storage area, there is hardly room to sit—no table, just a few gasoline drums filled with stuff. Under my sleeping platform was a pile of hundreds of cheap sectioned plastic plates, the kind used in prisons. These absurdly inappropriate gifts from the Alliance for Progress are stamped with the American flag and a handshake logo. The plastic plates have a round indentation for plastic cups, but the cups are missing. I noticed that here even plastic rots, like all the organic matter. In the morning I woke up feeling the silent eyes of children watching me at close range through the loose wall slats.

We discovered that Walter's tape recorder had been stolen, as well as all the money Vivanco had been carrying. Some other things had disappeared, too, and everything had been rummaged through. Vivanco said nothing had ever been taken from him in an Indian village, and for that reason we wondered at first whether the thefts might have occurred while our stuff was being inspected at the Teniente Pin-glo garrison or in Urakusa at the military outpost, where our papers had been checked, but we were soon able to eliminate that possibil-ity. Jaime de Aguilar discovered that five or six adolescent boys were probably involved, and later in the day some of the money turned up on a bench, folded into a page from a school notebook. We did not want to make a big deal of it, because our position remains delicate until we can explain our intentions at a community meeting. With all the rumors flying around, with the pressure created by the mili-tary presence, whose effect on the people exacerbates the situation, and with the problems the oil company has created with its pipeline project—what is going to happen to us? An additional factor is that the community here is very split politically and furthermore under pressure from a political alliance that wants to extend its influence to Wawaim by means of threats and acts of violence. I was so starved for salt that I ate a whole handful; then I sharpened a machete in the company of several young men who were sharpening theirs. One of them used his machete to shave his sparse facial hair.

Before the meeting got under way, a wild hubbub erupted. Viv-anco and I were told we had to present our wishes and our plan in tandem. Another argument broke out over who would translate, and eventually the translating was done by someone affiliated with the Indian council from farther downriver, who, as Jaime de Aguilar told us afterward, having listened from close by, had intentionally distorted the meaning of our words and even translated some parts completely wrong. He wanted to play himself up as a protector of the *comunidad*. It was crucial that we be prevented from digging a canal that would partially transform the settlement into an island. Among some in the crowd a brand of hostility sprang up that I had encountered previously only in the reports of early seafarers, except that now the natives were wearing "John Travolta Fever" and "Disneyland" T-shirts. It ended with everyone shouting at me and making menacing gestures, and one man brandished a spear and forced his way toward me, snorting furiously. He thrust the spear right at my belly, but retracted it with only centimeters to spare. Somehow I realized that this was just a sort of ritual attack, and to my own astonishment I stood there very calmly. A soft murmur spread through the crowd, expressing admiration, either for the fine pantomime of the feigned attack or for the composure of the apparent victim. Vivanco conducted himself remarkably in the situation, remaining self-controlled, friendly, modest. All of this has a long prehistory, of course: these people have been robbed and abused, their gold and oil taken from them. There have been border conflicts and political factions that aspired to impose an imported ideology based on the futile dream of a great revolution, an ideology making a last-ditch effort to find a home in this region. All fathers of families are eligible to participate in the communal deliberations, and I noticed that the overwhelming majority were boys, hardly older than fifteen. At that age most of them are fathers already.

After the meeting many of the participants came up to me and told me they would like to help with our project, and we would see that there would be a large majority in favor of a contract with us. Such meetings had always gone this way, they said, and in the reality of life things had never been changed by them. I wanted to retreat back down the river, out of the Wawaim region, and wait to see whether a contract was feasible and supported by a large majority. I felt somewhat encouraged and also took comfort in the simple fact that the Indian cook who had arrived from Santa Maria de Nieva was called Grimaldo. I find the sound of that name comforting somehow.

An agreement with the family whose *chakra* is located outside the

Aguarunas' territory. We can establish a beachhead here, and as soon
as we started clearing the underbrush people came from Wawaim and
asked whether they could work for us. I took a machete and joined in
for a while. Like a scythe when you are mowing, a machete has to be
sharpened constantly. For that purpose we use a large, smooth rock
on the riverbank, near where our luggage is strewn about: tools, chain
saws, kitchen utensils. White vapor streams through the Pongo,
floating upstream, and the sun shines on it from above and turns it
into a delicate, blinding web. For a while a dragonfly hovered in the
air in front of me, taking my measure. Now and then chickens flail
around as they lie in the shade with their legs tied together. A liberat-
ing feeling to be working in the brush with a machete; limbs falling,
lianas hacked through as if they were air. The lianas hesitate before
they fall. Every machete has its own sound, tuned like an instrument
in an orchestra; together they create a unique music. No one here
wears a watch; I gave up mine long ago because the humidity plays
havoc with the works. In the sand there are traces of gold. When
I stamp my foot, nearly transparent spiders with skinny legs dart
along the shore and continue their headlong flight out onto the river,
skimming along the surface of the water.

A *machetero* had hacked himself in the toe and was being treated.
Young women came with their infants, which they carry in a piece of
cloth slung diagonally across their chest. They shield the children's
faces with banana leaves. It seems almost deceptively calm, as if there
had never been any uproar about our project.

Saramiriza, 9 July 1979
A parrot at my feet is devouring a candle, holding it with the toes of
one foot. The people are rescuing their possessions from the huts,

because the riverbank has eroded even more. In some places the embankment protrudes far over the water, and you can knock off large sections with your foot. A hen and her chicks came into the store, a wooden shack with a corrugated tin roof, where we were having some food fixed for us, and attacked the almost naked parrot, tearing one of its last arse feathers out and pecking several times at its sore bald head. Afterward the hen wiped her beak clean on the ground. We are all still shaken from the terrifying impression of the rapids, and are behaving with almost mathematical correctness toward each other. At the military outpost of Teniente Pinglo none of the soldiers knew how high the water level was. They merely pointed out that a few days ago a boat with eleven men on board had disappeared without a trace. But the men had drunk too much *aguardiente*, sugarcane brandy, beforehand, and had not sailed into the gorge until nightfall. After considerable reflection we concluded that it had to be doable, because the Río Marañón was very shallow; the night before the level had sunk by a good two meters, and in the morning we had found our boats so high and dry that we could hardly drag them into the water. What did not bode well was the Río Santiago. There must have been terrible downpours along its upper reaches to the north, and where the river joined the Marañón it was alarmingly high. Before the first rapids, which formed an isolated prelude to the Pongo de Manseriche, a blast of bitingly cold air struck us, coming from the narrow passage between the mountains; here it would still have been possible to turn back. With the cold came a distant rumbling from the chasm, and no one understood why we sailed on, but sail on we did. Suddenly we were facing a wall of raging water, into which we crashed like a projectile. We received a blow so powerful that the boat went spinning into the air, the propeller howling in the void. For a moment we hit the water vertically, and I saw like an apparition a second wall of water towering in front of us, which struck us even harder, twirling the boat into the air again, this time in the opposite direction. Before we entered the rapids I had already secured the anchor chain so firmly that it could not fly overboard and get tangled in the screw, and the gas tank was fastened in place with iron clamps, but suddenly the battery, as big as a truck's, went hurtling through the air. Or rather, for a moment it hovered in the air on its straining cables directly in front of my face, and my head collided with it. At first it felt as though my nose were broken at the root, and I was bleeding from my mouth. Then came moments when there was nothing but waves all around and above us, but it was more the rumbling that I recall. Then I recall that we were through the rapids, drifting backward. On the steep jungle slopes to either side monkeys screeched.

In Borja at the lower end of the Pongo they did not want to believe their eyes, because no one had survived the passage when the water level was sixteen feet above normal, and our level had been eighteen. The village *pongeros* clustered around us, not saying a word. One of them inspected my swollen face and said, "*Su madre.*" Then he let me have a swig of his *aguardiente*.

The previous day we had sailed up the Marañón far past the confluence with the Cenepa. Several minor rapids. We registered with the authorities our intention of building a temporary camp. Returning only after nightfall; a white full moon shone enigmatically on the mist that had settled over the river. Several times we ran aground on hard gravel, but the screw did not break. We could proceed only very cautiously, soaked through, our hair dripping from the mist, and not until almost midnight did we reach our camp, where in the meantime a hut had been built, not much more than a sheltering roof. We all slept crowded together on the ground, freezing and fighting off the ants, which had a highway right by our heads. The situation seems completely free of tension. The Indios working here were very content, and Wawaim sent some extra men.

There is nothing to buy in Saramiriza but warm beer. The plane that supposedly lands on the river three times a week has been out of commission for a long time, but is slated to be repaired somewhere along its route. We assume, however, that the Estación Cinco, where the pipeline begins, needs to be supplied, and accordingly there will be a plane sooner or later.

Iquitos, 10 July 1979
In the afternoon a plane showed up with young pilots, quite bored, who allowed the plane to be even more hopelessly overloaded at every stop. We left Saramiriza behind, doomed to certain death, crumbling with its eroded riverbank into the water. Since there is almost no one left at the pumping station, the village hardly receives supplies anymore. But the tavern keeper at the shabby bar in the wooden shack tells himself that sometime a new boom will occur, and he is waiting for it languidly, without lifting a finger. In a month at most the river will have claimed his shack, too.

The city of Iquitos, although cut off from any connecting road, seems to take no notice of the ocean of jungle that holds it in a vise. Slow but visible progress on our work here. The members of our team are all over the place, in Lima, in Miami, laying in supplies–any sort of infrastructure is completely absent here. Uli's acquired a still young tigrillo, an ocelot, and a large, splendidly colored parrot. The mosquitoes right now are particularly aggressive; even repellent does not keep them away.

Iquitos, 11 July 1979

During the night Henning came back from Lima, bringing mail from Munich; life in the outside world does not stop. The boat, the *Huallaga*, is gradually taking shape; there are twelve welders constantly at work, and on land we have a field kitchen, operated by soldiers, who are earning some pocket money during their off-duty hours. From Lima, or rather from the port of Callao, where the more capable workers come from in any case, four carpenters arrived, sturdy as oxen, who are now working on the boat along with the welders. On the very first day they quit at noon because the food was not sufficient, and from today on they are going to have T-bone steaks every day, as big as wagon wheels. I went with Uli to the wood shop, an impenetrable chaos of trash, chickens, children, open fires, and pinups on the plank walls. Ducks and pigs wallow around in the dirt with the children. We ordered four wooden lifeboats for Fitzcarraldo's ship. In a workshop next door huge tree trunks were being stripped of their bark by means of crowbars, then loaded by crane onto trucks. Not far from us the wood is being processed into thin layers for plywood. The road to us and out to the Río Nanay is collapsing into mud, and the depth of the potholes is impossible to judge because they fill up with muddy water. At night Uli fell into an unexpectedly deep hole on his motorcycle and hurt his head. I dabbed iodine on the wound.

Every evening, at exactly the same minute, several hundred thousand *golondrinas*, a kind of swallow, come to roost for the night in the trees on the Plaza de Armas. They form black lines on the cornices of buildings. The entire square is filled with their excited fluttering and twittering. Arriving from all different directions, the swarms of birds meet in the air above the square, circling like tornados in dizzying spirals. Then, as if a whirlwind were sweeping through, they suddenly descend onto the square, darkening the sky. The young ladies put up umbrellas to shield themselves from the droppings.

Since I took Walter and Gustavo to the airport for their flight to Lima, the house is almost empty. Henning is painting sketches in watercolors, I am listening to music, and someone is feeding fish to the ocelot. You could be seduced into thinking all was peaceful. Luciano, our Indian houseboy, tried to sing along with Schütz's choral music as he swept the floor–"In the mountains a cry was heard, Rachel wept for her children and would not be comforted, for they were no more." Luciano is a reserved man who manages to make himself invisible, and I have become very fond of him. In the concourse at the airport a wounded hummingbird was fluttering along the polished floor, unable to get into the air. When it tired, the shoeshine boys nudged it with their toes, and it glided in crazed, whirring paths along the ground.

For days a dead roach has been lying in our little shower stall, which is supplied with water from a gasoline drum on the roof. The roach is so enormous in its monstrosity that it is like something that stepped out of a horror movie. It lies there all spongy, belly-up, and is so disgusting that none of us has had the nerve to get rid of it.

In Belén I was sitting in the marketplace talking with a boatman. A tarantula as big as a fist, all dark and hairy, emerged from the underside of the small table and scrabbled, as if in slow motion, past our beer bottles, disappearing under the table on the other side, where our legs were stretched out. We continued our conversation as though nothing had happened. On the filthy floor a woman was lying and snoring, drunk out of her wits. Her grubby skirt was hitched up, and you could see she was not wearing any underpants. I purchased a new net, woven of strong fibers, since I had hung mine on a post in the nonexistent village of Delfus and forgotten to take it with me, also a blanket, because it gets quite chilly at night, a large hammock, and two rubberized flour sacks as protection from the dampness in the jungle. Then I also found some sugar, which is not to be had anywhere, because whatever is left is being hoarded by the merchants. People stand in line to get it, but I found some and bought two kilos. Then alone in the house with the gangly young bookkeeper from the city, whose mere presence is death to any meaningful thoughts.

Henning drew the sketch for the figurehead of Fitz's ship, a naked Indian woman with a python curling around her and an alligator and a tortoise whose shell covers her pubic area.

Iquitos, 13 July 1979
The telex machine at the post office, the only means of communication with the outside world, was on the fritz again, and a repairman was taking it apart. No one can say if or when it will be working. At midday sultry, heavy, oppressive lassitude; it is hot, with not a cloud in the sky. With great effort I roused myself from my idle brooding and went out to the Río Nanay. Dust, heat. Empty sheets of paper staring at me. I returned to the house as the sun was setting. At every step mosquitoes flew up from the grass, glistening like gold dust in the evening sun. The chickens darted ahead of me toward their enclosure, followed by quacking ducks; the pig came galloping toward me, grunting, its legs stretched straight out, and it seemed as if these domestic animals were intent on getting a response from me. Only the tigrillo in its cage cautiously and dignifiedly approached the wire mesh, lowered its head a bit, and seemed ready to listen. A large squad of marines passed by on the street outside, in a sluggish jogtrot. They were holding their weapons at an angle across their chests, and were uttering deep, throaty chants in unison, answering their leader.

In the morning I went to the museum, where you can see a row of extremely depressing aquariums, filled with disgusting putrid water that has killed off any living creatures. In only one of them, which has no rocks, no plants, only stale water that has not been changed in months, a few miserable fish have survived. Then there were a few badly stuffed birds, most of whose feathers had been torn out by previous visitors, as well as snakes, turtles, and a few plaster Indians—Yaguas and Ashininkas—hung with Indian everyday-use objects from the souvenir shop at the airport. The taxi I took today was completely stripped on the inside and had holes in the floorboards, like all the others here. I cannot recall taking a taxi whose doors shut properly. The only striking thing about today's taxi was that it had no steering wheel; the driver steered it with a large monkey wrench, and did a good job. Even so, just the thought of what I have planned makes me dizzy.

On the little table, whose legs were cut shorter for me today because it was too high, a dim kerosene lamp is burning. Outside the sun is rapidly drawing the night after it like a curtain at the end of a play. The daytime birds are falling silent. For today the farce is ended.

Iquitos, 14 July 1979
On the way into town in the jeep, Uli picked up a marine who said he wanted to visit someone in the hospital. When they got to the hospital, the soldier had forgotten what he had come for, but he did not want to get out, and told Uli he should wait there with him. He sounded confused. Only then did Uli realize that his passenger was dead drunk, and he did not know what to do with the man. Finally he gave the soldier a friendly shove. The man tumbled out of the jeep and fell asleep then and there on the side of the road, in front of the hospital entrance.

This sultriness is deadly. Midday weighs us down. In his sleep Henning is caught up in some vague struggle, from which he will wake up exhausted. When he is asleep, he looks more grown-up and manly. They say you look like a child when you are sleeping, but here in the tropics, with the leaden atmosphere crushing everything, that is not true. The pigs are snuffling in the rotting garbage. Outside a small child is crying. An enormous insect, searching for a favorable angle of attack, is buzzing around; the feverish oppressiveness in my somnolent state makes it seem as large as a helicopter, and though I am watching it the whole time as if through billows of fog and know that it wants to destroy me, I cannot summon the energy to get up and murder it with a dull blow.

Iquitos, 15 July 1979
Last night Andreas came. I was already in bed at eight o'clock and was reading Gregorovius's *History of the City of Rome in the Middle Ages*, but was still intending to go to the movies. Not until several of us felt like going did I pull myself together. It was an Argentinean film, with one very thin man and one very fat one, blondes with bursting breasts and naughty lingerie, which was hanging up to dry in the kitchen belonging to one of the women. Because of his girth, the fat man could not duck down very well, so he kept bumping into the dangling panties and bras, rolling his eyes in ecstasy. Andreas's girl screeched with laughter. In one scene the fat man was also playing tennis.

We found our night watchman sound asleep, slumped down against the gatepost. He was drunk out of his mind. His head was sunk on his chest, his cap had fallen off, and he had thrown up between his splayed legs. He did not hear me, even though I had to stop the rattling motorcycle right in front of him, and I passed without being checked. Later, when Andreas arrived and was arguing loudly with the cabdriver, the watchman must have woken up, for he appeared, staggering, and aimed his flashlight in a slalom at our faces, although there were lights on inside the house, and joined in the conversation. Our watchman has only one tooth left in his mouth. In the morning Uli found him sleeping in the shed, lying on the boards on top of the ocelot's enclosure.

On the way to the airport in the morning, we ran into Huerequeque, who in spite of his big belly and his age was running with a surprisingly springy step. On the way back to the Nanay, however, he stops for a beer with each of his innumerable *compadres*, and often takes days to reach his house.

In Lima with Walter, Gustavo, and Janoud; the mood very glum. In the afternoon two men from some ministry or other showed up. They seemed to be quite reasonable at first. But in connection with our contract with the community of Wawaim they had worked out an action plan that was utterly pedantic, with Point A, Point B, Point C, and subparagraphs for each. The whole thing smacked of wretched manuals for provincial administration, and it is clear we must avoid working with the government bureaucracy if we do not want to see the project killed in short order.

At night waiting at the airport with torpid patience. The plane was supposed to take off at midnight, but when three in the morning rolled around, the waiter in the deserted restaurant showed us the empty room next to the bar where, he told us, he would lie down on the floor to sleep when no one was there but he was supposed to stick around. He had noticed that we had poked around the whole upper story looking for an unlocked office where we could lie down, but everything was shut up tight. We slept on the floor for an hour.

Lima—Los Angeles, 16 July 1979

The flight to Mexico lousy, hopelessly overcrowded. Sitting on the plane for an hour on the runway in Lima with our seat belts fastened. No announcements or explanations, and as always in such situations, the stewards here act as though they were not on board. Finally I got off the plane in my socks–it was already past five A.M.–and took a look for myself, because I had heard a racket from the luggage compartment. It turned out that there had been a leak from a toilet, and all the flushes had gushed into the luggage compartment and partially flooded it. A dozen or so airport employees and workmen were discussing whether something should be done, and if so, by whom. I saw one workman sleeping on a piece of luggage in the open luggage hatchway, and another who had slumped over in his vehicle, which consists mainly of a conveyor belt; slumped is putting it mildly. I saw that all this would take a long time, and, knowing the situation, accepted my fate somewhat less passively.

Los Angeles, 17–18 July 1979

Los Angeles, San Francisco. The management troika at Fox are going to leave Fox and start their own company. There are T-shirts with the motif from the *Nosferatu* poster, very nice. Tonight Syberberg is arriving from Munich, and I am masquerading as the chauffeur and I shall go with Tom Luddy to pick him up in Coppola's biggest limousine.

Two nights ago I had a kind of seizure such as I have had a few times before, once on the island of Kos, when I thought low-flying aircraft were attacking, and I roused all the others and made them get out of bed, and once in Taormina, when first the room and then the whole earth began to tilt, and I tried to brace myself, already awake but perhaps in a form of somnambulism even so. What happened to me two nights ago was so vivid and physical that I have not had the courage to describe it yet, because I am afraid it could have been something other than sleepwalking.

Larisa Shepitko is dead. Two weeks ago she was on the way to a shoot and lost her life in an accident. Her minibus with six passengers collided with a truck carrying huge precast concrete units. The concrete piers broke loose and crushed her vehicle, and according to what we were able to find out, all the passengers were killed. When Tom Luddy said he had something to tell me and I should sit down, I suddenly knew, before he opened his mouth, that Larisa was no longer alive, and I had a vision of that night in Mannheim when we drank champagne into the wee hours and knew it was the last time we would see each other. She was so sure of that, and so convinced that she would die soon, that we said good-bye to each other very calmly. She had called me up close to midnight, saying she would be there for only a few more hours before heading home from the festival, and I had to come right away. I grabbed a bottle of champagne from the refrigerator and drove to Mannheim, getting there around four in the morning. I stood up and left Tom's office, then paged aimlessly through the few books I have with me, Gregorovius's *History of Rome*, Chatwin's *In Patagonia*, the King James Bible, a Spanish grammar, Quirinius Kuhlmann's *Kühlpsalter*, Joseph Roth's *Job*, Livy's *Second Punic War*, but found no comfort.

San Francisco, 20 July 1979
San Francisco. Emptiness.

San Francisco, 21 July 1979

In the morning a thunderstorm. The Golden Gate Bridge mythically shrouded in fog. I got a tattoo; Paul Getty was my coconspirator. We talked about Rome, where he and his wife, Gisela, and her twin sister broke into cars with a gang, mine among them. One time they were shot at, and the racket woke me in my hotel room nearby. We talked about his ear, which the kidnappers had cut off. He got a butterfly tattoo, and without having planned this in advance, I sketched a singing death's skull for myself, using samples on hand. I almost fainted, as I invariably do when I have blood drawn, and that caused a series of episodes, since I am always having blood tests because of the malaria and the bilharzia; at any rate, everything went black before my eyes, and only then, because I was embarrassed, did I say anything, and the tattoo artist knew what to do right away, something I had never heard of: put your head between your knees, hold still for a moment, then have someone press a hand to the back of your neck, while you force your head back. That gets the blood flowing to your head; all you have is spots before your eyes, and then your sight clears. Drink lots of water. Death is wearing a tuxedo and singing into a 1950s microphone.

Napa, 23 July 1979

On the porch of Coppola's house in the Napa Valley. A winery, with a huge oak tree in front of the mansion, a footpath up into the woods, leading to the little artificial pond, cattle, dry heat. Syberberg said: like Russia before the Revolution. Rassam's little nephew boasted he was a pirate, and without further ado the other children threw him in the swimming pool.

San Francisco, 24 July 1979

A report by telex from Walter in Iquitos reporting on the situation on the Cenepa. The group of Aguarunas from far downstream, who want to call attention to themselves, informed Vivanco that our camp would be attacked, and journalists would be brought along. The people in Wawaim want nothing to do with the agitators' attempts to establish a political foothold there. Nonetheless Vivanco decided it was best to go to the station in Chavez Valdivia. Now the only person left is the agronomist whom the people here wanted to show them better methods for growing their cacao. Our medical outpost is also still active, and much in demand. By now over a thousand patients from all over the region have been treated. But that will not change anything; a firm decision has to come from me. At first it was just a geographical decision: two rivers that almost touch each other but are separated by a steep ridge, but now there is a political dimension, and possibly, lurking in the shadows behind that, a military one. For now I push aside the thought, hard to shake off, that on the very location chosen for our film a war with Ecuador could break out.

San Francisco, 26 July 1979

Money troubles. My left eyelid has developed a twitch, and when it is not twitching, it droops quite badly. Self-disciplined work in spite of that. I went to San Quentin. The walls of the gas chamber are painted linden green. I had to sign a release saying I had been informed that in case of a hostage situation there would be no negotiations on freeing me. Inside the prison walls there has been an unusually high number of murders and acts of violence recently, so they are concerned about liability if anything should happen.

Iquitos, 8 August 1979

Decided on short notice to fly to Peru. Mexico City, Lima, Iquitos. The situation in Iquitos has become highly dramatic, because there is no money left, yet we have the ships under construction–we will need two identical twins–and we also have to create an entire infrastructure and continue to maintain the camp on the Marañón, even if the future there is looking very uncertain. According to a list of the most urgent priorities, we would really need $300,000 immediately, but I am still completely alone, without any partner to help with the financing. These people working here seem cut off from one another and lack all sense of direction. The most recent arrival is Uli Graf from the University of Bremen, with his girlfriend. Space is getting tight. I have been quartered from the beginning in the little shed in back, next to the kitchen. It used to be the chicken coop, and the ceiling is so low and sags somewhat in the middle, so that my head hits it when I stand up straight. At night the rats romp around above me, and when I am half asleep, it is as though they were running right over my head. Every time I return, it takes me a while to get used to the mosquitoes. We sailed up the Río Momón for about an hour, turned off the motor, and let ourselves drift back down in the almost imperceptible, languid current. Such a sense of peace came over me that I felt I was discovering something that had been missing from my life.

Iquitos, 15 August 1979

While riding the motorcycle from town out to our place, I injured my foot. I rode into a piece of steel strapping that was sticking out of the mud on the road to the Nanay, and now the cut refuses to heal, like everything here in the Amazon. I saw a dog, the saddest of all; he was swaying on his feet, moving in a sort of hunched-over, squirming reptilian fashion. On his back and shoulders he had open ulcers, which he kept trying to bite, contorting his head and body.

These days an image keeps coming to mind, without any real reason: the rural inn in Slovakia, right on the Polish border, where we were filming *Nosferatu*. The building was occupied on a seasonal basis by Polish lumbermen, put up four together in the fairly small rooms, and in a rather large lounge they played cards, huddled around a little woodstove, smoked, and cooked bacon directly on the stovetop, which was sizzling with fat. They drank vodka, and were drunk from nine in the morning on. The women among them, sturdy creatures in worn padded jackets from Siberia, joined in the drinking. On a couch in their midst, one of the women had sex with one of the men, shortly after they had returned from their day's work–the others in the room did not let themselves be distracted from what they were doing. During this operation the woodcutter kept his jacket on and his rucksack on his back.

On the Río Cenepa the situation seems to be straightened out, at least in principle, because there is a detailed contract with the community and about a hundred men are at work building the temporary camp for us; they were the ones who were specially eager for us to stay. Walter, who takes a very legalistic approach, sees all this in a rosy light. He poured a round of whiskey, but I remain skeptical, because the contract cannot do away with the political dimension, which has nothing to do with us.

The ocelot has grown, and its beast-of-prey nature is becoming more and more evident, even though it can also be affectionate and playful, like a kitten. Today it pulled a pair of Andreas's underwear out of the laundry box, defending this booty with furious hissing, tossed it around, and then tore it to shreds. Then, when I wanted to get the rest of the laundry out of harm's way, it lashed out at me with one paw, leaving me with a cut that ran along the whole back of my hand. Our big parrot, with a yellow stomach, a blue back, and a white face with black lines, saw this happen and became agitated. He can actually blush when he is agitated.

On the way from the Río Nanay to town the rain has washed out the road by the gas station, leaving a small gorge that you can bypass by going inland. The road's new course is accepted by everyone; the damage will never be repaired. Near the fermenting San Tomás garbage dump my motorcycle had a flat. Hundreds of vultures poke around in the filth, and some came hopping ponderously toward me, until a man with an overloaded pickup invited me to climb up on top of his crates of oranges. Later Paul came and hauled the motorbike with his car to his bar. The mechanic who was summoned first fetched his assistant, then both of them got drunk and sat around on the ground singing; actually it was more a chanting without melody, which soon died away because both of them fell asleep. An hour later I woke the assistant, who seemed less drunk, but he just stared at me, as if from a great distance, sang the end of a verse they had not finished, and slumped over again.

Wawaim, 17 August 1979
Wawaim. Yesterday flying from Iquitos to Saramiriza. Upon landing on the river near Saramuro, the two young pilots, who take themselves tremendously seriously, almost destroyed the floating platform, and later they flew off course, and because they had forgotten to fuel the plane in Saramuro, the tank was almost empty, and they still had not found the Marañón. They turned to me and gave me an embarrassed grin. I was sitting in the aisle on several sacks of onions and politely pointed out to them that they were flying away from the mountains instead of toward them.

Huerequeque's boat was in Saramiriza, but the new gas drums were all gone. Huerequeque said that floodwaters had swept away the drums a few days ago. But we found the gas farther upstream, and Huerequeque had obviously sold it, though he still insisted that the river had taken it. He was impervious to the logic that flood-waters could have carried the drums only downstream. We drank beer together and got along better than ever. We were hungry, but found nothing to eat. No eggs, no yucca, no rice, nothing. Finally we located a rusty can of tuna fish, which I thought seemed question-able as we were eating it. During the night I developed diarrhea, the onset was so sudden that I soiled my pants as I was making my way into the forest. After that I swam naked for a while in the silent river, itself swimming in the silence of a pitch black night.

From Saramiriza on, I was asleep on the roof of the boat again, and stayed there for most of the trip. The water level in the Pongo was only a few feet above normal; I had never seen it so low, and at the worst spot, which was now completely harmless, we even throttled the motor so we could stop and measure the current. The *comandante* in Pinglo told me, with a certain zest in his eyes, how much he liked to fuck with people and how much he liked to kill people. Then, without prompting, he brought out one of his beer bottles, filled to the top of the neck with gold dust, and wanted me to weigh it in my hand.

Impressive progress on our camp. There are 130 people working on it now. On top of the hill a large round structure, the *comedor*, is almost finished. We call this building the Great Hall of the People. Huts, bridges made of lianas, a kitchen, which had to be staffed by four more men. On the riverbank a large wooden boat is being built by our carpenters, and according to the contract, the Aguarunas will be given the boat in addition to their pay. When it comes to transporting and selling their harvests, the Indians are exploited by other Indians, though recognizing that contradicts the prevailing ideology. The first-aid station is already functioning quite well as a medical outpost, and our doctor is training some of the local Indians as medics. A young lawyer from the Indian Affairs Bureau in Lima had come to have a look, because some newspapers were reporting that we were dealing in weapons, forcing Indians to work as slaves, and other such nonsense.

In the evening there was a heavy downpour, and everyone rushed to take cover in the sleeping cabin with the best roof. Next to me on the mattresses spread on the floor slept the agronomist from Iquitos who is there establishing a model cacao farm in collaboration with the Aguarunas. He snored loudly and farted even more loudly, but there was not a single other spot available where I could have bedded down.

The carpenters have suspended from a tree limb a wide-meshed basket containing a captured *chuchupe*, the most dangerous of all the poisonous snakes in these parts. Because of its coloration it is hard to distinguish from the lianas. It stared boldly at me with its pale yellowish reddish eyes; we took stock of one another for a long time. With a stick I cautiously poked its head from the outside, and it drew it back very slowly but did not strike. It must have seen that the splints of the basket were in the way.

Wawaim, 18 August 1979
With the three best *macheteros* I reconnoitered the passage where the ship is to be towed over the mountain. At a killer pace we went tearing steeply uphill through the densest jungle, and in no time at all I was so drenched in sweat that even the leather of my belt swelled

from the moisture. In spite of my neckerchief, fire ants slithered down my neck and got inside my shirt. As we descended to the Río Cenepa, I was staggering, and slid down the muddy slope through brambles. Once arrived at the river, I plopped into the water on my stomach and drank. Then we were caught in a powerful thunderstorm. As darkness fell, back at our camp. The clouds dispersed, and fireflies and stars danced around my head. Frogs croaking from the river, but the frogs sounded like sheep. At night shots rang out in the forest, and one of the Aguarunas brought the animal he had shot, allegedly a night monkey, but it looked more like a marten. That will be my lunch tomorrow. Time is tugging at me like an elephant, and the dogs are tugging at my heart.

On the beach by Wawaim, 19 August 1979
This morning the camp is quiet, because only thirty or so of the Aguarunas have stayed here; the rest left yesterday to go back to their families in the villages for the weekend. The river has gone down even more. From the gravel bank an enormous tree trunk is protruding, scoured by the water–it was never visible before. On the opposite bank rise slanting, polished, rocky cliffs. A barkless tree trunk that was washed up by the floodwaters has become jammed in the rocks on an angle. The cooks fry eggs for us, the pan directly on the fire. All day long and at night, too, large tree trunks that have been simply laid on the sand are glowing. The Aguarunas are roasting an alligator that they have cut in two. It was certainly no longer than three feet. They roast the animal as is–all they did was remove the innards. They leave the skin on and dig out the meat with their fingers. The *apu* is sitting with his tin plate, rubber boots on his feet, on two overturned

containers of Ideal brand condensed milk. Down by the river, the two boats that were in the water yesterday are now high and dry on a gravel bed. Just now the hunter came by proudly, his shotgun over his shoulder. Slowly the fog is lifting in the Pongo de Huracayo.

This morning I went looking for Walter in his bed in the little cabin next to mine, but all I found was his rumpled blanket. Later it turned out that he had been in the bed after all, but had made himself into such a tiny, inconspicuous ball that I failed to notice that he was there under the blanket. Yesterday he had talked for a long time about *Aguirre*, and a whole slew of horrible things came back to me that I had either forgotten or intentionally repressed. But there were also nice memories, for instance the time we both swam through a somewhat calmer spot below the raging rapids of the Urubamba, still rushing and swirling even there, as we tried to reach the gondola moored on the other side. With that gondola you could cross the river on a steel cable: the way we looked at each other when suddenly a huge funnel in the water came toward us on a semicircular course with a terrible sucking, slurping sound, then changed direction just before it reached us. The way I spent the night during the first week sleeping on the dirt floor of the hut belonging to the dwarfish, hunchbacked woman with her nine children, and at night whole herds of guinea pigs scrambled over me, which they kept as pets and roasted over the fire to eat. The way Kinski arrived in the jungle with tons of alpine equipment—down sleeping bags, ice picks, ropes, crampons—to take on the wild alpine slopes high in the icy Andes. He did not want to accept the fact that the opening sequence, with hundreds of pigs in the midst of an army of Spanish conquistadors who were staggering from altitude sickness high on a glacier, had been written out long ago, even though I had told him so in letters several times. During our first investigations in the vicinity of the Walla-Walla Pass, where a glacier came to within a few kilometers of the passable road, four of the six people with me developed altitude sickness, and the worst of all was Walter. The way Kinski at first growled that he, a child of nature, would not be caught dead sleeping in a hotel, but the very first night he got so wet in his tent from a tropical downpour that we had to erect a thatched palm-frond roof over it; and by the second night he was already in what was Machu Picchu's only hotel in those days, where night after night he flew into a rage and chased his Vietnamese wife through the halls, beating her in his fits of raving madness and hurling her against walls, until all the guests woke up and rushed to see what was happening, and only our bribes prevented the hotelkeeper from throwing Kinski out. Walter described how every morning at four he went around discreetly scrubbing off the splatters of blood that the madman's poor wife had left on the walls. Yet these were minor sacraments. To this day I have not dared to write down anything about those events.

A canoe passed by, with three men in the bow rowing in unison with long poles. Behind them the boat is piled high with freight, on top of which a woman and a child are crouching.

Afternoon: taking the speedboat to Pinglo, because a plane is supposed to be leaving from there. The boat's vibration kept me awake for most of the trip; I stared in amazement into the jungle as it whizzed by. In Pinglo, as I had expected, the plane was not there, and we went to the farm on the opposite bank of the Río Santiago to bargain for the cattle that a farmer wants to sell; he has lived here for twenty-five years and is starting to find it too lonely. A cloudburst drove me onto the porch of his house, where I played with two newborn puppies. Not even the death of a chicken shall have been in vain.

The Pongo was twelve feet above flood stage, but sailing through it was not difficult. I stood in the stern and held on to the roof for support. Saramiriza was as desolate as ever, and I fell asleep in the little shop with my head on the table, while between my feet hens rested, their chicks under their wings and their feathers all puffed up; one of the chicks stuck its little beak out through the feathers of his mother's wing. The dogs were sleeping, everything was sleeping. Toward five in the afternoon a vehicle was leaving for the Estación Cinco, but an officious little man who had recently been put in charge of security up there would not let us get on; claiming all the seats were taken. Nearby, where the Williams pipeline folks once had their camp, all that remains is a leveled gravel area in the jungle, and around it, where there were dozens of brandy shacks, shops, and brothels, what is left are rotting timbers, like the skeletons of animals not native to the area. Between this dead zone and the pumping station at Cinco are a few utterly wretched wooden shacks, and we were able to spend the night in one of them. It is going to be a night of fleas, bedbugs, and mosquitoes. In the sandy area in front of the shack are a few wobbly tables and benches. Five glum Filipinos who work up at the station are sitting around, drinking warm beer and speaking Tagalog with each other, while for half an hour the same scratchy John Travolta record is played over and over again. Our gasoline drums that supposedly drifted upstream turned up here–empty–and the shack owner served up a story according to which he had bought them from a man whom he indignantly referred to as the thief. The man had died two months ago, however, and was thus hard to get hold of, unfortunately. César is coughing. He plans to go to Cuzco because there is some problem involving his house to deal with, as he says, and besides his Corsican wife is very pregnant.

Saramiriza, 20 August 1979

Soon the small transmitter in Saramiriza will be covered in a tangle of lianas and vines. They are already creeping from all sides up the guy wires. As we got to the river, a helicopter was just landing, being greeted with barking by one of the most wretched mutts I have ever laid eyes on. The dog was chasing the helicopter the way dogs sometimes chase a moving car, even though the draft from the rotor almost knocked it to the ground and was kicking up gravel at him. Then, at a slight distance, the dog lifted one leg and pissed in the direction of the helicopter.

Spending the night in the utterly miserable and shabby shack that tried to pass itself off as a hotel. It looked like a bedbugs' ballroom, but was not so bad in that respect. The hotel had an upper story, but the walls were bare boards and the building was half open on one side. There were no doors, and the floor had a large hole, covered with a sheet of black plastic to make it less noticeable. In the dark I stepped into the hole and descended in slow motion to the ground floor, pulling the plastic with me and landing in the midst of the innkeeper's sleeping family. I climbed back up to my room by a ladder. The corrugated tin roof leaked, but it rained only briefly during the night. The next morning I was awakened by the call of the whistling bird that I remembered from *Aguirre*. They call it a *wist-winsche*. I was wide awake immediately, because there were several of them calling and answering each other at the same time.

Last night I went to the kitchen, located in a wooden shack, sat down among the women and girls, and listened to their stories.

The river flows fast here. On the gravel bank on the other side two black cattle are at the river's edge, gulping water. We are going to wait all day for the plane. There is not a soul in the Saramiriza school, a rickety wooden structure. The hastily nailed-together wooden benches are deserted, and on the walls hang posters show-ing the nervous system, the useful and the harmful animals, the muscles, the cow's stomachs. A child's pencil drawing shows a cow, and beneath it various products from the cow are nailed to a board: representing leather, a piece from a battered, decommissioned soccer ball, a section of a belt, a shoe brush, gummy with black polish, but no shoe, not even a small piece of one. Representing cheese, pieces of tins from New Zealand that once contained cheese spread; represent-ing butter, three pieces of some kind of tin with an Australian label, in several sizes, probably taken from the lid and the body, each with a red ostrich feather; representing milk, tins from Nestlé and Ideal. A dog ran by on three legs. In the general store I took two warm Cokes from the refrigerator, which was not working and had become a breeding ground for cockroaches.

In the store, which has a total of two shelves, there are some T-shirts in cloudy plastic wrappers, the shirts wrinkled and discol-ored from exposure to the climate; also some rubber balls, padlocks, flashlight batteries. The entire upper shelf is filled with pictures of saints, the cheapest kind of print, the last gasp of the Nazarenes. One of the pictures shows the Virgin Mary appearing to the chil-dren of Lourdes, and Leonardo's *Last Supper* is also there, tipped on its side.

A primeval tortoise came crawling through the store, rocking its head and its body like an autistic person who wants to have nothing to do with the world. Outside pigs were grunting. The tortoise got stuck as it tried to squeeze under a plywood partition; its shell, which it cannot visualize, is too high, but it stubbornly works away, scrab-bling with its claws in a futile attempt to move forward. The wooden floor is smeared with oil and smells of rancid grease. From the court-yard in the back, strewn with garbage, where dogs and pigs dig in the dirt, came the cries of an infant, and I went outside to check because the infants here never cry. The child was lying naked on a bundle of cloth on the ground, and the tortoise, which had somehow worked its way out after all, had been turned on its back by the mother, so it would not crawl over the child. It was lying there with its head and legs completely drawn into its shell. The mother, half Indian, came and picked up the baby, a girl, and showed me that she had just pierced her ears, but instead of earrings had pulled a piece of string through each hole and knotted the ends. Out in front a pickup was being loaded with green bananas and papayas. The crates of fruit were being pitched up. As the papayas flew through the air, the catcher in the bed of the pickup, who had to stack them, was singing, and the men throwing them were working to the rhythm of his song.

When the float plane arrived, the only noteworthy event in the entire week, a few people here were spurred into action, a lethargic, reluctant action, as if this were a disruption, the incursion of history into the sluggish slumber of time. Last night an announcement came over the radio, allegedly from Gustavo for us, saying that the *Huallaga* is on the move in the direction of the Pongo de Manseriche. That cannot be true; now even the radio is spreading rumors. Nonetheless, our transmissions between seven and eight in the evening are our only connection to the camp on the Cenepa. César listens every evening to the transistor radio, when there is an hour of announcements about people being searched for and messages for strangers in the depths of the jungle.

The amphibious plane flew to Andoa first, and will presumably return here and then continue on to Iquitos. By noon it was hot, and the wait seemed very long. We rolled the gasoline drums down the bank and pushed them into the water. There they were fished out and loaded onto Segundo's large boat. This time we will at least get the gasoline to its proper destination, provided nothing goes wrong in the Pongo rapids. Our speedboat is stranded with gasket failure. The boatman forgot to take along spare parts and tools and is now waiting for a miraculous intervention that might revive the engine. Sweat, storm clouds overhead, sleeping dogs. There is a smell of stale urine. In my soup, ants and bugs were swimming among the globules of fat. Lord Almighty, send us an earthquake.

Iquitos, 21 August 1979
In the morning the goats leap, in the evening they have to sleep, Walter said to me at breakfast. Despite the jolly rhyme, the general mood is irritable, and I am probably going to have to let some people go, chief among them Alban, the woodcarver, who said he would deliver the figurehead a week ago, promised to do so without fail, but it turned out that he had not even procured the wood for it. I went and confronted him angrily. Yes, he had the wood, he swore, and showed it to me. So why would he not get to work right away? The wood had to dry first, he said, but tomorrow he would have the figurehead done. So how long would the wood need to dry? I asked. A week, a month, two years? No, not that long, he said firmly. So what was the next step, I asked. First he would turn the wood on the big lathe. I had him show me the lathe, and one look told me that it was a complete wreck, with the main axle broken. I asked whether he could replace the axle. Yes, soon. What did soon mean? Well, the axle had to be shipped from Miami–that was where the lathe was from. But he could carve the figure without the lathe, it would just take a little longer, a very little longer. With a pencil we scratched days and weeks onto a piece of plywood, and I added them up. According to my calculation, the figurehead could be done in three weeks at best, but more

realistically in five or six. At that Alban looked at me with a somnam-
bulistic gaze and said, no, not that long, no way. So when would he
be done, I asked. He gazed heavenward, quivering with fervor, like
one of the Nazarenes' saints, and exclaimed, *mañana*, tomorrow!

Problems with getting authorization for shooting–demands for
money from all sides. The top army general informed us that first he
had to issue a ruling on our project, and he did not know yet what
he would decide; it depended on us whether he would be able to give
formal confirmation of the existing permits, and I was so fed up that
I promptly went to see him without an appointment. I let him have
it and spoke so bluntly of the telltale signs of extortion that he stared
at me in amazement and wished me all the best, as if I were someone setting out to swim the Niagara Falls. The time for diplomacy is
past. My left leg is so inflamed from insect bites that it is swollen.

Iquitos, 22–23 August 1979
Yesterday at four in the morning, while it was still dark, Walter
shook me awake to tell me that in half an hour a plane would be leaving for Lima. Still groggy with sleep, I jumped into my clothes, then
into one shoe, then the other. But there seemed to be a sock bunched
up in the shoe. I reached in to pull it out, and suddenly instead of
a sock I was holding a tarantula, as big as my fist and hairy. At that
moment my heart stopped beating. I hurled the spider to the ground,
thinking, how banal and humiliating to die like this, and I considered briefly whether I should sit down or be whisked away standing.
When I decided to remain standing to see what would happen, my
heart began to beat again, first unevenly, like an engine that does not
want to start in the cold. Unreconciled with myself and the world of
big spiders, I sat in the jeep, saying not a word, and after a few kilo-

meters of tearing along the engine overheated because our watchman had forgotten to put water in the radiator, though when we asked him as we were leaving, he swore he had done so. The engine got so hot that it blew the radiator cap high into the air, after I had taken the precaution of loosening it with my sneaker. We found the cap on the jeep's roof. The airport offered a ghostly sight: all the lights were on, the terminal flooded with neon, but not a soul to be seen; we were the only ones in that eerie setting. Finally we found a guard. The flight had been canceled because the previous day a transport plane from Miami had torn a hole in the runway. That had thrown all the flight plans into confusion. Supposedly a flight to Cuzco would be taking off very soon, and from there it was possible to get to Lima. But I decided to stay here, even though it is urgent that we hold a press conference in Lima, because the rumors and allegations about us that people are spreading are getting crazier by the day.

On the street outside was a porter with ulcers on one leg; he had wrapped a cardboard box around the leg and tied it with string. It went from his ankle to his knee. In the evening to the Chinese restaurant, and then I went to see a film from India, *El Huerfanito*, "The Orphan," but the film had probably been mistitled by the distributor, because the plot had to do with a very rich man who suddenly became poor. Nonetheless he went on living in his palace, unmistakably a cheap set made of papier-mâché, with garlands of plastic flowers for decoration. There was a daughter to be married off, and the prospective bridegroom, a sleazy fellow with a little beard penciled on, fell in love on cue. Then songs were sung. Then came telephone calls. What? Horrors! said the rich man, who had a good heart, I am ruined. From then on there was lots of weeping, usually by four or five people at once, and the tears flowed most copiously when one of the sons was to leave home to get a job. All the poor folk in the town had already been invited to the wedding, which was called off now because the bridegroom's parents refused to have anything to do with an impoverished rich man. The poor folk stood outside the former rich man's door, weeping for him, but they looked like middle-class people, poorly disguised extras: only the one in the very front had a few symbolic rips in his sleeve. The poor folk at the door demonstrated their good hearts by rejecting the rich man's last money, which he wanted to give them, and insisting that they would pray for him to become rich again. The rest of the rich man's extended family formed picturesque tableaux in the background, then suddenly took one step forward in unison, and stood motionless, showing their emotion. That was the end of the film.

At breakfast Andreas had remarked that he was missing some underpants; every time the laundry was done, a few pairs disappeared, and he wondered whether Doña Rosa, to whom he turned jokingly, was stealing them and secretly wearing them. Doña Rosa, the little old Indian woman, screeched, clambered onto the table, lifted her skirt, dancing and laughing, and demonstrated that she had no underwear on at all. Every time I leave Iquitos, she gives me a big hug, and I press her to me; she reaches up only to my diaphragm. The last few times I have lifted her up to hug her.

At the market I saw a fish that must have weighed 430 kilos, a wide-mouthed, pale, giant fish without scales. The woman who was carving it up took an iron rod and brought it down hard on the upper edge of her butcher's knife to hack off the head. When the head was finally severed, I could see the heart, still pulsing and quivering. It kept on pumping for a long time, even though there was no blood left. I bought four liters of *siete raizes*, containing an admixture of slightly fermented wild honey and essence from the *chusuhuasi* root.

Today I gazed down for a long while at the floating town of Belén, as if for the last time. The rats scampering across the boards that form the ceiling above my bed kept me awake most of the night.

Lima, 26 August 1979
A completely pointless press conference given by us, grotesque from start to finish. The *Lima Times*, a little paper published in English, had reported that we had four Indians thrown into jail, made a habit of abusing Indians, and had destroyed their fields while shooting, and the news services are picking these stories up. What we have to say does not make a dent, because it does not make for a good story. Evaristo Nunkuag, chairman of the Indian Council, whom Wawaim does not want to have anything to do with, is being played up as the savior of those without rights, but no one cares to hear that he works as a contractor for the oil companies, recruiting Indian workers whom he exploits, or that he openly demanded bribes from us. There is no logic to the charge that we had four Indians arrested (how? by whom? where?), when practically all we are doing is maintaining a medical outpost, and the fact that we are far from ready to start shooting does nothing to disprove the allegations that we are ruining the Indians' fields during filming. Fortunately the half-Indian waiters in their white linen jackets took pity on me during this absurd scene and kept slipping me one *pisco* after another. I barely made it out of the hotel–and after that there is a gap in my memory. Walter said I pronounced a passerby the president of Peru, and then I must have bumped my head very hard on something. For a good while I did not know where I was, who I was, or why.

Telluride, Colorado, 31 August 1979

When the penguins hibernate in Antarctica–how, I do not know exactly; at any rate, it seems to be like what bears do: when they wake up in the spring without having had anything to eat for months, sometimes the ice shelf on which they spent the dark winter months has changed completely, so they have sixty or seventy kilometers to march before they reach the open sea. Scientists are trying to study the phenomenon of the marching penguins, and I saw films of penguins who had been put on treadmills, like in a fitness studio, with a kind of helmet fastened to their heads that allowed their brain waves to be measured. They march along steadily, their broad feet tapping, straight ahead, undeterred, their rhythm as even as a machine's, with mournful seriousness.

San Francisco was not pleasant. I felt completely out of place, especially in Broadway House. Errol Morris was suffering even more, because his latent hostility to Coppola's empty promises is becoming increasingly obvious. In addition, he was uneasy to the point of complete panic because as usual he has too much material but still no plot for his story about a small town in Florida where dozens of insurance fraud cases are uncovered by a detective working for an insurance company: policyholders keep losing limbs in the most absurd ways so they can bring enormous claims, but every time the accident leaves them with a combination of limbs–missing a leg or an arm, or one leg and one arm–that still permits them afterward to drive a Cadillac with an automatic transmission. I suggested to Errol that in the first scene, set in the town of Vernon, which the insurance companies privately call Nub City, which Errol wants to use as his film's title, he should show Junior attaching a self-shooting device to a tree so he can shoot off his left arm. He has a pot of tar heating up, into which he can plunge the stump to stop the bleeding, has already fastened the device to a branch with a wire attached to the trigger, so he can explain afterward that he was planning to attack a nest of vultures, when he notices at the last moment that he is being watched: the insurance company detective has come to town. From then on, the cops-and-robbers game can get under way, with the insurance investigator as the bad guy, the cop who tries to prevent the "accident," which Junior tries to pull off with increasingly clever techniques. In the end Junior triumphs when he succeeds in losing an arm.

We have no dinosaur, it says on a hand-lettered sign outside a farm that puts on rattlesnake rodeos.

A long, good evening visiting Satty, the painter. He told me about experiencing the war in Bremen, about the nights spent in bunkers. One time a bunker was destroyed by multiple-strike bombs, the ceiling caved in in front of him and buried 450 people. He spent two days and two nights in the water with his aunt, who held him up the entire time to keep his head above water–the water pipes had broken. After a day they heard the rescuers' jackhammers, and that gave them courage. He also described the postwar period in Bremen, which was wonderful for him; he and his playmates ruled over the ruins like kings. Wherever he went, he took along a hammer and chisel and a length of rope so he could collect scrap metal.

Telluride, 1 September 1979
Abel Gance talked to me for a long time about his idea for a fifteen-hour film on Columbus, which he wants to pass on to me, now that he has seen *Aguirre*. He says he is ninety, and it is too much for him. Half seriously, half jokingly, he said that he would like to die here, if that were acceptable. We drank red wine to that, straight from the bottle, and he remarked that he did not take anything seriously; he took everything tragically. Last night I saw his *Napoleon* outdoors, on a triple

screen. I was wrapped in a blanket against the piercing cold, for five long hours. This morning Abel Gance blocked a screening of his film *Beethoven*; he had not seen it in forty years, and he remembered everything so differently that he did not want to believe it was his film.

San Francisco, 6 September 1979

Loneliness, huge problems with the finances. This morning a reporter from *Spiegel* phoned me from Hamburg and read me the most far-fetched made-up stories, which he wants to publish. I simply told him I had no desire to be a dancing bear in his circus. I had a reunion with Constance Carroll, who was with me fifteen years ago in Pittsburgh, and hid me in the library and let me sleep there for a week, after I had impulsively given up my scholarship and as a result had no host family. Today she is the president of the college in Novato, and I was very happy to see that as a woman, and a black woman at that, she has come so far at such an early age. I had only a vague memory of what she looked like, but a vivid memory of her gentle voice. The group that once coalesced around her literary magazine has dissolved, and none of its members has amounted to anything. They never made it out of Pittsburgh, and now they have children, are divorced, have become alcoholics, live in suburbia. On the campus here large herds of deer, with forty or fifty animals, roam about at night, stripping all the plantings, and the college is located right on an active fault; anything else she could deal with more easily, she told me as we parted.

San Francisco, 7 September 1979

Yesterday I had opened the window in the bathroom, and the evening sun was shining in, clear and bright. I took my shoes and put them on the windowsill to air out, half inside, half outside, with the toes pointing in. Later I forgot they were there, and as I was washing my face I turned toward the window and was filled with terrible panic at seeing the shoes standing there empty, as if *no one* was climbing in the window.

San Francisco, 10 September 1979
For my birthday recently, Kitty, the female sheriff, secretly made me copies of the crime-scene photos from one of the Kemper murders, because she knew I had visited Kemper in the Vacaville jail. I returned the favor by going to see her Sunday morning in the prison here where she is in charge; it is the women's wing on the sixth floor of the justice department building, and on Sundays she is pretty much alone there, and no one objected to my bringing champagne. We had a jolly time, and I laughed a lot with Gabby, the whore who has become a trusty there. I should have smuggled in more alcohol.

New York, 29 September 1979
After a dramatic blow-up with his wife, a man rushes into the bathroom, hastily weighs himself on the scale, then shoots himself.

Munich–London, 8 October 1979
Big organizational and financing problems. Jack Nicholson wanted me to meet him on the set of *The Shining*; he said he would like to do something with me, but does not want to go to the jungle and wonders whether we could not shoot the whole thing at home in a studio. Kubrick heard that I was on the set, and because it happened to be

the midday break, invited me to lunch. A bucket brigade of assistants with walkie-talkies passed me along to him. We were very respectful, but did not have much to say to each other. Since I knew hardly anything about his project, I told him that I found his set impressive, and we talked about how he had to open with long traveling shots, without cuts.

In Los Angeles, Sandy Liebersohn confided to me that he was going to resign as president of Fox; no one else had been told, and I should keep it to myself. But insider news like this does not mean a thing to me because I am going to be on my own as a producer. For a moment the feeling crept over me that my work, my vision, is going to destroy me, and for a fleeting moment I let myself take a long, hard look at myself, something I would not otherwise do—out of instinct, on principle, out of self-preservation—look at myself with objective curiosity to see whether my vision has not destroyed me already. I found it comforting to note that I was still breathing.

Iquitos, 12 October 1979
In the *jefatura* Gustavo and I tried to get onto the flight going to Teniente Pinglo tomorrow. The fat young captain took us to a reception area that was the most pitiful thing I have seen in a long time. It had a clumsily made kidney-shaped table and an upholstered bench, as well as two chairs, all covered in the same yellowing plastic, already killed by the tropics. Just as there is a clinical death, there is a tropical death. The captain was young and pudgy, and complained he had gained thirty kilos sitting around in Iquitos. He had unbuttoned his shirt at the bottom to let his belly fat spill out more comfortably. His hair was dripping with sweat. He offered us Coke and leaned back against the wall. When he got up, the wall was damp with sour sweat.

I had heard from Walter by radio that the situation on the Cenepa was critical. He intends to hang in there, however, because of the contracts, but all he sees is the formal legal situation, whereas I am in favor of a total break and a completely new start.

Santa Maria de Nieva, 14 October 1979
Seen from the air, the jungle below looked like kinky hair, seemingly peaceful, but that is deceptive, because in its inner being nature is never peaceful. Even when it is denatured, when it is tamed, it strikes back at its tamers and reduces them to pets, rosy pigs, which then melt like fat in a skillet. This brings to mind the image, the great metaphor, of the pig in Palermo, which I heard had fallen into a sewer shaft: it lived down there for two years, and continued to grow, surviving on the garbage that people threw down the shaft, and when they hauled the pig out, after it had completely blocked the drain, it was almost white, enormously fat, and had taken on the form of the shaft. It had turned into a kind of monumental, whitish grub, rectangular, cubic, and wobbly, an immense hunk of fat, which could move only its mouth to eat, while its legs had shrunk and retracted into the body fat.

Festival of the Virgen de Fatima in Santa Maria de Nieva, with a soccer tournament, a procession, and dancing. Les Blank filmed the photographer who sets up an ancient camera with bellows and does his developing on the spot. He took a picture of me. First he gave me a comb and said I should comb my hair, then sat me down on a stool. His shutter is the lid from an oil canister, which he pulls away with a flourish for a second, while with the other hand he shades the lens. The negative that he develops, poking around inside his camera, he then rephotographs with a frame of roses, birds, and maxims, which gives him a print. During the procedure he carries on a conversation with two voluble little parrots, which he keeps in a basketlike pouch attached to the tripod.

We traveled a stretch up the Nieva to see Grimaldo, the cook, where we were served fairly warm beer, and since I had already done some drinking at the fiesta, we went to the nearby waterfall and positioned ourselves under it. Les and I let the water pound down on us; it felt like a herd of cattle trampling me, but afterward I was quite refreshed and also sober.

The reports on us have stopped referring to jailed Indians; somehow that has been taken care of. I did some investigating in Santa Maria, checking on the names that had been mentioned. Three of the four who were named had never had anything to do with us and had also never been in jail, but the fourth had in fact been locked up here for about a week. He had run up debts in about thirty stores and bars and was on the point of making himself scarce, so a barkeeper had him arrested. He, too, had had no contact with us. In the meantime new reports are circulating to the effect that we are dealing in weapons and drugs. Tomorrow I plan to go directly to the Consejo de Aguarunas y Huambisas in Napuruka, even though they are warning me here that I would be killed there immediately. A political agitator, a Frenchman, is living there now, and in Wawaim two Germans have turned up, apparently from the Society for Endangered Peoples, who are handing around pictures of Auschwitz with heaps of skeletons, as an argument against me.

Santa Maria de Nieva–Wachintsa, 16 October 1979
After only two hundred meters we had to turn back, because the engine was not running properly. Walter had set out shortly before us in the

completely overloaded speedboat; he had invited the five musicians from the fiesta to go along, with their microphones, amplifier, and Hammond organ. Only the thrust of the engine kept the boat slightly above the waterline and prevented it from sinking. We managed to locate a replacement engine for our big wooden boat, and set out again. An Aguaruna woman with tattoos on her face and upper thighs spoke to me, gesticulating wildly and apparently asking to be taken along. I went to the bow and fetched the boatman, who had to sound the depth of the river in the shallower spots with a pole, and had him translate. Where did she want to go? To Pinglo, downriver, and from there to Iquitos, she answered agitatedly. She was very put out that I could not speak Aguaruna–she found that unnatural. I asked why she wanted to go to Iquitos; was not her family here, and what did she want to do in Iquitos? But all she said was that she wanted to go to the city of Iquitos; she did not know anyone there. I asked whether she did not have a husband and children here. At the same time I tried to make it clear to her that there was nothing for her in Iquitos, that they would not understand her, either, since only Spanish was spoken. With agitated gestures she then talked about her husband, and the pilot was reluctant to translate. Her story was as follows: her husband had run away with their eldest daughter; he did not want his wife anymore and had taken their daughter as his wife. When we pushed off–I had told her again that we were traveling in the opposite direction, upstream–she suddenly jumped into the boat after all. She wanted to get away, it did not matter where to. After a few hundred meters, however, she asked us to tie up again so she could get off, because on the bank she had spotted a woman with a baby whom she knew well. When she got off, she did not go straight onto land but hiked up her skirt first and washed her legs.

We made a stop in Napuruka, and I climbed the long, steep bank alone to the large village at the top, to see for myself how much truth there was to the story that I would be killed if I showed my face there. I was wondering what good it would do to kill me, but maybe such a question is too Western. When I got to the top, the children gazed at me solemnly in silence, as if a prisoner in shackles were passing by. Two young men with machetes in their hands approached me, and for a moment it looked as though they were prepared to undertake the fine deed that would bring them everlasting glory, the way in medieval armies the greatest honor accrued to the first knight to advance on the enemy. But I saw a few members of the Consejo whom I knew, and asked them whether I could confer with someone in their village so as to hear whether there were charges against me. For the time being that defused the momentary and perplexed tension. I asked whether it was possible to sit down at a table with the Consejo and talk. In no time people converged from all sides. Evaristo Nunkuag was there, along with most of the council members, and they asked me formally whether I was armed, whether I would permit a body search. That was mostly for the benefit of the villagers, to show that the council was exercising its authority here. Obviously I had no objection, I said, and they patted me down and turned my pockets inside out. Since all I had was a Kleenex, they confiscated the most dangerous object I had–my sunglasses.

The members of the Consejo de Aguarunas were enthroned at a table on a podium, and soon they had a thick packet of papers in front of them, whereas I was placed on a stool, with my back to the assembled villagers. Things took a wrong turn at the very beginning, starting with the reading of resolutions and communiqués in stilted bureaucratic Spanish. I was not really allowed to speak, which I did not want to do anyway; I wanted to listen. Interestingly enough, the resolutions had to do with demands for legal jurisdiction, to be exercised by an autonomous Indian administration, with a military presence and an appropriate share in the oil revenues. There were several references to unification with the Aguarunas' brothers and sisters over the border in Ecuador, an obvious provocation to the national integrity of Peru. They wanted to force me to sign a declaration immediately, to the effect that I recognized the sovereignty of the council over the entire region, including Wawaim, and that as a sign of this recognition I would withdraw from the Wawaim area.

I replied that most people in Wawaim had never heard of them, and from what I knew those who did know had rejected the extension of the council's jurisdiction to their territory. At that, the mood became menacing, and they locked the door and would not let me leave. All right, I said, if the assembly had more to say to me, I would be glad to take the time. Only then did a free exchange take place with the villagers behind me, with questions and fears expressed that actually had something to do with me: did I intend to settle here for good; they were having all sorts of problems with three Aguaruna families that had moved into their village. Did I plan to dig a canal between the Marañón and Cenepa rivers? Did I know what the military was up to with all the new garrisons it was establishing?

I asked them to explain the reports that on my instigation Aguarunas had been jailed. The council conferred for a while, whispering in Aguaruna, and then told me they had no knowledge of any prisoners. Yet this story had been given to the press by Evaristo Nunkuag. Altogether, the people here are very skilled in dealing with the media: when he is here, Evaristo wears a particularly fine example of a "Disco Fever" T-shirt that is very popular in these parts, and with it Ray-Ban designer sunglasses, but the protection-seeking Indians he brings to his news conferences in Lima have their faces painted, are wearing feathers, and carry their bows and arrows. After several hours of listening, which included hearing more communiqués read aloud, the assembly ran out of steam, and we quietly went our separate ways, after shaking hands. I had pointedly left my sunglasses there, and someone came running after me with them as I was heading back to the boat.

On the way to Wachintsa I used Maureen's umbrella to protect myself from the sun. Shortly before we reached the Urakusa military outpost, a gust of wind blew it out of my hand, and it landed on the water, with the handle sticking up in the air. This image impressed me so much that I quickly wrote a scene into the script. To round out the day, I had a confrontation at the garrison with the sentries, who wanted to confirm my personal information down to the smallest detail: hair color, race (!), number of children, mother's maiden name. I said I had supplied this information many times already, and lately people had simply accepted the form I had filled out previously. At that point the guard turned snotty, and I went to find the major, who had always impressed upon us that we should stop in to see him if there was any trouble; he knew us, and did not much care for bureaucracy. But the major was not there, so I simply went back down to the boat, but then realized they would shoot if I sailed on without registering. A soldier came running to say I should come back immediately; they had located the major, and he wanted to speak with me. I said the major should come to me if he wanted anything of me; I would go back only if they arrested me. Up above a palaver with César Vivanco took place, the major did not come down to the river, and I did not go up to the garrison. I went swimming in the river, and nothing happened. We simply sailed on.

This evening there was a strange bug crawling on my hand, like a primeval armored creature, one I had never seen before, and I watched it for a long time, fascinated. The frogs, the *ʒapos*, croak in querulous and mournful tones, and they all break off at once, as if there were a conductor among them. At night I had the feeling that there had been an earthquake in the distance. For a moment the countryside quivered and shook, and my hammock began to sway gently.

Wachintsa, 18 October 1979
As if the outside world with its commotion and earthquakes did not exist, as if an existence of insular harmony were within the realm of possibility, six Aguarunas from Wawaim are working in a zigzag with shovels and machetes to clear a firm path up to the *comedor*, up to me. They joke and talk about a girl they say is pretty. In the surrounding jungle the birds carry on their conversation without agitation, tranquilly. With his ax a man is hacking away at a felled tree trunk, which under his regular blows is slowly and willingly taking on the form of a dugout. Cows roam among the huts, large and gentle and slow-witted. The bull, an animal of immense proportions and colossal strength, stood next to me for a long time under a roof, letting himself be fanned by the wind and flapping his ears. He looked at me quietly and sadly, and when he left, he was limping badly. Apparently he got a large thorn stuck in his front hoof. In the kitchen beer and soda have run out. Les, who had hauled his camera up here and then did not find any beer, sat in silence for a long time, and when I asked him what was wrong, he said he had to get over this traumatic experience before he started working. He sat there for a good quarter of an hour brooding, then gradually came to life again.

Wachintsa–Pongo de Manseriche–Saramiriza–Iquitos,
19 October 1979

A confused day, which began with a visit from Nelson, the one-eyed Indian from Nueva Vida, who came to tell us about reprisals to which he had been subjected; allegedly, though I have my doubts about this, he had been summoned to appear before the justice of the peace from Chiriaco, who does not even have jurisdiction over his district, on a charge of high treason against his community, a crime that does not exist. His mother was with him and stood there on the gravel bank, crying, gesticulating, and afraid for her son, who has the reputation of being a *brujo*, a male witch, but because he was spurned by everyone I had felt bad for him and had given him a job.

We decided to sail downstream, showed our identification papers in Urakusa, where I had a bad argument with the major over the French agitator Eric Sabourin, whom the aliens bureau wanted to expel. Les filmed the confrontation, and the photographer from *Stern* magazine, who is with us, took pictures. The major had the film and the tape confiscated, but those involved managed to turn over only unexposed material. The photographer pulled a roll of unexposed film out of his camera and made a big show of trampling it as it curled on the ground, meanwhile managing surreptitiously to take further pictures of the soldier who was seizing a reel of Les's film. The major, who had been the boastful megalomaniac, claiming to be the king here, the one who made everything happen and solved all problems, shriveled in a matter of minutes, with the cameras running, to the sphincter of his own asshole.

In Santa María de Nieva an absurd discussion with the police *sargento*, who harrumphed that he would get the Frenchman, he would "put the kid in the shade for a while," and wanted to know if we would lend him our boat for the operation, and Walter, the fool, was all for lending it to him, but I said absolutely not. It turned out that the *sargento* actually wanted the boat so he could go and bring his deputy back from Saramiriza; the man had been lying around there drunk for the last two months, with all the wages for the police station here.

We spent the night there. In the evening the place was completely dead. My foot is badly inflamed, and there are problems. In one of the huts an older man was sitting with a book by a kerosene lantern, reading out loud to himself. On the grocer's counter two scrawny boys were sleeping, their lanky limbs contorted, as if an explosion had hurtled them into a terrible, everlasting sleep. I gazed up at the starry sky, and it seemed as alien to me as I do to myself.

We hurried the next morning (Saturday?) to get to Saramiriza with the boat, so as to make the plane to Iquitos. On the way we saw an exhausted deer in the river, and I grabbed it by the hind legs and pulled it out of the water onto the boat. It thrashed around, but we managed to tie it down. It sighed loudly as we were holding it down and tying its legs together. Its coat was covered with little burrlike leaves, which were stuck to it.

Iquitos, 21 October 1979
Waiting, glowering sun, inactivity. Last night I had a fever. I played Zapo and hit the frog several times in the mouth with the thick bronze coin. On the way to Belén I saw a procession following a statue of the Blessed Virgin. The music up ahead was provided by a small, flat drum, a conch shell, and a little tin whistle, thin and capable of only four notes. An Indian was playing it. He was wearing a plastic hard hat, with the logo of a local company.

There is a kind of uneasiness bordering on panic that does not have its roots in anything factual–unlike the situation in Wawaim, which actually would give reason for unease–but is completely illogical: I had received two telexes, one of them from the U.S., with mysterious content; I have the impression it contains an extremely important message, but I cannot find it. It is lost. I have looked everywhere, then looked again, but the message is gone. I sleep badly and wake up with a start at the crack of dawn, wondering where that message can be. The actual news coming from Wawaim, all garbled on the radio due to electrical storms, cannot be understood. When Walter speaks German, scratchy fragments come through that might just as well be texts in Assyrian cuneiform; only when he speaks Spanish does an isolated word make it through to us. Upon leaving Wawaim I had a sense I was seeing the place for the last time.

Belén caught up as usual in its comforting tropical chaos. Pigs in the bog, children in such large numbers that there might as well be no adults, games of Zapo. A man was unloading large fish, *dorados*, and told me he watched the surface of the water and could tell when the *dorados* were hunting smaller fish in the warm, brown depths; that was when he cast his nets. All afternoon a phonograph record kept playing the same scratchy song about *corazón*, the heart. Gisela told me the telexes had turned up on the bottom of the swimming pool, murky with algae. Since then the day has taken on a different coloration.

Iquitos, 23 October 1979

During the night from Sunday to Monday I developed a high fever. My leg was throbbing and hammering, and the lymph gland on the left side of my groin swelled up and got very hard. In the morning there was a lot of pus in my foot. I drove to the new production house because only one of the telexes had been found in the swimming pool; the really mysterious one was still missing. Because I assumed that the paper had not been thrown into the pool on purpose but had been picked up by a storm gust and blown there the day before, I hunted all around the garden and near the swimming pool; finally I remembered the direction from which the last storm had come, followed that lead, and found the missing piece of paper.

I received a telex describing what a cherub is. Then I realized that I was developing a high fever and lay down upstairs in Gisela's bed, hoping she would let me rest there. She made a poultice for my calf, and I started taking antibiotics. I was sick all day, and then the fever began to subside. I had received another telex, monosyllabic, saying it was the twilight of the gods, and I knew who had sent it and what the code meant. Then I was in the high mountains, Hindu Kush or the Himalayas, and at a great altitude I had to fight my way forward, sunk up to my chest in powder snow. I was going downhill to reach an enormous gorge where a stream was roaring. Two mountain climbers were roped below me and did not want to believe that I was following alone. The stream had eleven waterfalls. You could grope your way toward the first ones along a layer of ice, down the middle of which, a sort of groove, roared an open, foaming rivulet. The first of the waterfalls was the size of Victoria Falls–by moonlight–which made the proportions even greater. It cascaded straight down with a roar, and from below steam and foam billowed up toward me. I threw myself into the falls, but knew as I did so that there would be no going back, that I would then have to pass through the next ten cataracts. I had to rely on my hearing as my guide, because it was impossible to see anything amid the foaming vapors rising from those unspeakable abysses, but I could tell by the sound whether the waterfalls ended in a basin or struck rocks. I was spun around, weightless, as the water hurtled me downward, and then came the impact, as I was tossed hither and yon, the struggle against the massive wall of water that was descending on me. From the sixth waterfall on, still at least half the size of Niagara Falls, there was no more ice; and of course it must have been two or three thousand meters lower in altitude. Finally we emerged from under the eleventh waterfall, the mountain climbers and I, to find alpine pastures. We shook hands, for during the descent we had never been close enough to do so. We struck out along a path. Farther down we came upon an unoccupied mountain-patrol cabin, but we did not want to go in because it belonged to the Christian Socialist Union Party, which held socials there for the rural population. Finally we descended through a forest to a village. The first building was a musty stone goat shed. In the dim interior, damp and oppressively warm, sat my best friends from my childhood; they spent almost all their time there, pale, dirty, and pimply, almost rotting away from the bad air. They always sat half beneath a staircase, leaning against a damp stone wall and getting drunk on stale beer. So there they sat and stared at me, their eyes glazed and stupefied in their pocked, fleshy faces, and it struck me like a bolt of lightning that they had been sitting there just the same way when I had set out half a year earlier; they had not even left the musty corner to pee, but simply went on the shed floor. One of them was Kainz Ruepp, who had become a milker on the Fraueninsel in Chiemsee Lake and burned to death in his bed, presumably from a cigarette he had neglected to stub out.

A little girl led an even littler girl along a dusty road out into the world. A small green parrot was clinging to the older girl's other hand and was speaking. The girls said nothing because the dust was so hot and parched their throats. The dust burned beneath their naked soles. The first houses were built on stilts. Plowing the centuries, today a dark sun rose, solemn and heavy, above the jungle, which was full of poisons. Orchids in heat steamed. The jungle reeked of sweetish sweat and fornication.

. . .

Eight months expunged, as if I wished they had never happened. A year of catastrophes, personal and related to my work. After the camp on the Río Marañón had been abandoned, except for the medical station, it was set on fire by the Aguarunas of the Indian Council. Newspaper photographers from Lima were invited to witness the event. I was made out by the media to be a criminal, and a grotesque tribunal was convened in Germany to judge me. Nonetheless I pressed on, knowing, or possibly only hoping, that time would show things in their proper light, that the facts would ultimately triumph over all the rest. Money troubles. I was so broke that I had nothing to eat. In Iquitos I sold two bottles of American shampoo at the market and bought four kilos of rice, which would feed me for three weeks. My daughter was born; something beautiful will remain.

A loose, undated slip of paper tucked between the pages: life is either dead on or dead off.

Iquitos, 2 July 1980
Upon my arrival, several large pieces broke off my incisor, which had been knocked out and replaced by a crown. I kept the crumbled fragments because I associate them with the most awful dreams, namely that my teeth are made of limestone, hollow inside, and liable at any time to be chewed up and crushed, like the most fragile stalactites formed in caves.

When a massive rainstorm moved in at noon, the music on my radio was like the intermittent buzzing of many insects. All the cassettes I left here months ago have been stolen, with only a few of the plastic cases remaining. The news and the photos César just brought from the upper Ucayali are bad; there is almost no area left where we would have the geographical features I need for the film. Gloria, Walter's wife, is in her ninth month, her face so altered that at first I did not recognize her. I knew her, but I did not recognize her. W. is sure it is going to be a boy; the *bruja* prophesied that, the same one who magically healed his stomach ulcers.

Iquitos, 3 July 1980

Profoundly unreconciled to nature, I had an encounter with the big boa constrictor, which poked its head through the chicken wire surrounding its wooden cage and looked me fearlessly in the eye for a long time. Stubbornly confronting each other, we were pondering the relatedness of the species. Both of us, since the relatedness was slight, felt sad and turned away from each other. Out by the garden wall, in the direction of the banana plants, a washhouse had been built, with fresh concrete poured for the floor, but before the concrete had a chance to set up, ants had built canals and tunnels through it. Yesterday four motorcycles were supposed to have arrived from the U.S. by plane, but they are nowhere to be found. During my flight over the Andes I was able to see the Huascaran from very close up; its crevasses and glaciers were so forbidding and the mountain maintained its solitude so majestically that it took my breath away. Beyond it I saw the entire Sierra Blanca.

A plan to have a hut built for me on the edge of the jungle. I still have not found my way to the lagoon through the forest. There is a swampy area that can be crossed only when it is completely dried out. Walter's rice crop out there never amounted to anything, because although the rice grew, no one wanted to harvest it. Now weeds are taking over the rice paddy.

Iquitos–Pucallpa, 4 July 1980
News from Wawaim that the oil prospectors have established a major foothold with Evaristo Nunkuag's help, that he has signed a contract with them and is busy recruiting workers for them. It is possible that they have been planning for a long time to force us out because we would have tied up too many workers. Whatever the reason, it is not relevant anymore. I have to reorganize the entire production from scratch.

Iquitos–Pucallpa, 5 July 1980
Searching for a possible location. For reasons that could not be determined, we had been stricken from the train's passenger list, but somehow we managed to get on board. I sat on a fold-down seat next to an Indian woman with her one-year-old daughter, who clung to my finger for an hour and looked me fearlessly in the eye. Walter had arrived in the morning and brought aerial photographs of the entire Ucayali, Tambo, and Pachitea regions, pieced together from small individual shots. My collarbone, which is half separated from my breastbone, hurts. It was news to me that there is a kind of meniscus there. I am just lucky that the injuries to the vertebrae in my neck did not leave me a paraplegic, as Lucki was initially told would be the case.

Studied the aerial photos carefully with several pilots. They make no promises. I saw a child that had painted itself all over with green paint, and I saw a crippled young woman in shorts climbing into a tree with her crutches.

I have 450,000 *soles* on me, bundled tightly to form a sort of large brick. The packet is as heavy as a brick, too. When I went to lie down, the packet reeked so strongly of stale sweat that I wrapped the money in a plastic bag and tied it up tightly.

Pucallpa, 6 July 1980

We got up early and ran into the German, Maulhardt, who has a tourist lodge on the Yarinacocha lagoon. It turned out that he owns a small plane and has highly detailed maps. Mostly because of those maps we went out to his place and had a long talk with the pilot. Everything here is focused on tourism in the most appalling way. That is the real sin.

Before my eyes a painting was condensing into shape; it could not decide between a tropical rain-forest theme and an East African savannah, even though this blending appeared perfectly natural. So it was a jungle, and two elephants were tearing leaves off the trees with their trunks, and then on the riverbank were some antelopes and hippopotamuses. They stood there motionless: as in a painting. Through the branches, very clearly visible, shone the full moon. Then one of the elephants started, turned its head, and stared at the moon, so startled that the other elephant took notice. Now the antelopes also jerked their heads out of the brackish water and likewise looked up at the moon, and at that I became aware that it was not the moon but the earth which had risen. The entire continent of Africa stood out clearly. Next the first elephant broke into a gallop and fled, while the second, in spite of its colossal size, raced off in the opposite direction like a rabbit in flight, taking great leaps, whereupon the antelopes streaked in a panic into the forest. Only then did one of the hippopotamuses turn languidly, wondering where the other animals had gone; it stared at the moon, and because its mind worked slowly, did not realize that the earth on which it was standing had risen in the sky. It looked so helplessly stupid that you could not help being moved. The painter working on the painting swished his brush around in the dabs of paint on a mahogany board, and after I had watched him for a while, I knew that he was only pretending to be painting; in reality he would never paint, only mix colors, for all eternity.

Before sundown César and I rode to the other side of the lagoon to have a look at the lodge the American missionaries were having built. They are here under the pretext of doing linguistic research to further destroy the Indians' culture. From a distance the roofs with their stepped rows of skylights looked good, but on closer inspection the huts the people here build are much better. Many of the missionaries were out swimming and sunning their obese bodies like pigs on a small wooden platform, and German tourists were taking pictures. A woman photographer from north Germany asked me whether I was the *one*, and I said, yes, that was me, and then preserved such a silence that she did not dare try to make conversation.

The Río Pachitea is a disappointment–along almost its entire length up to Puerto Inca, just one *chakra* and cow pasture after another. The few steeper spots between bends in the river are all almost vertical with flattish tops like those of tabletop mountains. There is some hope along the Río Picha and the Río Pachitea, but the thought of building a camp there for the entire production team and almost a thousand extras terrifies me, because the nearest larger town, like Iquitos, is fourteen hundred kilometers away. Every nail, every gram of salt would have to be brought in from there.

Pucallpa–Yarinacocha, 7 July 1980

An entire school of small fishes leaped out of the water as our boat passed. I saw a stuffed alligator, standing upright supported by its tail and singing to the accompaniment of a guitar. The alligator was also wearing sunglasses. A young man was holding five small alligators by the head and wanted to sell them to me. At first I thought they were dead, because they were drooping, but it was probably from exhaustion, because the seller insisted on demonstrating how much life was left in them by holding his lit cigarette lighter to their tails, which made them writhe like snakes. A young woman was suckling a newborn piglet that had been orphaned. Once the pigs are fully grown, saddlebags are hitched to their backs for loads, and then off they go. The Indian women like gold teeth. The powers of heaven are powerless against the jungle.

Earlier, on Río Huallaga, the boat stopped where actually no village was to be seen. Other than a dock and a corrugated tin shed filled with broken engines there was nothing, but there must have been some huts farther into the jungle, because I heard chickens and the shouts of children. The captain and crew had disappeared without a word. At first no one noticed, but when evening came and there was nothing for the passengers to eat, anxiety began to take hold. This situation lasted for two days, and it turned out that the entire crew had got drunk on beer and was holed up in a village brothel.

In my French grammar book there was a picture of Camus engaged in a philosophical conversation with an intelligent, somewhat older man about human beings' right to exist on this earth. He was squatting casually, his weight resting on one knee, on a road that wound up a mountainside, and it was nice to see a philosopher speaking so spontaneously. He was squatting near a low stone parapet, whitewashed, obviously there to keep vehicles from tumbling into the ocean. The harbor in the background looked a bit like Dubrovnik or a small town on the Côte d'Azur. I heard the two of them talking, then laughing out loud. Then one of Camus's legs must have gone to sleep, and he shifted his weight. I could see the man he was talking to only from behind or at an angle over his shoulder. Then Camus straightened up from his squatting position. All the time while he was philosophizing, he had been feeling gas in his stomach and thinking of nothing else as he laid out his arguments. The dialogue was printed on the left side of the book. All the women and children gathered around a glowing fire nearby looked around. On the fire a fish was grilling.

At night it was quiet. Only the stars sang, far off. A few stars came shooting down. Wagner, a naked little Indian boy with a distended stomach, not yet able to speak, was pushed toward me among the silent observers. Another child, about five, asked whether I wanted him; little Wagner did not have either a father or a mother, only his shadow.

Yarinacocha, 8 July 1980
We are going to fly up the Río Ucayali/Urubamba as far as the rapids; there is still hope that the Río Picha, the Río Camisea, and maybe the Río Mishagua will work out. But if we cannot find a suitable place, there is nothing left in this country. The Río Pachitea and Río Huallaga can be written off, and that would be it. Weather: a little cloudy. We are not going to take off until almost nine, because the mist does not clear in the mountains until about ten in the morning. We buy a few cans of food, sugar, Nescafé, and three papayas, just in case there is nothing to be had on the Camisea.

I was told that the *Lima Times* of 20 June reported that I had almost finished filming without permission, and there was some nonsense about United Artists, probably that they were behind the whole thing as producers, but apparently no else is picking up that version. Maybe no one is interested in the story anymore. Otherwise the usual: on the back of a motorcycle a pole was fastened horizontally with a dozen live chickens attached by their feet, and also a tied-up hog. Their heads were dragged in the dust kicked up by the rear tire.

Camisea, 9 July 1980

Yesterday we flew over Atalaya, then over the secret penal colony on the Sepa, where dangerous criminals serve their time without walls and barbed wire, imprisoned by the jungle, so to speak. All of them have sentences of at least ten years. From there to the Picha, the Camisea, and the Pongo de Mainique. At the Pongo it took me a while to realize that what looked like clouds in the distance were actually snow-covered mountains. The Pongo itself, a good show, is not passable for us with a large boat, because when the water level is low, as it is now, the Urubamba is not navigable, so out of the question, and when the water is high, the current will be too strong.

In the village of Camisea the Machiguenga Indians had put up a soccer goal at the beginning of the runway, which made the landing somewhat perilous. The village consists of a row of about fifteen huts along the bumpy grass strip. Completely different types from those along the upper reaches of the Marañón, a friendly attitude, and children who crowded around us and reciprocated when we shook hands, except that this form of greeting is unknown to them, so they offered us their wrists, a little fist, or stretched out their fingertips toward us. We ate a few bananas that they brought us and recruited two guides with machetes so we could check out the ridge that occupies the isthmus of land between the Río Camisea and the Río Urubamba. A very arduous hike through the jungle until we reached the almost perpendicular spot from which the two rivers should have been visible, but the vegetation was too dense, and the view of the whole site will be accessible only from a platform built in one of the treetops. Exhausted and drenched in sweat, I threw myself into the Urubamba when we got to the bottom, and immediately felt little fishes swarming around my blistered foot and nibbling bits of skin. In the end, I was just panting and stumbling through the vines after the guide, but we got back to the village too late to fly on to the Picha. There was a chicken available, for an astronomical price, but no one to cook it, so we let it go and ate tuna fish with onions and lemon juice. I downed tea by the liter. The family who had given us a pot of hot water crowded around, and we fixed tuna for them and gave them tea; that is how it is done here–food is always shared, César says, which is why there is no word for "thank you" in their language.

At night I slept fitfully, plagued by worries and freezing cold. Also the bats, against which we had put up the mosquito nets, kept fluttering around my hammock. In the morning I saw that the pilot was sleeping in my blanket, which had disappeared suddenly, that is to say, he had it inside his sleeping bag, and during the night, when I was so cold that I got up to put on a long-sleeved shirt, César was lying on my duffle bag, which he had taken to use as a pillow. How and where are we supposed to set up a camp here and keep it going? No one has any salt, candles, or string–a man I asked for a piece so I could put up my hammock gave me the string from his bow. In the end I used a length of liana bark.

After eight in the morning we flew to Picha and met there the fat Dominican padre who looks more like a tavern keeper. Another man, a Spaniard, with a dark beard and smeared with oil, was working on a tractor, which was beyond repair. Later I saw him sitting on it, and thirty or forty children were pulling him with a rope across the cow pasture. The tractor was puffing white and black smoke from places where no smoke should have been coming out, and refused to jump-start. Inquiries about the Picha and the Urubamba, fruitless. From the fat man I purchased a *cushma*, one of the Machiguengas' almost ankle-length nightshirtlike tunics, woven from a nearly indestructible fiber, for Gisela Storch to use as a prototype. The two Spanish padres are quite obviously living in a marriagelike state with the two Indian schoolteachers; one could tell from the women, but not so much from the priests, who remained rather discreet in the presence of strangers.

Thought for a long time about the inertia and the unique rhythms of cultural history, for instance why the Middle Ages did not end in Serbia, Macedonia, Bosnia, and Albania until two or three centuries later than elsewhere, and in some parts of that region still have not ended.

Pucallpa–Yarinacocha, 10 July 1980
I got up very early because out on the porch mosquitoes and ticks were swarming all over me, and went down to the boat landing. I had a sense of great delight when I saw the lagoon. Some seabirds were fishing, an early *peke-peke* sailed by with a heavy load, and farther off the mist was rising from the jungle. I heard someone in the house laughing quite shamelessly and unabashedly, but it was such a strange laugh that I soon realized it was one of the two parrots here. Workmen were tossing boards from one pile onto another next to it, and even after considerable reflection I could not see any rhyme or reason to what they were doing.

In town several streets were blocked off. Indian schoolgirls were marching in Prussian goosestep, three abreast, practicing for the parade on the national holiday. They were wearing uniforms consisting of knee-length gray skirts and white blouses, with suspenders. They kept their hands flat at their sides to diminish any wind resistance and swung their arms, slicing the air to accompany their brisk steps. We rode to the Shipibo village of San Francisco, which is devoted entirely to the tourist trade. All the textiles look as if they were made in Hong Kong. I bought a few samples for Gisela and left the place feeling quite depressed. The harbor of Pucallpa, which I had a closer look at, is so chaotic and run-down that just the thought of ever having to ship anything from here terrified me.

Across from the wretched Pucallpa airport is a bar with a beautiful monkey, black, with limbs that go on forever. He looks very intelligent and would make the ideal companion for Fitz. A drunk spat at the monkey and almost hit him from behind. The monkey inspected and sniffed with great interest at this globule from the depths of an unhealthy lung, as it lay on the ground, greenish yellow and steaming. It looked as though the monkey wanted to eat the spit, or at least taste it. I said silently to him, Leave it, leave it alone, and he let it be. Now he is sitting with his tail wrapped around his buttocks like a rope, his knees under his chin, and his arms around his knees. That is how he sits when he is chained to a tree limb. I realized I was sitting the same way, with my feet propped in the rungs of a second chair and my knees under my chin. Does the monkey dream my dreams in the branches above me? I ordered a beer, and my voice sounded altered, like the voice of a parrot imitating operatic arias. The sun sank in an angry blaze. For a moment, and for the only time I think I can remember, the earth struck me as motherly, covered with a decaying forest that seemed positively humble. A large brown moth was boring into the smooth concrete floor as if it wanted to go down into the earth, and beating its wings so violently that the wooden sound it created blended with the electrical hissing and crackling of a dying fluorescent bulb overhead like a symphony from the depths of a ghastly universe, a universe readying itself for the final harvest.

Iquitos, 11 July 1980

We reached Iquitos at eleven in the evening. Walter had been sick for a few days. In the morning I sent off several telexes to Munich and Los Angeles, because of Mick Jagger. The young cat here has caught a lizard whose front third is green, the rest brown and spotted. The cat was tormenting the lizard to death, like a mouse, and in its terror it sought refuge in one of my pant legs, but I did not want that, either. When the lizard stops moving for a while, with only its throat sac pulsating, the cat stretches out, half on her back, striking out rapidly with her paws until the lizard darts off again. One of its hind legs is already dragging and does not work anymore.

I settled in for a stay in Iquitos and hung some of the Shipibos' textiles on the wall and over the window. Then I fastened two pieces of wood to the wall to serve as a bulletin board. I pinned up aerial photos of Camisea, along with photos of Burro, the ski jumper Steiner, and Lotte Eisner. I was mulling over plans for colonies in space, but aside from a few maneuvers in Antarctica there was nothing doing.

Iquitos, 12 July 1980

A dead tarantula, tacked to a piece of Styrofoam in the office, makes me uneasy, but especially when it is behind me. I have a hard time reading. Deep inside I have made the decision to shoot in Camisea, though not announced it yet. Walter also seems to favor this solution, but it is easy for him, and he seems less tense, only because he does not have any way of fully realizing the enormity of what lies ahead of us.

In the afternoon Walter caught a little green snake that opened its mouth wide in a threatening way but seems not to be poisonous. Later we stuck it in the cage with the smaller boa, which immediately began to hiss and thrash the end of its tail like a cat ready to pounce, while the rest of its body was as taut as a spring. Only once did the two involuntary companions go at each other in a brief, crazed dart, and after that they maintained an uneasy truce.

Iquitos, 13 July 1980
A beautiful, fresh, sunny morning. I read in bed awhile and listened to music on cassettes. The two newly hatched chicks had been put in an empty rabbit hutch to keep them safe from the cat. One of them drowned in a saucer containing only a couple of millimeters of water. The other chick slipped through the woven wire to one of the albino rabbits, which, murderous through and through, wanted to devour it instantly, and bit off a leg and a piece of its stomach. Gloria barely managed to press the bloodthirsty rabbit to the back wall of the cage with a broom and rescue the chick, which is done for, however. Why do these animal dramas preoccupy me so? Because I do not want to look inside myself. Only this much: a sense of desolation was tearing me up inside, like termites in a fallen tree trunk.

In the peace and quiet of this Sunday I intend to make my decision. The sultry heat is building gradually. In the slight breeze I see a plant with thin, sharp, lancelike leaves whose inner tension holds them upright in all directions. Only one leaf, its sharp edge slicing the rising wind, vibrates and quivers, while the others remain motionless in their taut strength. Nature here surrenders only after victorious battle.

Wind sprang up and whirled dust from the pores of the earth. The little boa and the green water snake escaped, resuming their place in the seething of the jungle. César took off, clinging to the big motorcycle, and when I asked where he was going, I was told "the hippodrome." I did not understand what was meant until they explained that was the brothel. Later, at supper, César was smiling quietly to himself. We heard the deep foghorn of a distant ocean liner blowing across the jungle, and Walter is excited: that must be the ship from Houston with our cars on board.

Iquitos, 14 July 1980

The whole town is on strike because of the redrawing of the *departamentos*, and everything seems dead. I have never seen Iquitos this dead; the sun blazed down indifferently and mercilessly onto the dusty, empty streets and revealed the shadows of things as never before. Nonetheless the mason came out to our place and worked with Vivanco to put up a roof for the motorcycles. The concrete had been covered with palm fronds to protect it from the previous day's rain, and once the concrete had set, they were removed. Underneath sat a large tarantula, and César unceremoniously stepped on it. It is lying there now, crushed, as big as a hand, and flies with plump green bellies are perched on it. This sight provides a handy trigonometrical focal point for my fear of spiders. In the grass behind the house two lizards were fighting, their speed breathtaking. I did not know that lizards fought.

Vivanco says that bureaucracy is not merely an instrumentarium,

an ugly form of organization; here, he says, it is a despicable disposi-
tion of the heart. The jungle growing riotously around Iquitos is on
strike against human efforts, in perpetuity.

Uneasiness because I have some blood in my urine. I noticed it
a few days ago but at the time did not take it seriously, but now it
is impossible to ignore. Maybe it is upsetting me so much because
I had bilharzia from my time in Africa, and the symptoms were the
same then. After I confided to Walter and Vivanco, I felt as though
the worry was somehow distributed over three sets of shoulders, and
we decided to send a Coke bottle with a urine sample to the hospital
tomorrow, though it is more than doubtful that they can do more
there other than the traditional taste test. Actually, they would simply dip their fingers into the urine and taste it. We laughed a lot, and
Walter gave me a big glass of bourbon to medicate myself with.

I wrote letters, including a long one to my little son, but when I
write, I always feel fairly certain these letters will never get there. For
weeks I have been sending mail without once receiving confirmation
that it arrived. Phoning Europe is practically impossible; recently I
tried for forty-eight hours to get through, without success.

Iquitos, 15 July 1980
In town, sitting on parked motorcycles, with people all around us,
I had a major blow-up with Walter on a matter of principle, which
continued later over lunch with great vehemence. The relationship
with Koechlin in Lima also needs to be recalibrated. Behind the
house, near the banana plants, growing toward the jungle, the construction of my hut on stilts got under way. It is supposed to have
a raised platform made of springy bark and a roof of palm fronds.
It has gotten too crowded here, and I need a place of my own. I

gave orders that they should procure taller supports, so I can see over the bananas somewhat. I also think the platform would have been too low when the river rose, because I remembered how high the water had been in our office. The telex machine's keyboard just barely showed above the brown brew, and it was a miracle that it still worked. I also remember the secretary, Nancy, rowing into the room in a canoe and lying on her stomach in the bow of the dugout to send a message.

Today Walter and I are going to fly to Lima to take care of the most important bureaucratic details. There is also an aerial photograph of the Río Camisea and the Río Urubamba waiting for us that will presumably provide more exact information on the terrain's geographical features. For the end of the week I have booked a seat on the plane from Iquitos to Manaus, and from there I will make my way somehow to Rio; it is not possible to reserve a flight to Brazil because there are no telephone connections. My urinalysis revealed an abnormally high number of leukocytes, which may indicate an infection.

Lima, 16 July 1980
Lima cold and awful, damp and foggy. Lunch in a pseudo-Florentine restaurant run by a Chinese. A blind beggar woman begged so insistently with her dead eyes fixed on me that I recoiled. She had a child in her lap who also stared at me wordlessly. From midday on, news began to dribble in that there had been a military coup in Bolivia, and soon the city was filled with rumors to the effect that in this country, too, the military were planning a coup because of the strikes taking place everywhere. Although we still have a number of things to

attend to, we decided to fly back to Iquitos before the airport could be closed, because Iquitos is an island in the jungle without any overland connection to the outer world. At the airport some army trucks were parked ominously, ready to be deployed. They were full of young Indian soldiers, who looked out from under the tarpaulins, silent and scared.

Met Janoud, who was allegedly out in the highlands for three months. We laughed a lot. Our friendship has stood the test of time. We talked about Munich, about the winter, about snow. I remember seeing Janoud sitting in my basement at three in the morning, with night and snow outside, and the cellar was freezing because he had mislaid the key I had given him, yet again, and had broken a window to get in. Janoud had pulled a woolen cap down over his ears and was bending over a light box, sorting photos, so absorbed that I had to call him several times from outside. Finally he looked up and stared at me with a face that was filled with the jungle and the Indian markets in his photos. He did not recognize me because I did not fit into the scenery of his images and thoughts. In the morning I went into his room. It seemed he had not gone to bed at all because he had to leave that morning. He was standing and staring motionless into an open wardrobe, which was empty. I greeted him, but he did not hear me. I tried to speak with him, but his gaze was stuck so far inside the dark, empty wardrobe that he did not register my presence.

Iquitos, 17 July 1980
In the afternoon a heavy tropical rain pelted down, and I was surprised to see that even during the cloudburst the vultures continued

to circle. As if felled by a fever, I could not shake off the notion that a press conference had taken place at which only three reporters had appeared, among them a shapelessly fat woman who tormented me with such pointless questions that I finally lost my temper and hurled my glasses into the grass. I knew this was the only thing that would be reported, and I sat there as if paralyzed and stared at my radio, waiting for the terrible moment when the incident about the sunglasses would be broadcast. I was damned to immobility, frozen, and the terrible thing was that now time also stood still, and the only thing that could get it moving again would be this report. Then Janoud sighed, the way dromedaries sigh in their sleep. Had his mother been on an oasis while she was pregnant with him, surrounded by sighing dromedaries? People do say that the Indians are certain that hummingbirds, which whir their wings unimaginably fast, have *more* than just their own life.

Bats are nesting in the top of the house, and before dark they fly out through the vents and flutter aimlessly around the house. We were sitting outside, batting silently at the mosquitoes all around us. A girl from the neighborhood came by and wanted Gustavo to see her, and Gustavo made a very indecent remark to the girl, barely fifteen. All she said was *ay diosito*, oh, lordy, and ran off, but she wanted G. to follow her.

In Belén a falling-down drunk followed me aimlessly, and I lost sight of him. As I was sitting for a while on the steps by the marketplace that lead down to the floating huts, suddenly he reappeared. I noticed him only because he urinated directly behind me, leaning on a post. The only reason he did not hit me was that his shirt was hanging out of his pants in front and diverted the stream. A tourist boat with blaring, overmodulated loudspeaker announcements passed by, but promptly turned in the Río Itaya and sailed away again, as if so much *pura vida* were too much to impose on anyone.

Iquitos, 19 July 1980

In Belén, which keeps exerting a pull on me for no reason, a woman was selling soup from a large tortoise shell. An older Chinese man was sitting nearby on a threshold and making frantic movements, as if he were drawing a thread out of the interior of his eye. He was insane, and thus cut off from all ordinary human behavior, and he was engrossed with such extreme exclusivity in what he was doing that he drew not only my attention but also that of all those who were eating the woman's soup. As if under a compulsion we all stole glances at him, embarrassed at the thought that someone might catch us looking. I have never seen anything resembling the intensity with which he was pulling that imaginary thread out of his eye, and later, when I passed him on my motorcycle, he looked up slowly and stared me so penetratingly and so insanely in the face that it scared me. On the way I lost the wicker hamper I had tied on to the back of my motorcycle, and never noticed, pursued as I was by that gaze. Later I did not want to go back and look for it. The sky turned black and flickered silently with distant lightning. Once at home I got everything lying around outside under cover. The sky is fomenting an angry battle, plotting something dark and dreadful.

One of the Brandenburg concertos that I sometimes play on a cassette always lures a little black bird to the window. It hops around on the wall outside, paying no heed to the fragments of broken Coke bottles stuck on the top to deter intruders, and woos the music with its song. For days I have apparently been writing the wrong date, but do not want to correct it, except that today the Olympics seem to have started somewhere, and then this: the bats are out, around the house and now close to my head as well.

Iquitos, 20 July 1980
Because of the strike there was a large rally today on the Plaza 28 de Julio, with speakers shouting and gesticulating the way Mussolini used to in the thirties. I went to the movies and saw a film in which a madman wanted to exterminate the race of blacks, but three muscular athletes stopped him. Toward the end, when a man burst into flames after being shot and ran off, a living torch, the entire movie house exploded in laughter. The cheering continued to the end of the film. On the way home, I stopped by a hut where a dark crowd of people was clustered outside a window. From inside came the sound of two thin fiddles, a rattle, and a monotonous flute. Dancing was going on inside, and when I cautiously pushed my way past the half-naked bodies to the window, I saw that the people inside were dancing around a seated plaster Jesus wearing a halo. Above him was a canopy made of mosquito netting, and around him were plastic flowers, stuck into the dirt floor. The dancers were holding handkerchiefs. I stared in through the window for a long time.

In the office I noticed new black lines along the crack where the walls and the ceiling meet. Upon closer inspection I discovered they were freshly constructed termite tunnels. I poked into one of them with my ballpoint, and termites came tumbling out; they were very surprised. Before I left the city, I was stopped on my motorcycle, which still does not have a license plate–I thought that was why the two policemen had stopped me. But one of them merely turned the key with an apologetic shrug, killing the engine. The big flag was being taken down, and a nervous honor guard fired a salvo, while two trumpeters tried in vain to blow a melody at the same time.

At dusk I rode the motorcycle to the airport, and, as usual at this time of day, flies, bugs, and other insects came to life and flew into my face, my hair, and also into my collar and down my shirt. Hours later on the plane I could still feel bugs scrabbling inside my underwear where I could not get at them. The flight was overbooked, and three passengers were assigned to the same seat next to me. Two of them were accommodated somehow, but the third spent the entire flight in back by the toilets.

Rio de Janeiro, 24 July 1980
At night I woke up in Cattaneo's apartment and when I saw that the clock was showing three-thirty had the dreadful feeling that it was afternoon already, and I had slept through the entire night and half the day, and had missed everything. In my confusion I was not sure what that everything was, but there was no question it was vitally important. I lay there with my eyes open, unable to move, and listened to the traffic streaming by outside. Then I peeked through the blinds and saw a deep blue sunny sky, rocky islands, and swimmers. The clock still mercilessly showed half-past three, and it was too late for everything. Why, oh why, had they shown so much consideration for me and not called me for breakfast? Finally I forced myself to get up and open the window. Outside it was night. My clock by now said four, but it was four in the morning. From then on I woke up every half hour; I had been warned deep inside, my leaden exhaustion disturbed.

Spent the actual day restlessly. In the evening I went to one of the finest hotels here and crashed the vernissage for a lousy artist. No one realized that I was not invited, so I drank several of the cocktails being served. I sat down between a large fern in a terra-cotta pot and a column, so as to be undisturbed. Tiredness. I felt a great weight dragging, dragging me down, and had the sense I was involved in something that exceeded my abilities and my strength, something I was not made for. This sense was so overwhelming that I was glad to be able to sit. I stayed there a long time, which seemed to provide some relief from the weight. Then an elegant young woman wanted to discuss art with me; what kind of art, I barked, and she said something confused about my hostility to art per se.

Rio de Janeiro, 21–26 July 1980
Very early in the morning the cripples bathe at the beach. Then young houseboys and nannies all in white take the rich people's babies out for a stroll. The baby carriages form clumps where the infants' employees gather to chat. Gisela Storch arrived, and we immediately went to check out the costume depot here, a thoroughly sobering experience. In the evening stayed late at Carlos Diegues's. Glauber Rocha was nowhere to be found, and Rui Guerra is apparently in São Paulo. I learned that Armando was still living in his old house, whose foundations the excavations for the new subway missed by a hair. All the other buildings around it were torn down, I heard, and he was killing himself with alcohol.

On the beach, boys launch kites that they let sail over the promenade and the street and flutter among the high-rises. One fell and got tangled in a VW bus, which dragged the nylon cord along till it broke. The kite was dangling from the front bumper and ended up under the bus, where it fluttered crazily, trying to break free. It was banging back and forth so violently that the vehicle stopped in the middle of traffic, and the passengers got out and cut the line.

São Paulo, 27–28 July 1980
At the screening of *Every Man for Himself and God Against All* the hall was so overcrowded that during the discussion that followed, to which even more people came, those trying to force their way in pressed so hard against those standing that people were fainting, and it was only with the greatest difficulty that they could be carried outside. Once it was all over, I went with some of the people to a house where they sang to drive away the shadows.

Belém do Pará, 29 July 1980
Into town with Gisela; because there is no sense of history, only a panting, sweating present, there is no hope of finding any historical costumes here. A sense of the uselessness of everything I am doing; the most important things are happening elsewhere. We went to the editorial offices of the *Jornal a Provincia do Pará* to get some information, but all we found were large fans, bored editors drinking *caipirinha*, and everything at a standstill. No one was working. The typewriters upended on wooden typing tables from the thirties, rather like beached boats. Then to the radio station, where many people were trying to get in for the live broadcast by the King of Radio, or at least that was how he was announced, though he looked more like a pimp, draped in gold chains, his shirt unbuttoned down to his waist, his hair pomaded. A woman had a seriously malnourished little child lying on her lap, wearing a woolen cap, its eyelids drooping. It was too weak to cry, and the infant's eyes seemed to express the knowledge that it was

going to die. The woman said into the microphone that her neighbor had simply abandoned the child outside. She was always drunk, and instead of her breast she had given the child *cachaça*. Brandy! Brandy! shouted the King of Radio, and punctuated the rest of the woman's story with the exclamation *Cachaça . . . Cachaça*. The studio audience, all poor folks, none of them wearing shoes, responded enthusiastically to the King's shouts, while the child unobtrusively died a bit more. Now the King, enthralled with himself, shouted, That whore! The woman who had taken in the neighbor's baby was barely given a chance to talk about herself–that she already had twelve children of her own–because the King struck up a rhythmic chant of The whore! The whore! Our appeal for clothes worn by people's grandparents was not read until after we had left.

Outside it was dark already, and on the street, where everything was still steaming from a hard rain, two cables belonging to a high-tension line had snapped and were touching on the paving. Sparks flew, there was a fierce cracking sound, and the cables sprang apart, thrashing in the air, and touched again. Amid flashes they jolted apart even more violently, and the people on the street were afraid to go by until the cables, more and more crazed, spewed forth flames and tumbled from the pylons.

Belém do Pará, 30 July 1980

I sent off mail, hoping for a change that it would not arrive, because this is a time of padlocked hearts. No one came in response to our appeals, and I said to Gisela, whose mere presence makes her a witness to such a defeat, that if here no one came, in Manaus we could not expect even half of no one to come. Toward evening lovers meet in the park by the bandstand. Night descends very quickly. The universe's light simply burns out, and then it is gone. The light just goes missing here. Under a fan a slight, dark local poet sat writing, but no one in this city ever seems to read; there is not a single bookstore for a million inhabitants. Life is dragging us down. I weighed myself in a pharmacy and found I was too heavy. The delicate needle on the scale moved more and more slowly, and it was almost a minute before it finally stood still, as if my weight were increasing the longer I stood on the scale. Maybe, I thought, the scale also weighs one's thoughts.

Belém do Pará, 31 July 1980
A touch of fever in the morning. We drove about eighty kilometers by car to look for an old locomotive that I need for the story. We found a few dilapidated railroad cars, rusting away, and later a locomotive, but it was mounted on a cracked concrete pedestal as a monument. The whole thing surrounded by high grass and brush, to the left and right concrete benches, also crumbling, painted in bright colors. There is also part of an old turbine, cemented into the ground to celebrate progress. On another pedestal was a plaster statue of an unknown, representing the heroism of the place. He was missing one arm. I fell asleep in the car, and when I woke up, my clothes were drenched in sweat. I bought a Coke, and I noticed that the people here have Coke dispensed into a plastic bag and take it home that way to avoid paying the bottle deposit. On two days in a row I was confused by the Amazon, which is so broad here that you cannot see the opposite bank. It was flowing briskly in the wrong direction, and at first I thought I had lost my sense of direction, until I realized that the ocean current was at work; here the Amazon flows backward and forward.

Manaus, 1 August 1980

The idea of having an entire opera performed in the opera house here, not just an excerpt for *Fitzcarraldo*, was well received. From my wretchedly noisy hotel room I see oceangoing ships going upstream as far as Manaus to be unloaded. A maid came and was about to steal something from the minibar when she noticed me, and pretended to be counting the bottles of cola and beer. Among the boats tied up higgledy-piggledy by the market hall, one had a tiny platform protruding from one side on which a large, sad-eyed dog was chained. The chain around his neck is fastened with a large padlock, and nearby lie drunken boatmen. A woman, likewise drunk, crawled onto land over a swaying gangway, ending up among the trash on the ground, and took a long time getting her feet into her sandals, while a man kept stabbing a large knife with great concentration into a tin can on the ground. A barefoot workman with a very heavy load on his back, held in place by a forehead strap, saluted me with a panted *capitán*. A paper cup that he kicked inadvertently whirled and was still dancing about when he disappeared onto a barge.

Manaus–Iquitos, 2 August 1980

Fever. The women on the plane fat, sweaty, inconsiderate; the children already the same. I flew to Iquitos with reluctant longing.

A stifling feeling of pressing forward with something that ultimately could not be done. If all of this were in another country, I would have fewer reservations. The greatest uncertainties: the actors, the new camp, the ship over the mountain, the scope of the undertaking, which no one has grasped yet, the Indians, the financing–the list can be added to indefinitely. Seen from the plane, the sheer expanse of the jungle is terrifying; no one who has not been there can picture it. We do not need virtuosos of syntax.

Two stops on the flight from Manaus to Iquitos. One of the landing strips was in the middle of the jungle, and I saw no signs of a settlement. The second was in Tabatinga, and I seemed to have a hazy image of the town, as if welling up from the depths of memory, as if I had been there before, but for a long time I was unsure whether it was not a place I had visited in my dreams. The stacked-up gasoline drums, the little terminal with its corrugated tin roof seemed as familiar as a repetitive dream. Walter was there to pick me up in the jeep, which was covered with dust inside, even though it is brand-new, and we stopped to see Gloria, who, as my intuition had told me, had given birth to a little girl on Walter's birthday. The baby had not been given a name yet. She looked very contented. Andreas was there, and we immediately discussed the new method he had suggested for getting the ship over the ridge. On the face of it, his system of inflatable pontoons seems to make good sense, but I am dubious, for one thing because you need to have some experience handling them, and for another it will not look good on the screen. It has to be basic, primitive, and obvious, as if each moviegoer had just come up with the idea himself. Andreas had brought along plenty of mail, half eaten by the parrot but still legible. Vivanco flew to Cuzco, and I hope he carries out his assignment well, though he is a magnet for bad luck and terribly indecisive. Walter's still dreaming of a decree from the Belaunde government, as if such a thing were thinkable outside normal official channels, and his insistence on that idea has a somewhat paralyzing effect.

According to an English scholar–and his view is shared by the majority of his readers–the opera house in Manaus, the Teatro Amazonas, is a spaceship, not built by human beings. He simply rejects all reports of its construction–the blueprints, the photos, all the supporting documents–claiming they are government forgeries. How, Walter asked, did the theater end up in Manaus? I told him it must have landed there. The entire theory is interwoven with the legendary figure of an Indian prince from Portuguese colonial times. Supposedly this prince appeared very openly in those days, and still appears, but only secretly, late at night, to stage his sexual orgies there, for only in that location does he succeed in having an erection. The beauty of all this is that a fever dream became a reality in the jungle and is now being transformed back into a pure jungle fantasy.

The enormous remaining boa constrictor will die in its cage, I think; it leans its ugly head against the wire and has a heartrending air such as you see only in the dying. I thought it must be thirsty and carefully poured water on its mouth and head, but it merely stared at me from the depths of a loneliness that had little connection left with earthly things. So we decided to release the boa. Walter and I shook it out of the cage, because it did not want to budge. The women watched from a safe distance, not looking happy. The snake crawled right back into its enclosure, yet when I checked later, it was gone, and there was a clear trail in the sand leading toward the jungle. At night the place where the snake had disappeared was thronged with twinkling fireflies, and overhead a clear, starry night sky. Andreas, our mathematician, was playing chess with his girlfriend, losing most of the games, but he accepted that with mathematical decorum. A white pawn is missing, and has been replaced with a bullet casing, much too large, which usually becomes the object of attacks early in the game. For the first time in my life mosquitoes are leaving me completely indifferent, not that I have accepted the superior power of nature. It is more of a dispassionate scorn with which I am leaving my skin and blood undefended. God grant us one good day, a single one, amen.

Iquitos, 4 August 1980

The *Huallaga* just returned from Pucallpa, and I spoke with the crew. The trip had gone well, but had taken a very long time because the water in the Ucayali was very shallow. What is going to happen, I wondered, if extremely shallow water in this mighty river causes such problems, and what can we expect if we encounter such conditions many tributaries farther upstream? Additional disquieting news came from César Vivanco in Cuzco; the bureaucracy there seems to have documents about the Camisea that are not even known in Lima. The carpenters are doing good work. The sun is hot. Our fate continues to be suspended in suspense.

A man was walking down the dusty road to the Río Nanay, shuffling a deck of cards as he went. On the plane a woman began to sing litanies, and then, her eyes growing wilder and wilder, to rail at evil spirits. Not until we had landed and taxied to a stop did she calm down. Am I in the wrong place here, or in the wrong life? Did I not recognize, as I sat in a train that raced past a station and did not stop, that I was on the wrong train, and did I not learn from the conductor that the train would not stop at the next station, either, a hundred kilometers away, and did he not also admit to me, whispering with his hand shielding his mouth, that the train would not stop again at all? Drastic measures, he whispered to me, were appropriate only for someone who had not set foot on this continent yet. To fail to embrace my dreams now would be a disgrace so great that sin itself would not be able to find a name for it.

. , ,

Fragments. Two weeks on the Río Camisea. Upon returning to Iquitos, I found the little bookshelf in my cabin encased in a termite mound; I had to peel the few books, the radio, letters, and journals out of the hard coating, and the most recent journal, which was on top, has been devoured, except for the cover, which is covered in plastic. One passage is left: ". . . broods a storm. Hate is seething over the rain forest. Where in the depths of history has the word 'reprobate' gone missing?"

Iquitos, 25 September 1980

Henning and Uli came back from Puerto Maldonado. There actually is a ship in the jungle there, and they brought photos. The ship is small, however, in terrible shape, and in no way suitable, so that puts an end to another wild-goose chase. I am still prepared to set out on any other that might present itself. Up to now connecting by radio to the Camisea has worked only once, and I do not have much confidence in our radio. Sometimes the men working on the ship come, and sometimes they do not.

Iquitos–Pucallpa–Camisea, 5 October 1980

Yesterday's flight almost ended in disaster. The plane had already attained a high rate of speed for takeoff when a strange cracking reverberated through the entire plane, and the pilot barely managed to bring the craft to a standstill before the end of the runway. We were told there was a small technical repair that needed to be done, and we should remove our carry-on luggage and also get all our bags from the hold; we would be taking off shortly.

Translation: this plane would never fly again. I walked around the stranded plane and saw that all the fins in the engine under the right wing had snapped. We continued our trip on a small Cabaña plane, which happened to be there by mistake, but upon taking off from Pucallpa we were so overloaded that we almost did not make it into the air. I have never experienced such a close call. When we landed on the boggy strip by the Camisea we were so heavy that we skidded past the end of the runway into grass as tall as a man, and mowed down a wooden post with one wing. It left a deep dent in the wing. Our party included the cameraman Mauch, Walter, George Sluizer, who will be a particular help in Brazil, and the more reckless of the two pilots.

Iquitos, 5 December 1980

Mick Jagger's assistant, Alan Dunn, arrived and inspected everything. He seemed to like what he saw here. Big problems with Walter, which I accept almost with indifference. Less panic than usual at the costume department. Lucki in Munich was supposed to let us know about the interim financing, but for days no news arrived. I know, however, that he will take care of it. The deadlines are inexorably closing in on us. As if describing a distant, unfamiliar world, Dunn told us there was a half a meter of snow on the ground near Cologne. Laplace Martin, the engineer from Brazil, arrived, his neck and wrists weighed down with gold chains; even his ballpoint pen is gold. Nonetheless he makes a solid impression. Almost all contacts broken off. Life is blowing away from me like fallen leaves.

In the costume shop was a carpenter who always looks at you strangely and distractedly. It took him six days to make two sets of shelves for the hats. For three of those days he was hammering on the wall, for reasons not obvious to me. When this job was done, he attached a molding to Gisela's closet, for which he had to climb into the closet. I saw him kneeling inside. Then we did not hear anything more from him and forgot all about him. When we got worried hours later and opened the closet to check, we found him asleep on his knees.

Outside the screened window of my cabin on stilts the banana fronds stand motionless in the steamy evening, and little frogs soar in long leaps from frond to frond, landing with a splat on the pale leaves. As soon as it gets dark, they begin their dialogue with the frogs perched on the thatched roof. I am at the intersection of their exchanges. In the last light, the frogs on the other side of the leaves show through as if the leaves were waxed paper.

Another strike is in the offing, and the post office is already closed. Soon the airport will shut down, too. How will we get all the urgent technical dispatches from Miami? Robards's and Jagger's contracts have not been signed yet, either, and even if they were, how would they reach me? It has been raining so hard that the road to the Río Nanay, where our headquarters is located, is like a mud patch for pigs to wallow in. I look at the pictures of my son, Burro, again and again; I have tacked them to a piece of plywood by the window. I also have pictures of Lotte Eisner and Walter Steiner, the ski jumper. I would like to fly myself now. The second, identical ship, on which work is proceeding at a crazy pace, still will not be ready in time.

Iquitos, 6 December 1980
From the brackish water of what must have been a swimming pool years ago, I fished out with a broom a thin, very lively snake, which immediately disappeared into the grass. I spent a long time admiring the anteater we have had around here recently as it used its unbeliev-

ably long, agile tongue to rake termites together on a board and then lick them off.

Almost all the people working here are on the verge of collapse, have reached the limit of their endurance. Izquerdo was throwing up all day, but probably more because not one of the extras we were counting on came to be fitted for a costume. Vignati's disappeared to Satipo and is over a week late getting back. Sluizer, who just joined us for the first time, is reorganizing some of the procedures and exudes human warmth. Laplace left us, headed for Brazil; he speaks Portuguese with me, and I answer in Spanish, and we understand each other. We bury everything important in casual asides, and when I explained to him recently why it had to be a full-sized ship that we hauled over the ridge, he smiled to himself, this man with the dark face and pitted skin who never laughs, and he shook my hand and said nothing. Then we nodded to each other, and he rode off in the jeep, while behind him a storm with horrendous flashes of lightning burst. It messed up my electric wristwatch.

Iquitos, 7 December 1980
Fiesta time in Pucuchama. All along the road into town stands had been set up, selling beer and grilled meat, and there was dancing everywhere. I played a game of chance several times and lost each time; the principle was like roulette, except that there were no balls but a live guinea pig under a small wooden crate, which was raised by a rope. Numbered Swiss chalets were set up in a circle, each with a dark entryway, and the guinea pig dashed around uncertainly for a while before quickly making up its mind and disappearing into one of the doors. The prizes were little bowls made of pink and light green plastic, and I kept on betting until I had no more money on me.

This morning I got up very early to try to put through a call on the phone. Two *campesinos* came and brought chickens into the office–Walter had ordered them. When they left, I knew that I would never be the same again. I looked out at the pale trees in the jungle and tried to imagine Munich in the snow, with my little boy celebrating Advent–without me.

A woman arrived from the Río Napo with her children; her husband is working up on the Camisea for us. She was in a hysterical state because she had heard that her husband had been murdered by Indians and eaten. I managed to establish radio contact, and because it was Sunday, her husband had the day off and was not at work in the jungle. He was called to the radio and could speak with her directly. She wept for joy and wanted to give me the two chickens she had brought along as provisions. I had to show her the chickens we had purchased that morning to prove to her that we already had more than we needed.

Still no news from Munich about the financing, but I am counting on Lucki, who is probably in Paris with Gaumont at the moment. At breakfast a bad mood in the house because of an overflowing toilet. I promptly took steps to solve the problem, because something like that immediately assumes an importance out of all proportion to much greater misfortunes. It was as if I had taken the house's temperature. Later I drove to Paul's bar. On the street outside a little procession was passing, led by a barefoot man carrying a white child's coffin on his shoulder, behind him several women with umbrellas to protect them from the blazing sun, while all around the horizon was a menacing black and gray. In broad daylight lightning was flashing silently all around, and a thunderstorm was swirling on the horizon, while up above in the middle there was just enough room left for the glowing murderous blade of the sun, toward which silent clouds of dust whirled and snaked, glowing and malevolent. The thunderstorm held off all afternoon, but then descended far off over the rain forest, sweating and steaming, as if out there an enormous, violent rape were being carried out.

At night the chickens, frightened by something, screeched like pigs being slaughtered. An airplane passed overhead, going north, and I have been lying awake for a long time, because I cannot suppress a voice inside me saying it is going to crash.

Iquitos, 8 December 1980

This morning, when I checked on the telex machine, Gloria was trying to make contact with the *Narinho*, the rusted-out ship that we had gotten to float here from Colombia made buoyant with six hundred empty oil drums, but the on-board receiver must have been turned off. A young woman had shown up; she had no way to reach her husband, an electrician, who was on the ship. In the morning her child had been throwing up for two hours, then went into convulsions and was suddenly dead. I did not know what I should say to the woman. She turned her face to the wall and cried; she had been keeping it in until then. I took her hand and held it, and when her silent sobbing had relaxed somewhat, I took her on the motorcycle and rode to the boat landing. The boatman did not want to set out because he was waiting for the cooks, but I hustled him off with the woman to the place where the *Narinho* was anchored. The woman was still very young, and it had been her first child, a son, only half a year old.

A still day, sultry. Inactivity piled on inactivity, clouds staring down from the sky, pregnant with rain, fever reigns, insects taking on massive proportions. The jungle is obscene. Everything about it is sinful, for which reason the sin does not stand out as sin. The voices in the jungle are silent; nothing is stirring, and a languid, immobile anger hovers over everything. The laundry on the line refuses to dry. As if part of a conspiracy, flies suddenly descend on the table, their stomachs taut and iridescent. Our little monkey was wailing in his cage, and when I approached, he looked and wailed right through me to some distant spot outside, where his little heart hoped to find an echo. I let him out, but he went back into his cage, and now he is continuing to wail there.

Mexico City–New York, 15–16 December 1980
In the waiting area for the flight to the U.S.; I spend too many deadening hours in airports–Miami, Kennedy, La Guardia, to name only a few of the worst hellholes. Bleary-eyed from a sleepless night, I let myself be cheated by the man at the currency-exchange counter; he seems to have developed an infallible eye for his customers' weaknesses. It was less than $20, but I felt like a dumb tourist, and brooded without much inspiration on ways to get back at him. The hotels were almost completely booked, and the only way I got a room was by taking one on the thirteenth floor. From there I saw hens on the flat roof of a modern building next door. I recall that in Tokyo once, in the innermost inner city, among the metastasizing concrete, I actually heard roosters crowing at daybreak.

In New York I went to the entryway, only two blocks from my apartment, where John Lennon was shot. In Central Park a crowd had gathered spontaneously for a silent vigil that kept growing and growing. The degree to which people were feeling genuine shock and dismay made an impression on me, even if the demonstration was plagued by all the inanities that also formed part of his era: joints were passed around, posters of gurus were held up in the crowd, and vague demands for peace were voiced–for what peace, where? A young woman wearing a paleo-hippie outfit held up a banner reading, "All he said is give peace a chance."

The Robards and Jagger contracts still not signed. In the afternoon a weather front with black clouds moved in rapidly from the west, and there was a shaking and howling around the building. On the thirty-fourth floor, where my apartment is, I felt a slight swaying and then saw driving snow out the window. It lasted only a few minutes, and then the whole thing was over. I have not seen snow in such a long time.

Iquitos, 17 December 1980
Landed in Iquitos beneath a massively heavy sky. As the plane glided in, the storm dumped darkness and pounding rain over the countryside. Powerful lightning. I still have 50 *soles* in my pocket, the equivalent of 15 cents, but no one has come to pick me up, probably because my message never got through. Outside the storm is moving away to the distance, leaving eddies of vapor rising from the concrete. I saw Gustavo drive by in the Bronco without a care in the world, never suspecting that I could have arrived. During the strike the tires on two of our motorcycles and one of the cars were slashed, and Gustavo, that idiot, drove into town with a gun in the car. Unthinkable what would have happened if a patrol had spotted it. Because of the precarious situation, the airport is swarming with heavily armed police, who brandish their submachine guns in the empty arrivals building, where there are not even imaginary enemies, and have riot helmets hooked to their belts. The mood is nasty; you can cut it with a knife.

Iquitos, 18 December 1980

A message about some emergency reached us from the camp on the Camisea, but only half of it got through before the power failed, and since then the connection has been dead. Apparently an Indian woman in the late stages of pregnancy came to our medic, with the child in her womb dead. She cannot deliver it, and, so far as I could make out, she will die if nothing is done. This morning our telex also gave up the ghost. All we can do is try to send a plane from Pucallpa, if we can get a connection somehow. Otherwise the only hope I have is that Cucho can bring the woman in the speedboat to the Río Sepahua or to the missionaries on the Río Timpia, because they are better equipped than we are at the moment.

From the few days of my absence, the costumes and props are in a mess, and so, according to Uli, is the entire production, because Walter is utterly disoriented and can seemingly focus only on the ship; otherwise he has lost all sense of continuity and perspective. Come what may, I will try not to put off the actual shooting; any other course would be psychologically catastrophic. To quote General Patton, the only direction is forward; the rear guard will fall in place in its wake; organization, logistics, and everything secondary will be swept up in the momentum.

I have a snake on my roof again. A little while ago I heard something rustling up there, and then something dark fell into the banana fronds with a thwack. I took a look, and it was a poisonous brownish snake that had caught a bird, which was still peeping. I tried hitting the snake with a stick, but it disappeared like lightning into the grass. Only now and then did a blade quiver, and from the piteous cries of the bird I could tell where the snake was. I did not follow it into the grass, because I discovered that another snake was on the thatched roof, and directly above me a third snake was trying to get from a banana frond onto the platform of my hut. I tried to strike it with the machete, but the snake was too fast for me.

The power is still out. Evening descended on the countryside. What would happen if the rain forest wilted like a bouquet of flowers? Around me insects are dying, for which they lie on their backs. A woman in the neighborhood is suckling a newborn puppy after her baby died from parasites; I have seen this done before with piglets. The current in some *malpasos* before the Río Camisea seems to be too strong for our ship. A voice saying, There goes the whole project, keeps droning in my head like church bells, while lightning flickers above the silhouettes of the trees. Henning was supposed to come tonight with money, but I hear he is not coming until Saturday. We have nothing left here, and it is urgent that we get food supplies up to the Camisea, buy tools in Lima, and pay the workers. Outside a bright moon is floating now above the treetops. The frogs, thousands of them, suddenly pause, as if they were following an invisible conductor, and start up again all at the same time. Their conversations come and go in curious waves. Waxy moonlight, as bright as neon, is shimmering on the banana fronds. I was called to the telephone in the house, and fell off the ladder that leads to my platform. It was one of very few phone calls that ever get through to us, and a stranger on the line was trying to make it clear to me that I was a madman, a menace to society.

Iquitos, 19 December 1980
In the morning a sinister-looking man appeared in our office. He was missing his upper front teeth and was wild and wily, and it seemed

to me he would be willing to commit murder if you made it worth his while. The thought had just crossed my mind when in an unobserved moment he darted upstairs and forced his way into Gloria's room, giving her a good scare. Allegedly he was just looking for an advance. A young captain is here from Atalaya, the first and only one who has impressed me as reliable. He calculated calmly that the ship might need twenty days to get from Atalaya to the Camisea, without counting on favorable conditions. That scared the daylights out of me, because the ship needs two weeks just to get to Atalaya, and there is no chance of doing better than that. Gloria's still crying hysterically. The telex machine has not been fixed yet, but for the first time in a long while the electricity is back on in the city.

Two thoughts that do not belong here have been preoccupying me amid the uproar of getting everything reorganized: how can it be explained that Latin left no traces in Germania south of the Limes, yet in England such lasting traces were left in English, even though the Roman occupation was far more fleeting there; and are not stars that are moving away from us at a speed near that of light also on a collision course with us, as in mathematical reality a bullet we fired on earth that flew around the globe would have to hit us in the back?

When I am in my cabin and toss the tea remaining in my tin cup out the window, the liquid spurts through the screen onto the banana fronds outside, but the tea leaves remain suspended in the window screen in a flat, strange pattern, harshly reduced by one dimension, betrayed. They stay there as a two-dimensional reminder of the turbulent way in which the tea went through the wire mesh.

I sent off my Christmas letters, knowing they would arrive late or more likely not at all. The Christmas tree in the post office, consisting of a few bare branches decorated with strips of silver foil and green cellophane, as well as a little package, touched me to the quick.

Outside I looked down at the river for a long time, trying to regain some composure. *Chatas*, flat barges, are chugging along, carrying pipes for distant oil-drilling operations. Belén is partially under water. Today at daybreak the birds were pleading for the continued existence of the Creation. For them, anything but the continuation of the status quo is deadly. My watch has stopped now once and for all, but for a long time I have been thinking in Amazonian terms anyway: before dinner, after the storm, toward evening. A blind, barefoot beggar was groping his way along the wall of a house. A woman was drinking water from an aluminum pot in which slimy fish from the river, with big eyes, were floating. One of them was dead, its underside white, belly-up. Then a child drank from the pot.

At the market in Belén I saw a young woman so beautiful that I was startled. In my bamboo room I used a boarding pass, which had yellowed quickly in the climate here, as a bookmark, and I saw that it was only from this past summer. I cannot remember why I took that flight. That piece of cardboard will soon disappear into a filing case, and only the tax people will be interested in it, but it was life, my life. I tried transcribing the tape of *Huie's Sermon*, but much of it is almost unintelligible, and there are large gaps. A rooster crowed itself hoarse, for hours on end. Oppressive heat. Sleepiness. Does the devil keep a logbook?

In Belén I drank sugarcane brandy with some of the porters, barefoot wild fellows, whom I took along later to the costume depot. One of them was wearing a decorative circlet around his neck plaited from a length of liana and was constantly scratching his balls. Big black ants were darting back and forth on mysterious errands along a beam on which my arm had been resting. When they began carrying their milky white eggs, I knew this was serious business for them. The men, drunk by now, were mindlessly intent on finding a woman for the night, as if there were no tomorrow, while the mosquitoes, impelled by a similarly mindless principle, paid no heed to whether a person was drunk, horny, or dying.

Iquitos, 21 December 1980

I was supposed to get Claudia Cardinale settled in her hotel suite, which extended over two floors. As we entered the room, we noticed that on the upper floor, which could be reached only by way of a spiral staircase, a horse was standing, one of those noble Thoroughbreds, its bridle held by its jockey, a skinny, gnomish man. Klieg lights were set up because a commercial was being shot in the suite. We were told the room would be available shortly; we should go ahead and drop the luggage there. The word was–a rumor was flying around the hotel–that Cardinale's bosom was the most beautiful in the world; this had been officially established by a legal decision. Outside the river flowed by, drunk for all eternity. Fall foliage floated away to the south on the water. At Christmas the rich folks of Iquitos go water-skiing on the Amazon. In the gold country of Punt, tonsillectomies are performed with a vacuum cleaner. Benjamin wants to find sun temples and hidden treasure when he is grown up. One morning an angry country woman sawed off her chickens' beaks with a fretsaw. I wondered whether a dog could be disguised as a pig. Then my ship dissolved in its reflection in the waves into slow-moving arrows. A sudden gust of wind woke me, and I noticed that the light was on and my mosquito net was billowing like a sail, trying to get away from me. Outside a fire was sending out sparks in the wind; our night watchman, César, is heating up tar to spread on our artificial rubber balls to make them look authentic. The sky lowering and black, the horizon shimmering malevolently as if with northern lights.

Iquitos, 23 December 1980

Henning's birthday. Chaos with the costumes. Izquerdo, whom Gisela screamed at in German, promptly quit; that way he will at least be home for Christmas. Bill Rose, obviously drunk, sent a confused telex from Miami full of dire insults aimed at Alan Greenberg, who quit before he even started with us. Alan had got word to me that Bill had called him without reason and without warning, threatening to murder him and making no sense. At the camp on the Camisea there was a terrible storm. It uprooted huge trees, which completely destroyed some of the buildings. In a play staged recently in a student theater by the initiators of the tribunal against me, with some Indians from Cenepa as actors, I was portrayed, according to Henning, as always appearing for shoots with a fat cigar in my mouth; it seems to have escaped general notice that I have not done any filming yet. All this is part of the daily dance.

Last night a bat got into the office, where it fluttered around desperately for a long time, unable to find the open windows. At the marketplace I saw a porter carrying a squealing pig on his back with a forehead strap and speaking to it in Quechua as he made his way down to the dwellings on stilts. I jumped out of my skin because the trees were yelling at me. Has it come to this–that the trees are yelling at me?

Iquitos, 1 January 1981

Brotherly love at midnight. In the meantime Mick Jagger has arrived with Jerry Hall. Two of his suitcases did not make it, because he had sent them to I-Quito. We had rented a car for him, but it turned out that the key did not fit; it actually belonged to a construction crane. Mick took a taxi out here, and because the driver did not want to carry him the last hundred meters through the muddy ruts, even for twice the price, I found him groping his way in the dark, in a tuxedo and tennis shoes. Shaking with laughter, he told me that Robards and Adorf had confided to him that they had both had wills drawn up because they were going to be working in the jungle.

Our lighting man had no compunctions about tapping into the electric feeder line out by the new equipment shed, for all to see. Suddenly everything out there had power. For weeks the electric company had been promising us every day that they would get us hooked up, but they had never sent anyone. Chaos in Mexico, out of the clear blue sky. The agent there dismissed all the actors and production team members, canceled the contracts, claiming she received instructions to do this in a telex from us. Lucki managed to get on a flight today from Miami to Mexico to sort out the mess. The Caterpillar is going to be shipped from Miami too late; from there it is supposed to go to Lima/Callao, then overland to Pucallpa on the Río Ucayali, and then on a *chata* as far as the Urubamba and the Río Camisea. From the point of view of timing, this can be a catastrophe in the making. For days the shipment with the lights and the camera was nowhere to be found, because the plane could not land in Iquitos during a rainstorm and was diverted to Lima. There everything was unloaded, then a plane broke down, and everything was stuck in customs because Faucett Airways could not locate the bills of lading. The Brazilians, actors, and sound team will get here too late, but the *Narinho II* is sailing upstream faster than we expected. And: the general strike has supposedly been called off.

Iquitos, 2 January 1981
Our monkey escaped from his cage and is stealing things from the set table when no one is there. He has taken possession of

almost all the forks. This morning he stole the milk bottle used by Gloria's little daughter, and Gloria saw him out in the bushes sucking on the nipple until the bottle was empty. She is convinced the monkey will rape the baby, and she wants him shot before he does so. Around his waist the monkey still has the piece of electrical cable with which he had been tethered, and when he climbs he holds the cable high in the air with his tail, with which he can grasp things as well as with a hand; that way it cannot interfere with his movements.

Behind my back, Walter has flown up to the Camisea, leaving the chaos in his wake. He has reduced the number of extras for the scene of the ship's departure from five thousand to half that number, and I went with Mauch to the boat landing and calculated how many we would need to have a believable number to distribute over the riverbank. If we also want to fill the road up above, it will have to be at least sixty-six hundred extras. No one should be scared off by the work involved. After all, I do not even have an assistant, and the hard core of the team will consist of about sixteen people. If the same film were being produced in Hollywood, they would not get by with fewer than 250.

Iquitos, 3 January 1984
Since yesterday everything seems to point toward the general strike as being on again. We received word directly from the strike committee, and George Sluizer has also heard directly from the general charged by the government with gathering enough troops to maintain order in case the strike gets out of hand. The *Narinho II* is stuck in Pucallpa; the gear mechanism (?), brand-new (?), failed, and it can take up to a week for a replacement to come from Miami, without figuring in

delays resulting from a possible strike. Supposedly five Mexicans, and from Brazil the sound team and the actor José Lewgoy, are to arrive tonight. It is unsettling that a queue stretching two hundred meters has formed outside the office of Faucett Airlines–people wanting to get out of Iquitos before the strike begins. Piercing heat, and no rain to cool things down.

Iquitos, 4 January 1984

The Mexicans arrived so late at night and on a plane that was not listed on any flight plan that at first I thought my brother Lucki had hijacked a plane just to get here on time. Claude Chiarini was with them–what a pleasure to have him back with me. Mick Jagger helped out as a driver to get all the new folks to their hotel. The sound people are stranded somewhere in Brazil; we will have to manage somehow. Things are still on hold with the ship, but we have to take the plunge. Wrangles over the costume shop, because the makeup people need to spread out in the building. An obstinate, whiny tone, always the signal that chaos is about to erupt, like a lava eruption. President Belaunde wafted in from Lima and spoke to a large crowd on the Plaza de Armas, and people seem to have calmed down.

Iquitos, 5 January 1984

Around midnight Lucki woke me with the news that the strike was happening after all; it would begin on Monday with a warning strike, and starting the following Monday would be a general strike, continuing indefinitely. An emergency meeting during the night. Walter and Vignati were in favor of not shooting, while I am in favor of going ahead, on the condition that if we run into resistance we have to be smart enough to call off our plans.

In the morning everything in town was closed, and our twenty-five people at the Safari Hotel will not have anything to eat for lunch or dinner. We are going to walk to the costume depot with spaghetti and ready-made sauce, and cook for everyone there. The mood is good; we will manage in spite of everything. To wait now and not work would be like a psychological avalanche, sweeping us all into a depression. It does not worry me that I have never worked with any of these actors before, or with a good part of the technical team. My composure is keeping all the others' chins up now.

Iquitos, 6 January 1984, second day of shooting
Yesterday afternoon we got started without fanfare by shooting an empty chair, everything purely mechanical at first, but at least the camera was rolling. Robards and Adorf, those cowards, whose real problem stems from their appalling inner emptiness, had refused to get into the car with Sluizer, terrified that the strikers might shoot at them. To explain to them that we had already put forty people onto the ship, that Mick Jagger had crisscrossed the city in his car shuttling people and was already at the shooting site, did no good, and I decided to shoot without them. A rainbow that suddenly appeared in the sky behind Mick during the first shots gave me courage. The Brazilians made it onto the ship in the nick of time, still carrying their suitcases, their personal luggage, as well as the sound equipment. They unpacked the Nagra tape recorder, positioned the microphones on the set, and everything got under way before I even had a chance to exchange more than a hasty greeting with them. Lucki flew back

to Munich by way of Miami to get money. He has a report on the first day, a personal report from me to the partners, and the medical forms for the insurance company; without those items there can be no action in the bank accounts.

Iquitos, 10 January 1981
Night shoot with the monks. Not one of them could get out a single coherent line of dialogue. The monk from Mexico, at night the pilgrim at his mission station, caused a scene this morning at the hotel, running down three flights of stairs to the reception desk clothed in nothing but his flowing beard, shouting and raving. Now, during dinner at Don Giovanni, he meekly asks if he can have a minute with me alone. The tropical humidity is so intense that if you leave envelopes lying around they seal themselves.

Iquitos, 17 January 1981
Shooting. The strike on again in the city, but none of this seems as bad as the feverish horrors the rumors had projected. The water rose so high that it came in through the floor of my cabin. A pillow was floating around. In the morning, when I put on my pants they felt cold and odd. I turned one pant leg inside out, and a frog jumped out.

Iquitos, 21 January 1981
A dream, not dreamed at night because I do not dream, but experienced while walking: when I saw snow falling over the jungle and

forming a soggy blanket over the huge, warm river, over the palm huts, the vultures' branches, I knew at once that an ice age had broken out in Europe, covering everything calamitously, and this could only be a long-distance effect from that. A large boa constrictor was also there, killed by a volley of buckshot to the head, but brought back to life with energetic massage. Then I was riding in a speedboat ahead of the steamer, and at a bend in the river let an empty yellow plastic bucket drift back toward the ship. I told the crew the ship would explode if it continued on and passed the bucket. They radioed back that if they stopped, the pail would drift by them. That my gesture had been recognized as an empty threat did nothing to change the fact that I thought I had demonstrated my resoluteness.

Departure for the Camisea postponed again, this time because Robards's lawyers are demanding that we install a heart-lung machine there. Then they demanded that Claude supply his medical license, but after a rather long discussion they realized that this would be difficult to do from the jungle; Claude suggested that they simply check with the Sorbonne administration in Paris. Next they wanted to know what the Sorbonne was. Claude got the idea of obtaining a broken heart-lung machine from a junkyard in Miami and having our crew rig it up in some imaginative way. We were amazed at how terrified Robards must be of the jungle.

Río Camisea, 2 February 1984
Continuing mutiny because of the heart-lung machine, to which has been added a demand for a defibrillator, which is supposed to get a stopped heart beating again. War preparations along the border to Ecuador. We . . .

Río Camisea, 3 February 1981

Last night a Campa woman died very suddenly. The whole camp is quiet, nothing moving. She had diarrhea, developed colic, vomited, and died. In the afternoon a boat carrying many Campas sailed past our ship. They had the dead woman on board, and we buried her on a bank in the jungle. Alberto offered a prayer in her language.

Now that the water level in the river has fallen dramatically, the ship can make it around only one more bend. We started work late, because we are shooting at night now, and drove down to Camisea to take Lucki and Alan Dunn to the plane that had landed there. After some difficulty we had just managed to distribute our weight evenly in the overloaded speedboat, and had reached the speed that holds it up and allows it to glide, when I saw that about a hundred of the Indians were standing on the bank by their camp, gesticulating wildly and pointing at the water. We did not see anything, and Alberto, who was sitting in the bow, had not seen anything, either. But I shouted to the boatman, who was glad the boat was gliding at last, that he should turn around immediately to see what was wrong. From the confused shouting we gathered that a child was drowning, and I pulled off my shoes and dived in. Others followed, and then we searched with a second boat, going far downstream, but we found nothing. It turned out that two young men, both married already, had defied the order not to use the dugouts, and had somehow pulled a canoe out of the large stack chained together and fenced off. They had paddled out onto the river and capsized. Neither of them could swim, and only one of the two had made it back to the bank, while the other sank, and our wake had apparently stirred up the water and made it murkier at this very spot, so that the drowned man disappeared completely. We searched until it got dark. In the space of twelve hours we have had two deaths. In defiance of all reason I kept diving in the dark, so the others would not see how depressed I am. The river is as amorally beautiful as ever.

The drowned man, whom we did not find, was recently married. People told me that at noon he had left all his food for his wife, saying he did not need it anymore, and then told her good-bye.

Río Camisea, 4 February 1981
The search for the dead man continued, without success, without hope. In addition, problems with the ship. The water level had gone down so much that we got hung up in the only river bend in which we could still move. With the help of ropes and speedboats we managed to tug the bow, which was still free, into the current, so that the ship, whose stern was aground, actually floated free.

The council of elders chose a new husband for the drowned man's widow. The jungle does not allow widowhood. The wedding took place in the office of the Ashininkas' camp, with our radio crackling and squawking in the background. The bride, about fifteen years old, seemed outwardly completely indifferent, but in her right hand she was clutching the large plastic comb she had taken out of her hair, and she kept playing a single note on its teeth, repeating it mechanically and thereby revealing her inner turmoil. Her new husband knows how old he is—eighteen. He wore a light-colored shirt.

As Henning was working to fasten the carved Amazonian female figurehead more firmly to the ship, he was asked by a Campa whether she was dead; it was the same Campa who keeps insisting that instead of pay he wants a Suzuki motorcycle from us. No, Henning replied, she was made of wood. So was the snake made of wood as well? Yes, he answered. So how was it possible that the snake had crawled up and looped itself around her?

Río Camisea, 5 February 1981

Klausmann is still more disabled than he cares to admit; he is getting around in the jungle on crutches, but with some difficulty. In the bathing lagoon near Iquitos, where children are always splashing and swimming, a piranha bit off half of his second toe. At the time there was much laughing and joking at his expense, but to Robards this is proof of how malicious and life-threatening the jungle is. I fished several piranhas out of the Camisea and right afterward made a show of swimming in the river, because piranhas are a threat only in stagnant water, never in flowing water. But Robards saw me pulling the fishhook out of the mouth of one of the creatures, and because it was still snapping its sharp teeth, I stuck a pencil into its mouth to block it, from which it promptly bit off several chunks.

Last night Lucki sounded the alarm from Iquitos: things could not go on. The second ship had been stopped, Laplace was not coming, ultimatums and threats from Walter, but it looks as though we will be able to meet each other halfway. Upon returning from the Indians' camp the actors fell upon me like vultures on a carcass. There was not enough mineral water on hand for them to wash with; where could water be found here? I pointed wordlessly to the river, where some of our people were swimming just then and washing themselves. Before the contracts were drawn up, I had described the camps in detail, which in any case are much better equipped than originally planned. Everyone has a washbasin, a porcelain toilet, and a shower, which, however, is supplied with river water when the little brook that flows into the Camisea dries up. None of the meals here has fewer than three courses, and fresh fruit, lettuce, and juices are always available. Several cases of illness in the large camp, which make me uneasy. But among the hundreds of Indians are quite a few who came to us suffering from anemia, because they depend too much on yucca as their main source of nutrition, and it is not easy for the cooks to give them foods they are not accustomed to. We let them decide for themselves what they want to eat.

A little farther upstream I shone a powerful flashlight on the opposite bank and made out alligators, their eyes glowing as if someone were smoking a cigarette over there. But they have been almost completely wiped out here, and are small. Recently Machiguengas shot one of them at night with a shotgun, and I saw them smoking it over a small, guttering fire; it was only half a meter long and tasted good, if a bit swampy.

Río Camisea, 6 February 1981
Later I took a boat to Sepahua to meet Walter. Prompted by César, Vignati, and me, the workers and Campas had put together a petition asking for W.'s return, to make it easier for him to save face. The question is whether he has the gumption to step back from a line he has drawn in the sand, as I have done. The fact is that he alone is to blame for many of the lacks and omissions, except for the absence of a helicopter for emergencies; the war on the border alone is responsible for the military's failing to live up to the agreement.

Yesterday, when the ship's crew, armed to the teeth, flees in one scene in a dinghy, the Campas stood on the bank and laughed and cheered. The extras joined them for a commemorative photo, and some of the Campas yelled, "Emiliano Zapata!" César, who always wants to see things as serious problems, spread the word that upon seeing the men armed with guns, the Campas in their camp had equipped themselves with bows and arrows. The day before we had explained our camera to them; there was lots of laughter, and everyone had a chance to look through the viewfinder. The ocular was so smeared with their red face paint that Mauch later had a red ring around his eye, which made him look very odd. Yesterday the water level in the river rose tremendously, up to a banana plant that serves me as a landmark and from which it is only three more meters to the platform of our canteen building. Thought a lot of my son, with a heavy heart. Otherwise numb, tired, lacking a sense of meaning, very much alone.

In the shed–with our wretched attempt at raising chickens–sickly, half-naked creatures vegetate; with some sympathy, they can be described as hens, barely hanging on. A captured tapir is tied up there, as big as a full-grown hog. It is still young and is said to cry at night, thereby luring the tapir mother closer, whom the Indians have already sighted once on the edge of their camp but could not kill. Today the tapir was missing. It had quiet, sad, desperate eyes. Most likely they slaughtered it.

Sepahua–Camisea, 6 February 1981
My dates have been wrong, but apparently I am on track again. Yesterday, as we were sailing to the Río Sepahua, the radiator failed, not far from the Río Picha. A canoe with a *peke-peke* motor towed us as far as the mission. Henning, Uli, César, and Vignati were along. While the repair was being done, I fell asleep in the boat, and the sun shone on me and actually burned my face. Mendoza and his son happened to come by, returning from looking for gold on the upper Picha, and young Mendoza gave us a ride. We arrived toward evening, and at that very moment the plane with Walter, Lucki, Sluizer, and Cucho was circling before landing. A rapprochement reached with Walter after a long discussion that we conducted on a tree trunk. Nine of the extras arrived an hour later in another boat. I slept in a hut that we call the Sepahua Hilton, next to a deep hole dug in the ground,

between rusting gasoline drums and plastic crates with empty beer bottles, but I actually had a kind of bed, from which I first shook the dried rat droppings. The rats darted like squirrels up the mats serving as walls. In the morning I woke up early and found myself staring a guinea pig in the face; it was looking at me dumbfounded. In the evening I had got through to Mauch on the radio and given instructions for the next stage of the job.

Big reception for Walter in Camisea. Women and children were there, drums, the men with bows and arrows. It did Walter good, and I drove around the last bend to our camp, a bit farther up the river, feeling the future was somewhat less uncertain.

Camisea, 7 February 1981

I saw a Campa woman sitting on a tree trunk. She was staring intently over her shoulder at something I could not make out. Her child of about three was standing in front of her. It worked her breast out of her *cushma*, grasped it with both hands, and nursed, without the mother's paying the slightest attention.

Last night the various groups of Campas and Machiguengas played the drums and danced; we drank *masato* with them. A boat-man had taken a plate of food with him as he sailed from one camp to the other because he had not even had breakfast, and he was so preoccupied with the food that by mistake he steered into a wall of overhanging jungle. Robards is disintegrating more and more. Adorf is revealing himself increasingly as a whiner, a stupid star full of posturing who cannot stand it that the Indian extras are sometimes more important than he is, the famous actor. Furthermore, he is simply cowardly, sneaky, and dumb, high-decibel dumb, as Mauch says. Yesterday Jerry Hall wafted into Camisea on a plane.

At night I had first the feeling and then the certainty that I was caught in a twilit prehistory, without speech or time.

Afternoon: the camp seems dead. We decided to enlarge the tree-top platform first and make it more stable because Robards, using Adorf as his spokesman, is calling for stuntmen. Walter, who was there with workmen, also reported that the pathway up the slope was nearly impassable. He was unable to clamber over a huge tree trunk knocked down in the storm a few weeks ago and extremely difficult to go around. Before he had even seen it, Adorf, almost dying of cowardice, pronounced the scene on the lookout platform danger-ous, unsafe, and superfluous without even having seen it, and he is talking about doing the whole thing one meter above ground level, now using Robards as his spokesman. But in the film the geography has to be visible: two rivers that almost touch, with only a mountain ridge between them, over which the ship has to be hauled. Without that understanding the point of the story is lost.

The rain pours and subsides, and Mick is taking photos for *Vogue* of Jerry Hall in leopard-patterned bathing suits, with a backdrop of rain forest and wild Indians; it is disturbing to me to see our back-ground used for commercial purposes. Mick told me he would earn $4,000 for the photos, and laughed himself sick. I washed my socks in the river because too many of them disappear when I put them in the laundry. The river's sluggish whirlpools pass by, following the bidding of a distant fate. In the forest behind me the birds are cursing each other. Nothing ever gets properly dry here, shoes or clothing. Anything made of leather gets mildewed, and electric clocks stop. In two weeks we have not managed to get the steer to the ship; he is impossible to control, and no one was in a position to get him onto a freight boat. The leaves in the forest gleam and drip, and from time to time very large fish break with a smacking sound through the sluggish surface of the river and leave widening rings behind, as mighty as if a prehistoric dinosaur had dived in, smacking its lips after a good meal. When the rain lets up and there is just a gentle dripping from the trees, something resembling peace descends on one's soul for a few moments. A bug came toward me, of terrifying size. Far off in the forest chain saws are working at some job I don't know about.

Then an unbelievably powerful and steady rain came down over the jungle; language itself resists calling it rain. Foamy white brooks formed in the sand along the riverbank below my cabin and streamed into the brown river, which pulls everything to it and carries everything away: tree trunks, broken-off limbs, the drowned man, earth, pebbles. The pebbles clunk and roll and bang against each other, as if the entire base of the earth were washing away. In the meantime an immeasurable misty vapor spread among the treetops, which stood there rigid and patient, from time immemorial. All the birds are silent; the rain is having the last say. On a branch floating downstream, many ants; the rain forest has such an extraordinary surfeit of life. On the swaying liana suspension bridge wet leaves are lying, stuck on after being ripped from the trees by the rain. Little reservoirs form on the slope side of the path, next to rounds cut from trees and placed next to each other, and overflow between them. These round stepping-stones are partially submerged, the rest poking out as if they were drowning.

During the dance of the Indians, who resemble drunken birds displaying their tail feathers, the men and women do not touch. I drank *masato* till it tasted good. Little girls open the tough peels of green bananas with their teeth, just the way animals do. I have also seen animals lying and sleeping as they do. This morning, when we assembled all the Indians on the path in the rain and mud and saw that we could not shoot the scene without lights, and it was clear that it would take over an hour to get the ship with the generator in position and to lay a cable up the slope, I asked them all to go back to their camp, but they wanted to stay and wait. When I came back almost two hours later, most of them were lying on large leaves on the soaking, rotting forest floor, sleeping, wrapped only in their *cushmas*.

Nature has come to her senses again; only the forest is still menacing, motionless. The river rolls along without a sound, a monster. Night falls very fast, with the last birds scolding the evening, as always at this hour. Rough cawing, malevolent sounds, punctuated by the even chirping of the first cicadas. From all this working in the rain my fingers are wrinkly, like those of the laundresses. I must have a hundred bites on my back from some insect I never did see; all of me is rotting with moisture. I would be grateful if it were only dreams tormenting me. Across the table came a strange primeval insect, with a thin, lancelike, excessively long proboscis and feelers on both sides. I could not make out any eyes. It was dragging a dead insect of the same species, and disappeared through the cracks in the bark floor. Then caterpillars crawled toward me from all directions, brainless but unstoppable. I thought intensely of the great moment when I showed my son, five at the time, the mountains of the moon through a telescope.

Camisea, 8 February 1981
Robards demanded that he not be required to drink *masato*, because he knew it was made from yucca fermented with saliva; no further discussion was possible. He was sure he would catch tuberculosis from it. He hates the jungle because he finds it unhygienic, and dirty as well. Yesterday he ate steak, flown in from the U.S. packed in Sty-

rofoam and deep-frozen. Outside the river is rising more and more; its color has changed to a fresh brown, and it is flowing appreciably faster. Large uprooted tree trunks and pieces of wood are carried along. It is raining without pause, and I like the sound, the taste, the feel of the rain. The floating platform, consisting of a balsa raft with a *pona* bark covering, that serves as a mooring place for our boat tore loose. Someone saw it happen, and one of our boats took up the chase. Janoud, Silvia, and Alan Dunn arrived. They set out yesterday from Sepahua, but soon saw that with all the driftwood they could not make it. They spent the night in Nueva Luz and started out very early today. Their expressions did not bode well. Everything still vague, to be worked out—maybe—only with wrenching effort.

The rain has stopped, but the river continues to rise. Only now does real sadness settle over the land, rigid with silence. What today was murder will be called an emergency slaughter tomorrow. The camp is sinking into a deep depression. Now and then a boat arrives without any purpose, bringing nothing, and disappears again. Someone was poking around in a pile of rotting branches, looking for nothing in particular. The day has the aura of nights haunted by fear. I found myself wishing intently and completely in vain that an Indio would sharpen his machete on a flat stone, and in the process make a hundred years fly by *in no time*.

In an old newspaper that Alan Dunn brought, I read about a skiing competition that took place four weeks ago, four weeks that had slipped by, passed in no time, long-ago weeks. Mauch wanted to cheer me up with nonsense poems, of which he keeps a supply for such moments. He said, "A fool sings every type of song, sometimes right and sometimes wrong. A wise man sometimes sings at night, but always short and never long." I borrowed a bow and arrow from a tattooed Indian and shot an arrow into the sky.

Camisea, 9 February 1981

Comings and goings of boats with no particular purpose. Our land-ing platform is gone for good. As we were filming last night, the river was going down so fast that we constantly had to maneuver the ship to keep it from running aground by the bank where only a little while ago deep, gurgling water was streaming. Robards is being flown out today. Claude examined him before lunch and is now writing a report for the insurance company in French. I had seen Robards at the crack of dawn, when it was actually still quite dark, hurrying through the camp without his dentures, his hair flying and his eyes crazed, like King Lear through the deserted chambers in his castle.

*And this is how things seemed to end for the film at that time: as Jason Robards took off, the Machiguenga children in their threadbare cush-*mas *stood behind the plane in the whirlwind caused by the propeller and let their clothing billow. When the plane turned in place, they ran like fluttering birds in a half circle, still blown by the propeller's blast. Grass tufts were flattened, and bits of damp earth were churned up. By one of the huts the children had tied a length of sound tape, prob-ably lost by our soundman, knotted together in several places, between a post and a tree. It was so taut that it continued to hum and sing long after the plane could no longer be seen.*

Nonetheless: whatever I can still do, I must do. When I got into the boat again, there was a swarm of butterflies glowing in brown and yellow around me. The sun glitters on a silent river, which, though falling, is still much too high and seems to be slithering up on something that must be far off, hidden in the mighty landscape.

All the bushes are still under water, up to their highest branches, saying no to the current and standing up to the flood. I tossed a crumpled paper handkerchief into the river, and the next moment a very large fish snatched it under the surface, but let go of it right away, so that it popped up again briefly. The Indian boatman was playing the harmonica as he transported me back to the camp.

Jerry Hall gave me a piece of chocolate with a filling of brittle, half melted but so delicious that it rendered me speechless, and an Indian gave me a jaguar's large fang to wear around my neck as an amulet. We shot some footage with Mick and the little Indian boy who is called McNamara in the film, and both of them did such a good job that the team broke into applause. During the scene Mick was bitten on the shoulder by one of the monkeys and laughed so uproariously about it afterward that it sounded like a donkey braying. Whenever we take a break he distracts me with clever little lectures on English dialects and the development of the language since the late Middle Ages.

At night I brooded for a long time and quite unsystematically, trying to recall where I once saw a dinosaur footprint in petrified mud. Then I thought of my father, who had told me during the summer on the phone that he had recently almost been *blackbirded*. Then I thought about him and my mother. My life was handed to me between somewhere and nowhere.

Camisea, 10 February 1984
Very early in the morning I climbed with César to the highest point between the rivers, then up onto the platform. About halfway we heard a plane overhead that we could not account for. I was shocked again at how steep it was and wondered how a ship could ever be hauled up and over the mountain. Back down at the river I washed

the sweat off my body, being careful because scores of large, cobalt blue butterflies had settled on my skin, and I did not want to scare them off. A large wasps' nest with hollow chambers bobbed lightly by on the water, like a cotton ball. Chunks of earth gently break off the bank and plop into the water. Mauch was trying to cheer me up by telling jokes. Someone asked a lumberjack who was looking for work where he had worked last. In the Sahara, he replied. But there are not any trees there, he was told. Not anymore, said the lumberjack.

We filmed from the small plane that had come; securely tethered, Mauch leaned out the open side door, and I served as his focus puller; it would have been too risky to put any more people on board with the landing strip so muddy. The aerial shots were rather disappointing, though. There was too much turbulence, and even if it had been calm one could still have had the impression that the shots were taken from an express train. Mick, Jerry Hall, and Adorf left us right after dinner; they are flying out to Lima.

Camisea, 11 February 1984

Waiting on a sandbank that is normally firm but whose edges are so sodden that you sink way in. The ship, with more than a hundred Indians on board, is not in position yet. Over the walkie-talkie by which I communicate with the woodcutters on the other side of the river—where they are using chain saws to notch a series of big trees, which, we hope, will fall down in succession like dominos— I suddenly heard radio traffic from the U.S., from Kansas City. A woman was talking with her husband, on the road as a trucker, and the conversation sounded strangely artificial. The woman especially was speaking as though she were in a TV commercial, yet it was a private conversation, overheard in the depths of the rain forest. I wanted to break in and say hello, but my transmitter is not nearly powerful enough. Vignati came out of the forest, his hair matted and full of black flies. He was flailing at them, and we picked the nasty things out of his woolly hair.

Trees falling all the rest of the day. When these giants fall, the sound is the exciting part. The mightiest tree of all sighed, then screamed, then farted, then crashed with incredible force into the forest. Long afterward large limbs continued to snap until they finally fell silent. A bat colony fluttered off in confusion, along with swarms of wasps, birds, a cloud of small flying insects. Tiny, thin caterpillars flee, humping their midsection, then throwing their front section ahead, rushing along in a caterpillar gallop.

The jungle is steaming now as if after a thousand years of rain. The river flows aimlessly along. A shadow, rising from the forest, darkened the sky. The moon, tentative today, will not dare to peek behind the horizon. Tonight I am hitching my boat to barren, fainthearted stars. Once the sky turned pitch black, unfamiliar fruits from an unknown tree plunked onto the damp ground around my hut.

Camisea, 12 February 1981
In the morning a Cabaña Airlines plane circled over the camp. People were all in a tizzy as to who would get to fly out first. In the meantime this question comes to mind: is it worthwhile to live out there in a decoded world, inhabited by decoded people? The Mexicans are roaming around restlessly, the way Robards did earlier. At nightfall, when it is pure insanity to land, another plane circled over us—it can only be Pino from Cabaña, no one else would be that reckless. The

plane, whatever it is, has to land because there is no illuminated landing strip for eight hundred kilometers around. Quiet voices in the camp. Half-asleep, I kept listening to the calls of the nocturnal birds and changes in the atmosphere. I wanted to record some of the sounds, but could not drag myself out of bed.

My cabin: several steps, consisting of a sturdy tree trunk into which treads have been sawn as the natives do here, lead up to the platform that serves as a porch. There I have a crude table, roughly hewn from boards, two benches, and a hammock, as well as wooden hooks where I hang my raingear. Behind that a single room, which you enter through a swinging bamboo door. There are three windows, all fairly small, two of which can be closed with bamboo blinds that roll down. A bed with mosquito netting, the mattress stuffed with sea grass and hard; it has peaks and valleys, into which one has to fit one's body carefully. The room also has a hammock, hung diagonally, and a primitive wooden shelf for my tapes, the two books I have with me, and some odds and ends. By the entryway two small wooden shelves, one above the other, where I keep my toiletries. Underneath them, hanging from a nail where I can find it always by feel, the flashlight. Toward the foot of the bed, i.e., on the side with the door and the porch, which faces the river, two poles are braced in the corners of the room at chest height. Over the left one I drape all my clothes, over the right one my towels. But so much dust and loose fiber drifts down from the thatch of palm fronds that forms the roof that every day there is a layer over everything, which, however, can easily be shaken off. I have three stools, each knocked together from a thick slice of tree trunk and three legs. The floor is springy *pona* bark held up by posts that raise it about a meter above the ground. On the floor stands my radio, with a cord long enough to let me take it out to the porch. The toilet and washroom are in a two-stall outhouse about fifteen meters behind my cabin; half the camp residents use it, and usually there is a line. My lightbulb, mounted in a basket, provides too little light for reading. When I am lying down, I brace the flashlight between my shoulder and my neck so it will shine on the book. Usually the only time I can read is at night, but I soon get tired. When I go to bed, I always put my little travel alarm clock, my flashlight, and a book next to and under the pillow. The clock itself is silent; the alarm peeps like the insects outside, and only when I have it right by my head do I realize that it is meant for me. During the day I carry the alarm clock folded up in a small leather pouch on a second belt around my waist, because I do not have a wristwatch that works anymore, and hardly anyone else in the film crew has one. In the pouch I always have writing material, the notebook, the clock, a penknife, and sometimes my Minox or a compass. In Iquitos I always have my sunglasses in the pouch to protect my eyes from the dust when I am riding the motorcycle.

The river has fallen to its lowest level, but now it began to rain hard again, and from the sound I can tell it will continue through the night. On my mosquito net, in the light, sits a green, prehistoric-looking animal, motionless, gazing down at me.

Resortes keeps asking me what time the helicopter is coming, a highly doubtful proposition because of the war along the border with Ecuador. He practically ambushes me so he can fire the question at me. Sarah, who has worked herself all the way up the launchpad for discontent, spoke in all seriousness of the helicopter and commuter planes, four of them today alone. All I said was: the helicopter is not coming, but when it comes, it comes, and the flights will take off when they take off. Despite my explaining the situation to each of them before we started the project, many people do not want to grasp that we are at the headwaters of the Amazon, and that it is often not possible to land, even if one wanted to. Recently, when we packed the body harness into the small plane in Camisea, removed the door, and strapped Mauch and me in, a two-engine plane was circling overhead, from where I do not know, and wanted to land but then flew off again. Meanwhile in the camp Adorf had shouted that there was a big plane coming in, and they all threw their heavy luggage into a boat to get to it, Adorf leading the pack like a shipwrecked passenger ruthlessly pushing everyone else off a plank into the water. Walter told him the plane was not ours, and besides, it had not landed. No, no, it was there, Adorf shouted at him. Walter shouted back, asking whether he had actually been at the airfield. No, it was there, Adorf shouted, he had seen it. But because the airfield is several kilometers away, he finally believed Walter, who had just come from there.

During breakfast all of us had still joked that I should, like Pizarro, on his wretched island off the coast of Peru, draw a line in the sand, step over it and ask who would stay with me, who would step over the line. Even without Robards we still have enough work left, for a while at least. My thoughts are occupied by the image of the first man who stepped over the line. He was a man from the island of Crete, Pedro de Candia.

Janoud will remain in the camp, after everyone has left. Janoud told the story how he, at the age of six, together with his family, had climbed a hill in the Vogtland and watched the blazing glow in the sky, and they all knew that Dresden was burning.

Camisea, 13 February 1984
A bad night with little sleep. Incessant downpours, rumbling thunder, and my roof is not completely watertight. I rigged up my rain poncho to protect me from a leak. Now in the morning it is a heavy,

steady rain, everything gray on gray. The jungle has become dark and colorless, and stands there motionless. Now the river is rushing by twice as fast, angry, a gleaming brown, full of dark dirt and fast-moving driftwood. From yesterday's low-water mark it has now reached the highest level I have seen yet. One minute a post where canoes tie up was still sticking up above the surface by about a hand's breadth, and the next it had disappeared altogether. The mood is good; we are resigned to our fate. Every leaf is dripping, and the drops crash like meteors into the puddles out in the open. A great, steady rushing sound has settled over the land. The jaguar I thought I heard during the night was probably a howler monkey, which has now fallen silent. The Cabaña plane certainly will not be able to take off from the muddy airstrip today, and there will not be any helicopter, either. The camp is very quiet, as if dead. No motion, no sounds, no birds in the jungle, nothing; only rain, which refuses to stop. The forest is keeping still as if in ardent prayer.

Looking into the river is like gazing into a flickering fire; you cannot take your eyes off it. Without pause whole islands of decaying branches and wood drift by, everything that was rotting on the floor of the rain forest. Around large, uprooted trees, tangles form of old branches and all the stuff that was decaying on the ground. An endless layer of wood and detritus drifts along on the surface of the water. To travel by motorboat or take off or land in a hydroplane would be impossible because of all the drifting debris in the water. The water is creeping closer and closer to me. The bushes along the bank are now out in the middle of the stream, with only their crowns poking out, battered by the force of the current. The banana plants farther upstream are already under water. In the small bay right in front of me a powerful counter-current has formed. Along with the drifting wood, there is more and more white foam now. Several enormous trees, tangled in each other, drifted by like swirling islands. The rolling of heavy rocks on the river bottom. Has anyone heard rocks sigh?

Río Camisea, 14 February 1981

The river somewhat lower today. Mauch, Vignati, and I made our way up the slope with machetes and at the highest point between the rivers scrambled up onto the platform and let the wind rock us. We were all alone with the jungle, floating gently above its steaming treetops, and I was no longer afraid at the thought of hauling a huge ship over the mountain ridge, even if *everything* in this gravity-ridden world seemed to argue against it.

Iquitos, 15 February 1981

Dissolving the camp. The airfield in Camisea was so soggy that the pilot, coming to his senses, did not dare to take more than two people on board, so Miguel Ángel Fuentes, Klausmann, and I took a boat down to the Picha, to board the plane there, where the runway is much firmer. But the plane had trouble gaining altitude, and shaved the tops off some bushes at the end of the runway, so that even Pino, the pilot who will take any risk, broke out in a sweat. Refueling in Atalaya, and from Pucallpa on to Iquitos with Faucett.

The house that serves as our headquarters was deserted, with only Gustavo and Claire still living there. When I went to my cabin, a sense of desolation seized me. The bed full of dried rat droppings, dust everywhere, no running water. The banana fronds rustle in the wind, but none of it pertains to me anymore. No mail had come. I found an unwashed undershirt of mine hanging over the porch railing. The things I collected here in Iquitos now seem useless. As I approached my hut, the path was almost completely overgrown with brush; I was like a stranger, and the house did not recognize me. A man was hacking away at the yucca plants with his machete. My frying pan is all rusty. On the wall hang things that seem to stare at me in bewilderment, wondering whether I still belong to them. In the afternoon I fell asleep in the hammock on my porch, my limbs heavy. Several times I tried to get up, until the setting sun reached me under the palm roof, and burned me in the face, as if filled with hatred. At that point I withdrew into my four bamboo walls and tried to take in the situation. I ate a few cookies that I found in a tin. Unmoved, the birds in the forest were exchanging information. A twig cracked, but no one was coming. It is a hot, sultry afternoon, drained of meaning.

In the evening, I was invited by Henning and Uli to have dinner at their house. It was a nice, quiet evening, and it did me good to be with them. It is dawning on me that I am done for, even if I forbid myself to think so. Rats scurried across my room when I returned. I changed the sheets in which the animals had been living and felt my helplessness. Then, even though it was late, I washed my hair in my shower—the night watchman had turned on the water for me. So here I am. The nocturnal cicadas are sawing away at time. The sky hangs there, helpless and silent. The night is forcing its way in through my window with its blackness. A bird has strayed under my roof; it betrayed its presence by rustling. I pointed the flashlight at it, but that only confused it more, and I let darkness take over.

Iquitos, 16 February 1981
A storm sprang up very suddenly and blew the pages of an old letter against the window screen. The rain came in horizontally under my

roof. I made myself a cup of coffee, strong enough to knock a person dead. Outside the rain is raining, pouring off the roof. The large fronds of the banana plant bend reverently to receive the rain. The forest stands there, the soul of patience. The description of the rain sums up an entire continent.

After the rain the earth's smell was so overpowering that I felt dizzy. In the west, when darkness falls, there is one spot in the sky without clouds that has a pale, unreal glow. The sky heaves like the waves in the ocean.

The news I received today is unambiguous: Robards will not come back to the jungle, under any circumstances. Medical reports, legal mumbo-jumbo to stake out a position against any possible breach-of-contract claims. Contacted Lucki in Brazil, Walter at the Camisea. Walter insists I should seek a legal ruling in the U.S. to force Robards to fulfill his contract, but I do not need any legal ruling to know that I am doomed. In the house I went, now completely alone, through all the abandoned rooms. With their bare mattresses they stared at me and I stared back, devoid of emotion, simply into the void. Gustavo and Claire now sit with me at night beneath the fluorescent lights in the office, besieged by mosquitoes. We say nothing. There is a whistling and crackling in our radio, but sometimes music floats in, like a xylophone from ethereal spheres. For a brief time a station from the Soviet Union came in quite clearly.

Iquitos, Lima, 18 February 1981
As Gustavo was driving me furiously through the potholes to the airport, and I was being bounced around in my seat, the idea came to me: why should I not play Fitzcarraldo myself? I would trust myself to do it because my project and the character have become identical.

Lima. I drove straight to the country club to see Mick, and spoke with him, then with Adorf. It is clear that if the whole undertaking is to go on, everything will have to start again at the beginning, because we cannot excise Robards from the existing negative. There are no halfhearted or considerate solutions. I raised the question with Mick as to whether he would play Fitzcarraldo, but he does not trust himself to do that, even if the character were to be approached altogether differently. Furthermore, his stop-date is coming close because of the world tour with the Stones. Adorf heard from Mick what ideas we had been playing with and is trying to curry favor, but he does not have what it takes, and he drew me into a rather stupid discussion about acting, claiming that as an actor he would have made a much better Kaspar Hauser than a clumsy amateur like Bruno S. Without even trying to be polite I told him I did not see it that way, I saw it differently, and I also told him he was out of the question for the main character. Now he is deeply offended. So be it.

I am thirty-eight now, and I have been through it all. My work has given me everything and taken everything from me. No one and nothing can throw me off course. The only other one who could also be Fitzcarraldo would be Kinski; he would certainly also be better than I, and after all, there was some discussion with him in the very early phase of the project, but it was always clear that he would be the last one who could see such an undertaking through to the end.

Later to the beach south of Lima with Mick, Adorf, and Joe Koechlin's brother, who is a race-car driver. Stupid girls in bikinis, tanned surfers who had nothing to do and were revoltingly vapid. The sea had a strong smell, and the sky overhead was colorless and hazy. Next to a surfboard, a cormorant popped up from the water, looking so out of place and artificial that for a moment I thought it was plastic, like the fake ducks that hunters put out on ponds as decoys, but then it suddenly dived so elegantly that I gained confidence in cormorants. Disco music was blaring across the beach. Joe's brother kept bending my ear about an auto race he had wanted to take part in but which was called off. In the evening with a larger group to a Chinese restaurant. We were in a sort of separate niche, as were the other guests in the place. There were eleven of us, ten, that is, plus me. I was the primary number. I wanted to steal away into another era, quietly and without creating a commotion.

Lima, 19–21 February 1981

. . . flat, swept bare, as if made of concrete. Unwavering, pressing onward. Praised be any tree that takes pity on me, where . . .

Lima–New York, 22 February 1981

The pressure on me even more intense. We could not make the planned stopover in Guayaquil in Ecuador because suddenly the airport has been closed to all civilian air traffic, which can mean only one of two things: the Ecuadorians are preparing for a military confrontation with Peru, or a military coup is taking place, both equally plausible since a Peruvian helicopter was shot down in the border region two days ago, despite the ceasefire, and the unrest among Ecuador's military on account of the drastic price increases imposed by Roldos to finance the war effort. A combination of a military junta and an attack on Peru would be a third possibility.

In Panama the plane filled up with braying Americans. I could not see the canal from the window. As we flew over Cuba I saw a huge fire down below, certainly a kilometer long, an enormous, glowing worm.

New York, 23 February 1981

I phoned Kinski and got together with him at one in the morning. He ordered a bottle of champagne from room service, and that did me good. At noon today on the phone he said our nighttime conversation had been like too much potato salad: you felt stuffed and belched and it was better to forget the whole thing the next day. If I had debts of $20,000, I should be worried, but at $3 million in the red, the worries cease. I think he is right.

My personal affairs also in a deep crisis, at the breaking point. In the apartment near Lincoln Plaza, to which I still have a key, I carefully swept the crumbs from the table, straightened the cushions on the couch, placed the photos in their envelopes where they belonged, turned off the lights, and left the place with no sign of my having been there, as if I did not exist. In this state of inactivity, of waiting, of uncertainty as to how the insurance company, which is playing for time, will respond, I kept remembering how as a fifteen-year-old I played hooky with Till; at the time I think he had just finished his apprenticeship, and it must have been November. We hitchhiked to North Germany, and he wanted to go to Helgoland. We went our separate ways somewhere because he had picked up some girls and wanted to party with them for a while. In Düsseldorf, in ice-cold rain and fog, I broke into a cottage in an allotment garden and spent two days and two nights there, most of that time in a mildewed lawn chair. Then I broke into a fancy villa through a window and spent almost two more days in a young girl's room. She still had dolls on her bed, but on the walls she had posters with rock stars, and among her clothes were minuscule beginner's bras. Downstairs in the house, in the kitchen, an alarm clock was still ticking; the owners could not have been gone that long. I examined the house for hours, trying to find indications of how long they would be away: the date of the last newspaper in the wastebasket, how tightly everything was locked up, any written clue that might be lying around, how much food was in the refrigerator. There were eggs, milk, and vegetables, and anyone who leaves such things in the refrigerator is not away for weeks. Once, on the first evening, I had a terrible fright because the phone rang. I slept on the bed half dressed, with my shoes next to me so I could get them on quickly. When I ate, I collected the crumbs on a piece of newspaper. The second night it was about eleven, and I was already sound asleep, having not dared to turn on any lights, even though at that time of year it got dark around six; suddenly lights went on all over the house, there were voices, and the garage door opened. My room was above the garage, and there were people down there, so I could not escape out the window and over the garage roof. Nor was it possible to use the stairs. Breathless with fear, I locked the room from the inside. Soon after that someone pressed the latch. Mommy, did you lock my room, the girl on the other side of the door asked; who locked my door? Just then it grew quiet in the garage, and a man's footsteps came up the stairs. I climbed out onto the flat roof, jumped down into the garden, and scrambled over the hedge into the neighbor's property. For a while I crouched motionless under a damp, cold, dripping tree and then sneaked out of there without a sound. I still remember the next morning: fields shrouded in November fog, crows, and cars passing by that had destinations, were coming from somewhere and going somewhere else.

I tried to phone M, but the phone rang twelve times and no one answered. I could hear crazy people shouting in the street below all the way up to my thirty-fourth-floor apartment. From the window I can see New Jersey being pummeled by a winter storm. Many people here talk to themselves.

New York, 24 February–4 March 1981
Very difficult days.

New York, 5 March 1981
Driving snow, everything white on white and gray on gray. Far below me on the streets, the traffic almost inaudible, even the fire engines' sirens muffled.

New York, 6 March 1981
Among normal human beings again finally, not just lawyers and insurance adjusters, or so I thought. In the evening with D. at de G.'s place, where a little Italian colony was gathered. But the conviviality fell apart as soon as people began doing drugs. The whole thing seemed to have no purpose, other than that there was a meal at the beginning. A young woman who spoke German pulled up her skirt and showed her legs. Prela, the Albanian who claims he is a much better actor than Marlon Brando, dragged her with loud curses onto a bed that was heaped with coats, pulled down her pantyhose, called the rest of us to see, and dragged her by the legs over the mountain of coats, showed us her bare abdomen, and then, with even worse curses, left her lying there. The guests then made a big show of sniffing cocaine, after which any conversation collapsed, like a poorly constructed house of blocks thrown up by a cranky child. When I left the party, it was snowing hard, and on the Henry Hudson Parkway the cars were at a standstill in a hopeless traffic jam.

. . .

Then I flew to Munich. Meeting with all the partners and backers. Lucki had worked out a pitiless document in which all the eventualities were calculated down to the penny; even the unthinkable was expressed in numbers. But the question that everyone wanted answered was whether I would have the nerve and the strength to start the whole process from scratch. I said yes; otherwise I would be someone who had no dream left, and without dreams I would not want to live.

Iquitos–Miami, 26 March 1981
After having only a day and a half to keep things in Iquitos from collapsing completely, I am flying back to the U.S. already. As I was packing, I heard something rustling above me, and saw a large spotted snake on the wire mesh that serves as my ceiling. Whenever I got close, it thrashed the tip of its tail very fast and frantically, vibrating like an engine. With Walter's help, I drove it toward my porch, and tried to kill it with an iron rod, but it took off over the roof. The cabin is now standing on its stilts in water, with swamp all around. Frogs, even small fishes around me. When I arrived at night, everything was deserted, not a soul anywhere, deathlike silence, the house abandoned. Suddenly the Indian night watchman came toward me, noiselessly, with his light. I looked through the office for signs of life. All I found was the telex machine, fried by short circuits, the upper plastic parts melted as if after a war without witnesses. The number dial is punched in, like an eye into its socket. I groped my way to my cabin and found myself surrounded by bog. Frogs swam away as I approached and dove down to the bottom. I found the ladder lying on one side, among the banana plants, and as I put it

in place, I stepped into a hole originally intended for a differently positioned support post and now full of putrid water. I felt utterly out of place, the more so because I was still wearing the black pin-striped suit and black oxfords I had put on for meeting with lawyers in New York.

New York, 27 March 1981
I was picked up at La Guardia by a limousine with darkened windows, and felt as though I were in a movie. The woman who picked me up was wearing a mink coat, and as the car rolled along she revealed that she had nothing on underneath. Evenings with Mick; it will not be possible to arrange the whole schedule around him in such a way that he will be done in time for the tour. Telephone calls. Adorf is making shameless demands, such a vain, stupid, devious person. He has to be removed from the film.

New York–Miami–Iquitos, 28 March 1981
In Miami I caught up with Mauch and Beat Presser. George Sluizer and the Brazilians came from Río by way of Manaus. In Iquitos angry mists drifted across the landscape, that was good.

Iquitos, 29 March 1981
Lunch with Huerequeque; we drank the Chivas Regal I had brought along. The water level in the Río Nanay is so high that it almost reaches the porch of his bar. The busted construction crane is still rusting on the scruffy lawn out in front. Apparently Huerequeque took it as collateral from a debtor, and on Mother's Day, when he

was plastered, he made the grand gesture of giving the wreck to his wife as a gift.

Iquitos, 30 March 1981

The dates we want at the opera house in Manaus are not available, because that is when a ballet company is having a guest appearance. We studied the dailies of the Río Camisea. Still many uncertainties. I found a frog under my pillow. In town a policeman stopped me on the motorcycle on some pretext and wanted to extort money from me, but I stepped on the gas and sped off. Now it is evening and the sky has opened up. Rain is streaming under the door and into the office, collecting along the wall on the garden side. In no time the stream has grown to a width of two meters, and in a matter of minutes the room will be under water. The water is pulsing under the door in bursts. Polyplike eddies of swiftly flowing water snake around the legs of my chair and reach for each other, soon combining to form a single surface. Around the pathetically small drain in the middle of the room cigarette butts are swirling. The screens at the windows have turned into walls of water, pulsing downward. With a push broom and other tools we tried to direct the flood onto the vacant lot next door. From the thicket over there lightning flashed toward us, raining down from the sky.

As I was walking to my hut I observed some disturbing creatures that resembled eels, reddish brown; presumably they are a kind of very large blindworm, though they seem to dry when exposed to the air. I saw two of these weird animals, looking as though they had slipped out of an enormous cadaver. One of them was trying, with swimming movements, or perhaps they were also drowning movements, to burrow, to snake its way under a dissolving strip of *pona* bark in the water. I cannot imagine a more deadly, naked, wormlike eelish parasite to have in my own innards.

Waited for hours for a phone connection. First I was told it would take an hour and a half, and once that passed, two more hours, and so forth. The radio meanwhile was emitting an unending jumble of incomprehensible, distorted voices. One time I heard the whistle we had always used as a signal in Camisea, but after that our camp in the jungle remained silent. Today the rushes seemed like something I had dreamed, or rather, like something someone else had dreamed and I had merely been told about. Being wide awake at night now seems natural; I hardly sleep. I do not know what real sleep is anymore; I just have brief, strenuous fainting spells.

I followed an electrical crackling and found in the wet wall little metal doors that were wide open, inside them a tangle of cables installed by the confused man from the electric company. They are all insulated poorly or not at all. Here we have the portals to death by electrocution. Today there is supposed to have been an attempt on Reagan's life, according to the news from the local broadcasting station. In Poland Russian tanks are rolling toward Warsaw.

Iquitos, 31 March 1981
Massive burden on me; everything is too precarious: organizationally, financially, timewise, in human terms. In town I purchased a *Commercio* to learn more about the assassination attempt on Reagan. At breakfast, without knowing any details, we had speculated as to whether he was dead and how it would look if Bush became president as a result.

Yellow birds laid siege to me. Last night I had to combat a fresh invasion of army ants in my cabin; they overran me with their larvae, but they were easier to fight because they were so unusually large. First I tried spraying Baygon, but that did not work, and finally I swept the raving warriors off my platform into the swamp. Our work is not compatible with nature Amazon-style. The weather is bad, the chickens are not doing well, ditto the rabbit. The vermin in the earth is thriving. It is happy. The Chinese wok was filled with a jellylike, almost transparent mass, sticky and tough, and in its midst was a broken-off lizard tail, as if the poisonous bite of some nasty creature had melted the lizard into a tough, gluey mass. I set the wok to soak overnight, but even with scouring powder and a wooden stick for scraping I cannot get the disgusting stuff out. Tumors form on the trees. Roots writhe in the air. The jungle revels in debauched lewdness.

No one was affected by our problems as much as Norman R. from the lab in New York, the man who looks like Nixon's vice president, Spiro Agnew, and who greets his visitors by projecting porn photos on the wall. He called all the department heads into his office, and technical experts crowded in. He made a short speech and bowed to me, and it did my heart good. The second one was Schlöndorff, who reached me by phone and told me that he had gotten my letter belatedly after his return from Lebanon. He had prayed again for the first time since his mother's death.

Iquitos, 1 April 1981
Walter was back from Camisea, had got drunk at Paul's on his way to the house, and once here screamed and shouted for a long time in his most vulgar manner. He seems burned out, disoriented, disheartened. I will see what I can do for him. We made a video test with Paul and Huerequeque, and it is clear to me that I will have to be very patient when I work with the two of them; Huerequeque espe-

cially comes across as inhibited and awkward, contrary to his nature. For José Lewgoy I will combine the characters of Borja and Don Aquilino into one; there are too many minor characters in any case. Wilbur, Mick Jagger's part, I will remove from the script altogether. I do not want to look for a substitute for him.

Iquitos, 2 April 1981

A day fraught with struggles. W. wants to send everyone home Saturday, the team and the actors; his internal compass has stopped working. Today Vivanco is also arriving from the camp. He has closed himself off completely from the others and is acting weird. For a long time he was suspecting Cucho of conspiring against him, was seeing plots everywhere, and was blaming us for the failure of his marriage; yet we had sent him off quite early to have a vacation in Cuzco with his French wife, but he got hung up with some random women in Lima and told us later they had refused to let him go. I discovered that bizarre power struggles had occurred in the camp, of the kind that can happen only in the jungle. They involved the prostitutes that are part of the amenities of camps in the rain forest, because otherwise there would be problems with all the loggers and boatmen going after women in nearby Indian settlements. One prostitute had played Trigozo, Cucho, and Vivanco off against each other, letting them go at one another so she could move up the ladder to get the position of deputy camp administrator. A clever story, but I promptly and unceremoniously had her shipped back to Iquitos on the first available transport.

Paul told me how a friend of his had been attacked one night. He had married a native woman, but after a while all he did was drink; he stopped working, which annoyed the woman and her secret lover, who had been living well off him. He was found murdered in his bed; they had given him one on the noggin, Paul said, and the guy had promptly kicked the bucket.

Under the blazing hot corrugated tin roof of the house out in front, hundreds of bats have taken up residence, and at night they swarm out through the angled vents in the gable window. The washroom on the second floor has a hole in the ceiling, which has gone unrepaired all year–the only thing that would be needed is a piece of ugly pressed cardboard. One of the bats must have come down through the hole. Yesterday it was lying, gleaming black in the white sink, its wingtips with their grappling hooks and its legs slightly extended, and gazed at me with its black eyes. It did not fly away, it was dying, very quietly yielding to its fate, and also entirely without fear in the midst of this tremendous event it was experiencing. Today the bat was still there. Someone had neatly laid a strip of toilet paper over it. It was dead, its position unchanged. I left it there and did not use the sink, not out of disgust or hygienic considerations but out of an unarticulated sense of respect. One of my favorite words in Spanish has always been *murciélago*, bat. My life seemed like an invention to me, with its pathos, its banalities, its dramas, its idling.

Mauch, whose birthday is Saturday, which is why we were speaking of his parents, who lived in Württemberg, described the death of his father at the age of eighty-two; when someone dies at that age, he said, there is a folk saying in his region to the effect that you can no longer blame the midwife. We talked about the sphinx by the Cheops pyramid in Giza, which the Ottoman Turk artillery had used for target practice. We talked about how simple mathematical rules can be translated into language, but I have long been preoccupied with the question of how Zorn's lemma could be translated into prose.

As I was on my way to the costume depot on Calle Putumayo,

word came from Lucki that we are in the clear as far as the Second German Television Broadcasting Company is concerned. The others would probably follow suit, he said, and the insurance underwriters would most likely support the decision. Franz at the costume depot was visibly relieved, speaking of prayers that had been heard, and I responded, half jokingly, that our prayers resembled intense comments directed into a darkened room from which no answer came and which we had to assume was completely empty, not even occupied by a large, taciturn guy on a throne, who might be able to hear us but did not even bestow on us so much as an echo from the void, other than the echo of our stupid hopes and our self-deception. After I had got that off my chest, we laughed and had a beer.

Iquitos, 3 April 1981
Preparations for the trip to the Camisea; under pressure to get started there before the level of the river sank too far and made it impossible get the ship back to Iquitos. I became lost in imagining an unknown river with headwaters in dreamed-up mountains of alabaster and sapphires and ending in a sea of emeralds. Lord, grant me to see an unknown fish at my feet. Was not a scaly, breathing animal caught off the coast of West Africa an actual fish that otherwise exists only in fossilized form? A Chinese general had his troops assemble and summarily baptized two hundred thousand men with a garden hose. In the depths of my heart I decided that my favorite plant was the fern, and not only because of its name: fern beaded with rain. I carry my world with me in a little net made of liana fibers. Death is hereditary.

Paul unloaded six Broncos from his freighter. One of the Indian workmen climbed into the driver's seat and out of curiosity tried out the steering, the windshield wipers, and the gearshift. In the process, he backed the vehicle into the river. It sank, but he was rescued. Later Paul managed to pull it out with a tractor. Today several men attacked him with knives in his bar, something that almost never happens here. They took a case of champagne. In the evening the drug dealer came by, having bought his way out of jail after two days, and returned the case of champagne, saying his people had misunderstood his instructions. He apologized and paid twice the value of the case. He then proceeded to booze it up, celebrating his freedom in Paul's bar with his boys, in the course of which he grabbed a machete and with a few powerful strokes beheaded all dozen champagne bottles.

Iquitos–Camisea, 4 April 1981

Flight from Iquitos to Pucallpa with Faucett, and from there with Aguila's small plane by way of Sepahua, where I handed over 4 million *soles* to Trigozo, compressed as usual into a brick, before we flew on to Camisea. The airfield was dry and firm.

Camisea, 5 April 1981

Jorge Vignati came to pick us up yesterday with the boat. Walter was busy with the slaughtering of a cow at the Indians' camp. The camp peaceful and nice; they were all happy to have us back. The first thing I did was put my radio on the rough-hewn table on my porch and play, very loudly, the cassette with Vivaldi's *Dixit Dominus*. I noticed that two large ants, affected by the vibrations of the mighty tone, were acting like mad creatures, doing a rhythmic St. Vitus' dance in front of the loudspeaker. They writhed, raced around crazily in a circle, and whirled as if an electrical current were running through them.

The water level is extremely low; the river is flowing quietly, and the camp seems sleepy, like a dismal tourist locale in the off-season, or rather like a place that never has visitors, never experiences a high season, yet continues to wait for something. The events of the past have vanished, like bad dreams. It has not rained in days; it is dry and hot, and the river continues to go down, threatening to dry up altogether.

Yesterday at the airport in Pucallpa two scruffy four-year-old Indio children asked me in all seriousness whether I needed a taxi, and presented themselves as drivers. I responded just as seriously that I needed to take another flight; was not one of them a pilot? No, they said, neither of them was a pilot. So there they stood, the two miniature taxi drivers, barefoot, smeared with mud, which had welled up between their toes, their bare bellies distended above the elastic waistbands of their gym shorts, their hair wild and black. They were very sure of themselves.

In the camp there is now an athletic black man with a large gap between his upper front teeth. In Oventeni he was a cattle driver for the Campas, and came here with a group of them. He is always chewing on a matchstick, and usually carries several of these toothpicks stuck into his nappy beard just below his ear; they stay there even in the strong breeze created by the speedboat, as he proudly pointed out to me. With Beatus, or Beat Presser, the stills photographer, I took the heaviest nylon string, certainly heavier than the strings on a tennis racket, and attached the largest and most fearsome fishhook with a knot. Then I tugged on the string as hard as I could, and the third knot finally turned out to our satisfaction. We fetched a chunk of meat from the kitchen and threw this bait into the water. I have a running bet with Klausmann that during our time on the Camisea I will catch a fish at least one meter in length. The agreed-upon prize is five *pisco* sours; I have already lost ten in a similar bet.

In Camisea I waited with Mauch in the sweltering heat, which brings everything but the flies to a standstill, for the plane that is to take us to the Pongo. Pale coffee beans are lying in the sun to dry, and around me children are talking softly in Machiguenga. Walter flew on ahead, to track down Trigozo somewhere along the way, to whom I had handed the 4 million *soles* yesterday, as agreed upon; W. thought I should have kept some of the money for him, Walter, because it was essential that he appear up by the Pongo with money on him. Except that he had failed to breathe a word of this to Trigozo, Chavez in Pucallpa, or me. As his plane came in for a landing, I saw that it had a bit of green brush caught in the landing gear, and upon closer inspection I saw that a lot of long, green grass was caught in it. W. told us he had landed with Pino in a village whose landing strip was overgrown, with meter-high grass to the left and right of the runway, which had become narrower than the wingspan. Before takeoff the two of them cleared the strip with machetes.

When the water is low, the Pongo looks pretty harmless. We found the *Huallaga* in good shape, already past the narrows we dubbed the Gate of Hell. Something is broken on the rudder, and Laplace has brought along steel cables to secure it, but they do not seem strong enough to me. Laplace is confident he has things under control, however. There is a pregnant woman on board with a two-year-old daughter who is very trusting. On the steep bank the crew has used a piece of tin bent into a channel to divert a clear, cold waterfall, and under the cascade of water the woman was bathing her child in a plastic pail. On deck, on the large mirror behind the bar, the crew has taped a tropical pinup, a vulgar blonde, kneeling, with her voluptuous ass straining toward the viewer.

From above the Pongo Mainique, where there is another world, inaccessible and unknown, a fourteen-year-old Campa boy ran away from home, I was told, and took along his three-year-old sister; he wanted her to share his freedom and the new experiences he expected to find below the rapids. They passed through here on an improvised balsa raft, barely large enough to carry them, passed through the Pongo, then Timpia, Camisea, and the Río Picha. They did not stop till they reached Sepahua. There their story is lost.

As we were landing back in Camisea, the sun was going down and the moon was rising, a sickle moon, skinny and as sharp as a knife, like a glowing thread of steel. It had rained briefly and violently, and over the forest hung delicate white swaths of vapor, as fine as veils or spiderwebs. The rain forest took on a virginal cast, hiding the silent murders in its depths beneath veils that seemed to have been tossed over it by fleeting dreams. Above the whole scene, the sun, already out of sight, caused the narrowest strips around rapidly darkening clouds to glow, making all the contours blaze, as if marked by brilliant fire.

Camisea, 6 April 1984
This morning I woke up to terror such as I have never experienced before: I was entirely stripped of feeling. Everything was gone; it was as if I had lost something that had been entrusted to me the previous evening, something I was supposed to take special care of overnight; I was in the position of someone who has been assigned to guard an entire sleeping army but suddenly finds himself mysteriously blinded, deaf, and effaced. Everything was gone. I was completely empty, without pain, without pleasure, without longing, without love, without warmth and friendship, without anger, without hate. Nothing, nothing was there anymore, leaving me like a suit of armor with no knight inside. It took a long time before I even felt alarmed.

While getting into the boat, Mauch slipped, fell, and dislocated his shoulder. We immediately drove him to the other camp, where the medic was, but the old cook was also sent for; he was said to be a specialist, for births as well. When he arrived, at first we looked at each other apprehensively. His fingers were bony, with nails like those of man who has been felling trees in the forest. His face very Indian, a few lone hairs on his chin, a woolen cap on his head. In the meantime, Mauch, whose main problem was his tendency to faint, had been given a shot in the shoulder by the medic. Now the cook dipped his fingertips in the fat he had brought along in a greasy piece of newspaper. With extraordinary caution he began to feel Mauch's bones, checking the position of the shoulder blade, the collarbone, the humerus, and then gently massaged the muscles, which had gone into spasm from the pain. I tried to tell him it was not the shoulder blade that had been injured but the shoulder. He looked at me with perfect composure, indicating that I should be still; we were sure that soon he would bend M.'s arm and with a large rotating motion snap the bone back into the joint, but nothing of the sort occurred. The cook massaged and tapped the shoulder area with his infinitely careful fingers, then exerted a slight pressure, which hurt Mauch for a moment. Something had shifted, Mauch said, but that could not be it. Yes, it was, the cook gave us to understand, as he simply walked away. In fact the shoulder was back where it belonged, and Mauch, who had dislocated it before, simply could not believe it.

El Tigre, the toughest and most daring of our woodsmen, who always hides his shoulder-length black hair under his blue hard hat–I have never seen him in a shirt, but never without his hard hat and machete, both of which he probably takes to bed with him–showed me his ring finger, which had been crushed when he was felling a tree and almost torn off. Our cook, the medic's assistant, had set the splintered bones in the shape of a finger, stitched the tendons together, and saved the digit. It looks impressive, although, as El Tigre told us, he can no longer put a ring on it. Another man got caught in a boat's screw, and our cook stitched together his severed Achilles tendon. He also saved a woman who had been carrying a dead baby for days, unable to deliver it. He had managed to extract the baby. I recall Robards's arrogant disrespect for everything Peruvian; he demanded American doctors, considering even our French-educated doctor inferior.

We let Mauch, who was pretty exhausted, sleep it off, and scrambled with El Tigre up the cleared pathway to the vertical gravel bank. By itself the lane looks boring. Banal details and slovenliness preoccupied me for the rest of the day, things brought about by W.'s cynicism and dismissed by him as inconsequential. We are out of toilet paper, and that immediately makes the general mood very bad. In addition, we had promised, in response to numerous requests, to bring back a considerable amount of honey; I had ordered thirty one-liter jars in Lima, but W. had decided it was not important and canceled the order. When we arrived, he told us the honey was still with the rest of the groceries in Sepahua, but today, when two fully laden boats arrived, there was only a very cheap jam that no one wants. In itself the honey is not that important, but since it had been specifically asked for and had also been promised, and everyone was looking forward to it and asking about it every day, our organizational skill loses credibility more rapidly as a result of such small details than if something abrupt and serious had happened. So much for life in a rain-forest camp.

The razor-sharp sickle moon rose with mathematical precision above the rain forest, still rejoicing steamily, and then it was the cicadas and nocturnal voices that quickly pinned down the darkness in the great abyss of the night. Now and then a fruit falls to the ground with a thud. A strange Indian woman has arrived at the camp; no one knows who she is or what she wants. She does not speak either Ashininka-Campa or Machiguenga, and she has twins with her, about three years old, who also do not speak. They came and watched me as I hauled in the hook, from which the huge piece of bait had been nibbled away by small fish. Then they came into my cabin without any inhibitions and looked around to see where I kept all my things. They checked out my few possessions, their faces stony as they remained silent. The children look very Indian, but their clothing is quite urban. The woman no one knows moved around the camp as if she were planning to settle in.

Walter and Huerequeque got hung up in the Pongo de Mainique. They managed to get through the first *malpaso*, but then the water rose so fast in the course of three hours that they did not dare take the speedboat out of the Pongo. Pino, the pilot, reported this over dinner. We talked about two Swiss mountain climbers who play mental chess while roped together on a rock face. They are climbing the north face of the Eiger and calling out their moves to each other. Very far away, off to the east, we can hear persistent thunder, a constant soft rumbling, almost inaudible, but we all prick up our ears because it must be an unbelievably terrible storm coming down. Here it is perfectly dry, but a cool, gentle wind has sprung up, and the Camisea's beginning to rise imperceptibly. At the moment it is lower than I have ever seen it. The moths and insects buzzing around the light are more restless than usual. A rushing sound can be heard from the river and the trees on the opposite bank, and in undue haste one fruit after another tumbles out of the big tree and rattles into the motionlessness all around. The forest is perfectly still. I brought in everything from outside because I am afraid the river will rise fast.

As I was scanning the area with my flashlight, without warning rain began to pour down. The thunder is edging closer over the forest. Everything seems to be holding its breath in anticipation of something terrible.

Camisea, 7 April 1981
During the night rain leaked through the roof at the head of my bed, and I dragged the bed to another spot, but water was dripping in there, too, so I rigged a canopy with my oilskin and a stick and in that way managed to stay fairly dry. An animal ran across my hand; it looks like a little tuft of wool, or, more precisely, a cotton ball, but it actually has six little legs and darts as quickly and evenly as if one were carefully blowing a fuzzy piece of cotton across the table. The river rose a bit, but the extreme conditions we were expecting did not materialize. The day is starting out quietly and sleepily, and I hope it will end the same way. Birds in the depths of the forest are responding to others even deeper in the forest. The carpenter is planing and pounding away, and the echo of his work reverberates back to me from the other bank of the river.

I had woken up around three in the morning. The light was still on, and I was surprised that our generator was running all night. It felt as if an enormous butterfly had struck my head with its wings, as the imperial eagle is said to attack human beings with its pinions and beat them unconscious so that it can carry off lambs and little children unimpeded to its cliff-top nest, where its half-naked, screeching young are demanding to be fed.

Off in the distance, past the bend in the river where we want to haul the ship over the mountain, I heard the men working in the forest, and then with a tremendous roar, like a distant disaster, a huge tree fell. It sounded as if all of nature were rising up in rage at some infamous deed. Long afterward there was silence in the forest, as if it were holding its breath, and only then did the men start calling to each other again.

(I wondered at the way a brief moment of insight, of registering a particular image, can bring such consequences, with an almost inescapable mercilessness that grips me as much as all others who are involved, a pull that generates both joy and terror, determines the course of lives, brings children into the world, and causes deaths. Yet today the giant holds still for one last day. And all those who were riled up, who could not take the heat? The whole Bremen crew, with Andreas in the lead, who hung in there for so long and saw ever more clearly that he was not equal to the task, Izquerdo with the costumes, Adorf, that cowardly schemer, Arnon Milchan, the wheeler-dealer: behind each of them stands a small legion of those who have stumbled, suffered shipwreck, lost heart. I thought about the fascination of ski jumping, which persists in me like a dream without end. Is the desire to fly innate to all creatures? One should take a closer look at cows, dogs, lizards. Is not the ostrich, with wings that cannot carry it, the most unredeemed of all living beings?)

All morning a very large moth sat on my dirty laundry, its proboscis bent forward as it feasted on the salt from my sweat. It flapped its wings from time to time, and, when it folded them upright, rubbed them against each other like two plates until they were even; the impression was one of ecstatic well-being, and outside by the porch green fruits fell to the ground. I collected a few of them and went at them with my penknife, because I had seen the Campas open them with their machetes and eat them. They resembled unripe walnuts, with a green, fleshy husk, and inside a hard, wrinkled wooden shell, enclosing a milky-white kernel. I found two delicate little feathers that had blown onto my porch, with light and dark brown horizontal stripes, and they seemed to me like souls that had wafted there. Then I explored the area behind the camp for the first time, penetrating far into the jungle. Today part of the technical crew is scheduled to arrive by way of Pucallpa.

From Lucki in Munich I received a text consisting of only seven lines, so laconic that it made me worry all the more that I may not see my mother again alive. She refuses to be operated on. I went off by myself and stared into the river, which is smacking its lips lazily and happily, satiated with mud and leaves and rotting branches. The forest was filled with rich, sweetish rot. Footsteps make hardly any noise.

I hide my troubles behind joking, and had a good laugh with some local children, whom I told that in Germany bananas had zippers, the fish died in the rivers, and the cars stood still because there were so many other cars they could not move. That really amused them. Then I told them that hammocks were hung up vertically so you could lean into them from a standing position when you wanted to sleep. The working girl from Iquitos, who plies her trade with two other young women from Iquitos, came to my table at dinner and gave me a message from El Tigre, whom she had just seen: he had finished the new treetop platform. When Mauch wanted to know what she had said, I gave him a translation to the effect that she had reported incidentally, if also rather hesitantly, that El Tigre, armed with his chain saw, had tried to rape her, but she had successfully warded him off. That, Mauch said, was much worse than Jack the Ripper, whereupon I replied that for a London city dweller it was unimaginable what barbarity a person living out in wild nature could be capable of. So much for the tone of the conversations over dinner this evening, accentuated by something truly bizarre: a small electric heater, which had probably been delivered to the camp in error, turned up on the table and elicited much interest.

Camisea, 8 April 1984

With the veins in my temples throbbing, I hurried up the steep slope to the tree with the new platform; the tree is not suitable for ladder rungs, and I arrived just as they were installing a block and tackle. Tigre was working bare-chested, and on his back were hundreds of yellowish flies, to which he paid no attention; he looked spotted. A delicate cloud of the same insects was buzzing around him. From atop the tree it was immediately clear that this lookout point is far better than the one we had chosen initially, and I gave instructions to enlarge the platform. Some of the Campas came down to the river with me, and I tried to match the Indios' running gait, but no matter how fast I moved, I could hear the men's breath right behind me and the smacking of their toes as they pulled them out of the bubbling, waterlogged clay. I have often paid close attention to the way they move: it is a bit like a slalom, in which they have already spotted the next obstacle–a protruding root, a dangling liana, a thorny branch–and circumvent it with a graceful turn of the entire body that starts two paces in advance and merges with the rapid trot, never interrupting the overall movement, whereas Europeans stop, advance in fits and starts, stumble, hesitate. Once an obstacle has been smoothly skirted, the next one has already been registered, and the steps toward it all contribute to a flowing, economical circumvention. Their torso bends, and their feet, I noticed, tend to go up onto rather than over an obstacle, provided it is stable. It is better to step onto a loop formed by a vine than to get one's foot caught in it, and meanwhile the eye remains fixed on the objects one can grab onto in steep, slippery places without being stuck by a dozen thorns. One time I had grasped hold of a smooth sapling without noticing that a multilane highway of fire ants led up and down it. Then I made the mistake of trying to cut down the tree with my machete to protect those following behind me, but my blow was not strong enough and merely shook the sapling, sending fire ants raining down on me, getting under my shirt and in my hair, and for two days I was climbing the walls. That was during *Aguirre*.

Upon reaching the Indians' big camp, I greeted the old cook/medic who had set Mauch's shoulder, and told him how happy we all were to have him with us. He maintained a proud silence. By the fireplace in the kitchen, the little monkey who answers to the name of Tricky Dick Nixon ran to a guinea pig for help, clinging to its neck and pressing its face against the guinea pig's head, chattering with fear. A peaceful evening had settled over the camp, full of quiet people and quiet conversations.

For the last few days one thought keeps presenting itself: why can a four-legged stool wobble, while a three-legged one never does, and: if a person hangs himself in the attic and a breeze is blowing, how many additional ropes would one need to prevent the hanged man from swinging, or more precisely, from moving at all? The answer: one additional rope stretched from his feet to the floor and another from his belt to a wall, so the corpse cannot rotate around its own axis. But how many ropes would one need, if necessary infinitely long ones, to fix oneself in the universe, definitively and unchangingly, and free of rotation? Is a fixed position in the universe even possible?

Camisea, 9 April 1981
Mauch's birthday, Bubu Klausmann's birthday.

In the morning we went out to start shooting; twenty Campas had already built a light, very temporary scaffolding around the gigantic tree near the old platform. We filmed eight of them hacking away with their axes at the mighty roots, which extended like ribs up the trunk to a height of five meters, supporting the colossus. I carried the tripod and camera up to the old platform, hanging on to the rungs with only one free hand, and remembering Adorf, who had screamed for stuntmen. From now on I can safely call my rump zone Adorf.

Later, after lunch, I scrambled up the steep slope to the plateau in a mere 180 seconds; Beatus, who did not think it could be done, hurried along behind me, keeping time. Once at the top, we threw ourselves down panting on the moldy ground, our hearts pounding wildly, and waited for the others. Felling the huge tree proved a challenge. It resisted and resisted, as the light slowly and relentlessly faded, and then the tree began to list to the wrong side, jamming Tigre's chain saw, and the chain remained stuck deep in the wood. We hastily relocated the camera and equipment to a spot that seemed safe, but then, when I saw that the saw's spark plug was not working, that the gas was contaminated, and that the chain had to be painstakingly freed with axes, I called the whole thing off, hoping no wind would spring up, not even a breeze, because it could seize the tree's enormous spreading crown and bring the whole thing down. The ax blows echoed through the forest, and the mighty trunk sounded liked the resonance chamber of a gigantic musical instrument.

In complete darkness a plane passed overhead, probably W., making one of those unnecessary and senseless blind night landings again. His absence makes a greater difference now, and when it is critical to keep several organizational threads in order, the task falls to me in any case. With all the work I already have, most of the time I am also the head of production. I doubt Walter was really indispensable as a mechanic's helper on the *Huallaga* in the Pongo, though it is also true that anything involving the Pongo is risky. The largest wooden boat, with a seventy-horsepower engine, which was roped to one side of the *Huallaga*, was smashed in minutes by the rising waters, and the pieces sank, along with its engine. Cables snapped like violin strings, and the ship crashed into the cliff so hard that rivets on its hull went shooting out, and water rushed in, having to be pumped out constantly, but Laplace has fifteen men on board who know what they have to do.

Waiting for a boat, we all went for a swim in the river. I swam in my long pants and tried to wash out the sticky resin from the tree. The giant tree, which twelve men would hardly be able to span with their outstretched arms, had oozed milky, sticky juice where axes and chain saws had sliced into it. It made a great impression on me the way El Tigre walked around the giant tree for a long time, measured the limbs with his eyes, estimated their weight, and with great precision and forethought notched some of the root ribs, depriving the tree of their support. It was like the preparations for imploding a Gothic cathedral.

Camisea, 10 April 1981
In the Pongo de Mainique the ship tore itself loose with a crew of sixteen on board and was almost destroyed. W. reported that the rapidly rising water caused a whirlpool to form by the edge of a cliff, which in turn drove the ship forward against the current, and that loosened the lines and steel hawsers, some of which were a good two inches in diameter; then the current seized hold of the ship with full force; the ropes snapped, the ship ended up at an angle to the rapids and listed so steeply that the second deck was touching the water.

The boat banged into the cliff on the opposite side and thus righted itself somewhat, but the prow was bashed in and the *Huallaga* was tossed from wall to wall of the cliffs.

Anja brought disturbing news about my mother. Because of the situation, Lucki will stay in Munich till the end of the month. An inexhaustible, indifferent sky is raining itself empty. It is getting grayer and grayer, not less and also not more, just all-encompassing. In weeklong slow motion beer cans are digging themselves into the sand. Flat patches of white foam try to come together as they drift by, but they are driven apart by the eddies in the water. The mournfulness of cardboard boxes soaked through days ago: I sense a great metaphor there.

Yesterday a moribund infant died in the Indians' camp.

At noon, after more than a day and half's resistance, the tree finally fell. Suddenly there were shouts–Quick! Get the camera out of the way. Mauch did not want to take it seriously, thinking he could duck behind a nearby tree if necessary, but in retrospect we realized that we would not have had a prayer, because the other tree he thought would shield him ended up smashed to bits, as if by a giant fist. I asked whether our work platform was in danger. Yes, said El Tigre, it is in danger. We evacuated the area immediately and took up a position on the opposite slope. Seconds later El Tigre, Huerequeque, and another *motosierrista* fled in our direction. The giant creaked and groaned, then there was a sound like an explosion, as if something inside the tree were tearing, but after this terrible inner shock it was still standing, and leaves and shredded lianas came raining down on us. Then the tree fell, a terrifying drama, a true cataclysm of the world, dragging everything nearby down with it, like a gigantic avalanche. It was a long time before things were quiet again. Bats flitted around, leaves continued to drift down, wasps had been dislodged from a nest in the crown, branches continued to fall from the surrounding trees long after everything seemed to be over.

Camisea, 11 April 1981

There is an amusing detail from the *Huallaga*'s accident in the Pongo: the Brazilian Ephraim, who was hurtled back and forth on the lower deck, was so terrified and in need of something vertical to hold on to that he wrapped his arms around a half pig's carcass that was suspended there. People saw him hanging on to it and swinging back and forth.

Today a seven-year-old Campa boy with an intestinal blockage was flown out to Atalaya. Dr. Parraga went along, and will operate on him there. The flight to Pucallpa would have been too strenuous and too risky; it is possible the boy would not have survived the transport.

The helicopter of the Bolivian president, Barrientos, flew into a power line and crashed from a low altitude. He had suitcases full of money with him, presumably from drug deals. The helicopter immediately caught fire, but although people were there and tried to rescue him from the blaze, no one could get close, because the heat made the submachine guns carried by the president and his entourage start firing wildly, and in the hail of bullets no one dared approach.

When the *chata* arrived with the two tractors on board, Campas with red painted faces and coca leaves in one cheek stood around and watched what we were doing. On the small barge women had built a kind of playpen among cables, oil canisters, and bunches of bananas, and a small child was playing in it. In the fenced-off area a little girl of about five was also standing. She did not speak, but stared at us unabashedly in a way that suggested we were all crazy.

What I love most here is the brief stretch of time that represents evening in the camp, after the sun goes down and the sky is still bright and one or two stars begin to twinkle, though it still seems to be day, when the birds fall silent and the nocturnal animals gradually begin to make themselves heard, when the boats return, when the stillness becomes audible, before the Brazilians crank up their tinny cassette players to top volume in the dark. Today the river is completely hushed and glides by weightlessly, keeping to its laws and spaces; yet it always seems to me as if the river were secretly flowing much faster beneath its surface.

Camisea, 12 April 1981
Paul, Miguel Ángel Fuentes, and Miguel Vasquez arrived yesterday toward evening. Paul reported he had lost a workman while his barge was being unloaded. The stupid ruffian, he said, had slipped in his rubber boots on the slick, oily metal deck, fallen overboard, and never surfaced. It had happened in the middle of Iquitos, and, Paul added irritably, his disappearance had caused all sorts of paperwork at various official departments. We drank some of the whiskey they had brought along and played cards, and without really knowing what I was doing or how, I kept winning madly.

Huerequeque has come up with the ultimate card game: each player receives one card, which he is not allowed to look at. He sticks it on his forehead where the other players can see it; so you know what the others have and begin to bet on your own card, sight unseen. If one of the other players has a high number, you are going to be more cautious, of course, from which the other person can draw conclusions about the value of his card. On the other hand, you can bet an insanely high amount, and that is what Huerequeque almost invariably does, with the result that the opposite player immediately folds, even with an ace on his forehead, because with such a high bet on the table he has to assume his own card has a very low value. The best moment came when I was merely observing, and the improbable occurred, namely that all three players had a three on their foreheads. This made the chances extremely promising from any point of view, since each player could see two others with low numbers. It was a delight to witness how each reacted in character, showing joy or acting cold and indifferent so as to lure his opponent with a low bet into taking a reckless, ill-considered step. All of them eventually wagered everything they had, borrowed money, bet their houses, children, lives, but when the cards were revealed there were no winners, the bets were kept by the house, and not until the next round did everything fall to Huerequeque, of course.

The most lethargic sleepyhead among our boatmen, who always crashes into something when mooring his boat and misunderstands instructions, keeps reading and rereading, whenever he gets a chance, the same increasingly tattered letter, which he keeps under his sweat-drenched, sour- and rancid-smelling shirt. Every time he reads it, his face clouds over. Today his reading got us in trouble: he ran aground on a sandbank. But I gave him to understand that because of the letter he has my friendship and sympathy. In the morning Huerequeque swam by me, going upstream in baggy underpants, and Fuentes was pulling on a chest expander with alarmingly powerful springs, while on the opposite bank of the Camisea something was thrashing around oddly in the underbrush; from the way the branches were quivering, I guessed it was not a bird, but the invisible creature was squawking in a way that did sound like a bird after all, until finally a monkey appeared, swinging unmistakably into sight. I was surprised to see a monkey come so close to our camp. Maybe it felt safe because of the river between us. It began to rain. The river is a brownish green, staid and shallow. The banana fronds to the left of my hut are bursting with growth, shamelessly sexual. In the peace of the falling rain the landscape is practicing being submissive. The forest seems to be breathing deeply, and everything else holds still. Ferns are unfurling hesitantly, having kept their most delicate tips hidden. Flesh-eating flowers oozing oily invitations lure insects to their death. On rotting wood, slimy fungi brood poison. Today the forest's travails seemed less burdensome, with decaying, rotting, and giving birth occurring with less effort. The jungle, existing exclusively in the present, is certainly subject to time, but remains forever ageless. Any concept of justice would be antithetical to all this. But is there justice in the desert, either? Or in the oceans? And in the depths? Life in the sea must be pure hell, an infinite hell of constant and ever-present danger, so unbearable that in the course of evolution some species–including Homo sapiens–crawled, fled, onto some clods of firm land, the future continents.

I climbed into the *Narinho*'s clumsy little dinghy, and as I pushed away from the bank noticed that I had no oars in the boot, but by then it was too late. So I drifted downstream, passed the anchored *Huallaga*, and knew they would pull me out there. But when I shouted and whistled no one responded, and I found myself drifting faster and faster into the Pongo de Mainique, which looked brown, with white foam marking its terrifying rapids and cascades. I got caught on a slide of rushing boards and tree trunks, so slimy and smooth that I was soon moving much faster than the current itself. Up ahead, at the end of the boards, high above the most terrifyingly seething spot, I would be hurtled into the air as if from a ramp, but I jolted the boat with my body and slid sideways off the boards, flying high and far through the air, at which the bow reared up steeply against the cliffs, causing the broad stern to land hard on the raging water. The boat immediately filled up with water, and inevitably would have sunk at once if I had not thrown myself forward to prevent the stern from going under entirely. Half submerged, I raced and thrashed through the Pongo, and at the lower end I was thrown onto a Bavarian alpine meadow. I ended up lying half underneath the boat, and saw people approaching, a peasant woman in the lead. Since I wanted her to use her phone to call my crew, I pretended to be unconscious. That did me good. In the place on the meadow where I had vomited somewhat later, large, exotic moths congregated; or perhaps I had only urinated, and it occurred to me that maybe I had sugar in my urine, because otherwise why would butterflies have come from so far away? In fact the cows were also staggering, and even a herdsman, with a scythe over his shoulder, was tottering. I walked away, and the mountaintops bowed to a world that lay there shimmering in a trance.

Yesterday the Ashininka-Campas' top chieftain appeared, preceded by the rumor that he was Japanese, married to a Campa woman. The man is highly intelligent and clearheaded. We persuaded him to stay for the day. There is going to be a fiesta in the big camp tonight, at which the men plan to let themselves be shot at with arrows, and those being shot at have to catch the arrows in midair, a practice I always thought was just a legend.

In the administration building in the Indian camp all the ballpoint pens are tethered with liana fibers. As for the Campas, we have to hurry to get the work done, because many of them want to get home in time for the coffee harvest. Over everything hovers a Sunday stillness; the men are lying all around, one arm crooked under their heads. The thought thrust itself upon me, at first only a faint note from afar, that historically speaking the last trumpet is sounding for the Indians—in my lifetime. One of them had skinned a gleaming blue bird, its feathers more blue than anything I have ever seen. He told me he wanted to attach the feathers to his *cushma*, as decoration. Some of those lying down are picking lice off others as they lie there. From far upstream a dugout came by, accompanying a small, heavily laden balsawood raft. The man, woman, children, and dog on board stared at us without moving a muscle. The dog had scratched itself so hard that its ears were hairless and pink. Its scrawny shoulder blades protruded from its skeletal back.

We climbed up to the new platform and pronounced the verdict on those trees that had to be felled and those that could be left standing. In this baleful moment, when I was up in the tree's crown, a little primeval lizard approached me on the mighty trunk, like a messenger from the depths of nature. It stopped right across from my face and stared at me intently in that motionlessness that only lizards can achieve, while it inflated its reddish throat pouch several times.

A small Campa boy of maybe seven is always sneaking around us in our smaller camp. He helps the boatmen by sitting in the bow, where he is the first to leap to the shore and tie the boat up. Since he turned up, everyone has been calling him *comandante*. *Comandante*, how are you? Laplace asked him today. I do not know, the *comandante* replied, and without another word went into the kitchen to watch what was going on there. Above the ship, which is tied up in the bend, I saw an eagle circling, the feathers at its wingtips spread wide. Half the underside of its wings was white, and it soared majestically.

The people who were due to arrive from Miami (Kinski, two lighting technicians, Bill Rose) did not make it to Iquitos because the plane could not land in the bad weather and was directed to continue on to Lima. From there they flew to Pucallpa and spent the night. Maybe it is not so bad if Kinski is to be prevented from cherishing any illusions as to the way our staging area looks.

Camisea, 14 April 1981

Big costume try-on yesterday. Paul's hair was cut, and we tinted Kinski's hair a bit. Several times Kinski threw a tantrum, once because someone touched his hair. Not even my hairdresser is allowed to touch my hair, Kinski screamed, completely out of control, but when I adjust his hat and his hair, he accepts my touching him. As he was bellowing about some other petty matter, mist quietly filled the valley, eating its way gently into the depths of the forest. Alan Dunn, as I recalled, had a talking watch that announced the time in a flat robot's voice, and I wished I had it here.

I was reading the translation of Piave's libretto of *Ernani*, published in Zurich in 1952, and in the foreword I came upon the breathtakingly idiotic comment that the most blatantly unbelievable passages had been deleted–when in fact it is precisely the incredible elements that account for the beauty of the story, or rather of opera as a genre, because those elements that cannot be accounted for even by the most exotic probability calculations appear in opera as the most natural, thanks to the powerful transformation of an entire world into music. And the Grand Emotions in opera, often dismissed as over the top, strike me on the contrary as the most concentrated, pure archetypes of emotion, whose essence is incapable of being condensed any further. They are axioms of emotions. That is what opera and the jungle have in common.

Camisea, 15 April 1981

Yesterday Gustavo arrived with the helicopter. We got up very early to make test flights. In the meantime the actors were hoisted into the treetop by pulley. Kinski played the suffering invalid to the hilt; supposedly he had a fever and had been vomiting all night, but that is just what he says to call everyone's attention to himself. From Pucallpa a message came by radio, garbled and almost incomprehensible, to the effect that the Cabaña plane had crashed in Oventeni with the pilot, the tall, thin one, and two or possibly more Campas on board. Two of the injured had been flown by way of Satipo to the intensive-care station in Lima. Kinski, realizing he was no longer the focal point of attention, began to bellow like a madman: his coffee had been lukewarm. There was no way to calm him down, which we desperately needed to do, since we were straining to hear the fragments coming over the shortwave radio so as to know whether we would have to organize further rescue efforts. After hours of his incessant ranting and raving, I ate the last piece of chocolate I had been keeping hidden in my cabin; I ate it practically in Kinski's face, which he was holding very close to mine as he screamed his lungs out. He was so dumbfounded by my act of self-indulgence that all of a sudden he fell silent.

In the evening the Campas held their fiesta, to which I went, filled with dark thoughts. My collarbone was extremely painful, having almost completely separated from my breastbone when I was helping Vignati work the block and tackle. The cook came, but he could not help me. Eventually he and the doctor put a bandage around my chest and shoulders, so tight that at night I could take only shallow breaths. What is the next thing that will happen? Will there be an earthquake? Will the *Huallaga* sink? Will K. die?

Hunters had gone out and brought back rodents the size of guinea pigs, which the women roasted on a wooden spit, fur and all.

They looked like rats but were tasty. During shooting yesterday, the Campas were distracted, shooting with arrows at something on the slope. I ran over and saw that they had shot a snake. It was pinned to the ground by several arrows, which it snapped at. We quickly filmed the scene, and once the poisonous animal had been killed, we went back to work.

A Japanese doctor operated on his own appendix.

Camisea, 16 April 1981
Early in the morning Walter dragged me out of bed, because he had heard over the radio that the Pongo, which already had high water, had risen another fifteen feet and was rising crazily at the rate of a foot per hour. We did not wait for the two supplementary cameras, supposedly arriving in the morning, but quickly packed our two ARRI cameras into the speedboat, and Mauch, Klausmann, and I set out at once. Les, whom I would have liked to have along because of his additional camera, even though it was only 16 mm, was slow to catch on, as is often the case with him, and stayed behind. Walter plans to fly up to Timpia later, in case the additional cameras do arrive, and then Les could go with him, but because it is raining steadily, I doubt it will be possible to land near the Pongo. I will do the sound, but whether the ship can be kept in place until we get there is highly uncertain. The seventy-horsepower engine started to go haywire, rhythmically rather than irregularly, and now we are stuck. That is the only reason I am able to write; it would be impossible with the powerful shuddering of the boat when it is running.

We got stuck four or five times, again and again. The fuel pump was shot. It was raining hard, and the jungle slopes were wreathed in mist. On a sandbank I found two sets of footprints, one barefoot and the other in shoes. I also found a raft made of heavy tree trunks tethered with lianas to pilings rammed into the sand. These bollards were already almost under water–that was how fast the river was rising. Wood and newly torn-off branches, their leaves still green, were drifting in the river current, which was picking up more and more speed. Small white birds fluttered agitatedly over our boat. There was a pervasive sense of expectation. The gravel on the river bottom was rolling as loudly as if the entire earth were in motion. There was a surging and thrumming and whooshing, and stones, hissing in their rage at being jolted out of their inertia, rolled toward the sea, which they would reach only once they had been ground to sand. It seemed like recalcitrance, a refusal, like a violation of the stones' very nature. During one of our stops to repair the boat, I noticed heavy, black stones that gleamed out of the sand like eyes. They were heavier than all the others, and contained iron ore, as I could tell from the traces of rust on them. I found two stones, one of which was almost perfectly round, as unique as if it were a sacred stone, which hundreds of millions of believers had shaped to a perfection with their fervent kisses in the course of millennia. The gravel bank became transformed into a place of pilgrimage, the place of the sacred stones, which the river sought out in an everlasting pilgrimage, dispensing brownish watery kisses in its passionate piety. I should have a skilled goldsmith set that perfect stone in twining gold ivy, or in the arms of an octopus. Yet the river was wild and angry today, like an animal normally thought to be gentle.

For the Indios, the world ends at the Pongo; no one from here has ever gone upstream from the rapids, although sometimes trimmed tree trunks from rafts and other signs of faraway human life come floating down from an unknown world on the other side. At the edge of a sandbank I saw a corpse that had washed up and was partially buried in the sand. It was obviously a soldier, for the swollen body was still wearing army camouflage pants. He was lying on his back, his flesh waterlogged, his stomach distended. He was also wearing the tattered remains of an olive green undershirt and no shoes. No one dared to touch him. A grisly mystery surrounded him.

I recall experiencing a similar shiver of awe as a child in Sachrang, when I found a frayed piece of bright blue plastic that had floated down the brook and got caught on an overhanging branch. At the time I had never seen anything like it, and I kept it hidden for weeks, licked it, found it slightly stretchy, full of miraculous properties. Not until weeks later, when I had my fill of owning it, did I show it to anyone. Till and I discovered that when you held a burning match to it, it melted; it gave off black smoke and a nasty smell, but it was something we had never seen before, an emissary from a distant world high in the mountains along the upper reaches of the brook, where it vanished into gorges and there were no people. So where did it come from? Had it been blown into the mountains by the wind? I did not know, but I gave the plastic a name—what I do not recall. I do know it had a nice sound and was very secret, and since then I have often racked my brains, trying to remember that name, that word. I would give a lot to know it, but I do not, and I also do not have that delicate piece of weather-beaten plastic anymore. Having neither the secret word nor the plastic makes me poorer today than I was as a child.

My mother mentioned one time that sand was good for scrubbing rusty pans, so for her birthday I got my brother to help me fill several sackfuls with wet, heavy sand from the bottom of the brook. We gave her this extremely heavy gift, which we had managed to transport to the house on a handcart, an operation that took us almost all day. I cannot recall seeing my mother so pleased and moved ever again in her life.

For the film, the Pongo was a major and bitter disappointment. The water was very high, but that did not make the waves any more spectacular. For the entire time, the captain kept the ship facing into the current, with the engines at full throttle, and it did not wobble or crash into a cliff; it came pitching past us rather drearily in a sort of slow motion. They had forgotten to remove an old automobile tire from the prow, and from the railing hung a life jacket made of fluorescent orange Styrofoam or something similar. In our speedboat we would probably have been able to get close to the *Huallaga*, which was moored, but in the rushing river it would have been impossible for us to tie up, so we decided to set up the cameras and make contact with the crew somehow. From the frantic waving on the steamship I had concluded that any minute now they would have to cut the cables, or the ship would be jammed against the cliff and would sink. Finally a man came scrambling toward us along the extremely steep, slippery cliff, and I crawled toward him and managed to hand him a walkie-talkie, a fairly dangerous maneuver. In the process I slipped, but caught myself on the wet cliff, overgrown with algae and moss, because I was able to grab on to a tiny, scrawny shrub growing timidly out of a crevice in the rock. Our boatman reacted with such alarm that only then did I notice how terrifying some of the maelstroms below looked.

I radioed the crew to ask whether they could keep the ship afloat through the night, because I had not completely given up on the arrival of two additional cameras. No, the captain replied, he did not think he could keep the ship in position any longer; it would snap its cables, because the water kept rising. I decided to have it set free at once, but what we saw then turned out to be quite boring. As I later learned, the pregnant woman was still on board, having now sailed through the Pongo twice in each direction.

Right after nightfall we turned back toward Camisea. I was completely drenched, because I had used my shirt to keep the rain off the sensitive directional microphone, which made raindrops sound like gunshots. The Plexiglas window at the front of the boat had broken in the Pongo, and I was sitting in the cold draft. We had to sail by moonlight. The moon was already quite full, and glowed through the wispy mist over the Urubamba. The mist had dug its claws into the jungle slopes with a beauty such as I had never seen before. A large bird of prey was perched in a bare tree, its prayerful posture resembling that of a heraldic creature. Gray herons stood motionless, as if carved of wood, on a gravel bank whose gray matched theirs. The river was rushing, and since it had no knowledge of anything beyond its own reality, it simply did its thing.

Camisea, 17 April 1984
(It is Good Friday, I have just been told, but no associations occur to me.) The flower I planted in the sand in front of my cabin is putting out small, fleshy blossoms, like fatty boils, which fall off after a day. I have not *apprehended* any bug at work today.

Shooting on the platform proved difficult, because it swayed in the wind and gave us so little room. To stay out of range of the camera, I clung to the underside of the platform or crouched in a corner. Kinski became nervous, but today my arguments with him were actually productive. Three large parrots flew over, keeping to a straight line and screeching. The wind carried off a couple of loose pages from my script, never to be seen again. Today I found my thoughts often dwelling on home, though I am not sure anymore where and what home is. People are probably sitting by the Chinese Tower in the English Garden, and on the autobahns traffic is at a standstill. Today the Camisea looks greenish and calm, exuding a delicate melancholy. Boats ply the river quietly.

At night working on a scene that takes place on board. When I finally headed to my hut in the wee hours of the night and was crossing the bridge woven out of lianas, I was taken aback when next to me something dark-colored that I had not seen suddenly made a noise. It turned out to be two black hens that had been sleeping on the railing. I shone my light directly into their eyes at close range until I felt sorry for them.

Camisea, 18 April 1981

There was much talk of Pucallpa today, for no particular reason, and I found myself wondering why that town existed at all. Why is it not gone? I listened to the entire *St. Matthew's Passion*. For Burro in Albersdorf it is evening already. All the mothers are dying now. There is a trembling in the air. The valleys are swaying. Stillness above the mountains. In the jungle the leaves of the soul are stirring, leaf by leaf. Today many things are dropping from the trees. Wind springs up and carries away the last remaining prosaic things. The trees turn their leaves up, confessing. Heavy logs come drifting through the Pongo rapids' pipe organ.

Kinski was complaining and wanted to move out of his hut immediately because a trail of ants has formed nearby. He never knows his lines, either. I took him with me to inspect the ant trail and make it clear to him that he is in no danger. We followed the trail through the entire camp; it had no recognizable beginning, and the end was lost somewhere in the void of the jungle, where the trail branched off and came back together in a broad, bustling stream. In some confused spots knots of ants were battling each other furiously. Many of them had white larvae clinging to their underbellies that seemed larger than the adult ants themselves, although the larvae, already fully developed, with all their limbs, were folded up and looked like unborn mummies. This species of ant is about the size of our forest ants, perhaps a bit larger, with firm, knobby heads and very prominent biting apparatus. Under a piece of floor matting that had blown away from a cabin, a two-dimensional colony of larvae had formed, and when I picked up the mat, the ground beneath turned into a battlefield.

A man who had become a billionaire in Zurich by playing cards (!) purchased a beautifully curved Art Nouveau bridge made of copper, with a patina and age spots that made it seem even more valuable and significant. The billionaire had hidden his money in two secret bank accounts, whose numbers he wrote in pencil on the wall next to his telephone. But over the years so many telephone numbers and other scribbling were added that he could not make out his secret accounts. Half impoverished, he had to sell his bridge back to the city of Zurich, and with part of the money remaining in the other account he bought himself a sailing yacht, planning to set out into the wide world, to drown his disappointment. But the first time he took it out, the yacht capsized, in perfectly calm weather. All this happened very close to shore, yet no one noticed the accident. After swimming to shore, the man made several attempts to be washed up like a corpse on the sand and gravel, because he wanted his misfortune to appear dramatic. By mistake he actually drowned. As a result, his story ended up in the newspaper. My friend's name was Djibril Diop Mambeti; you could let his name melt on your tongue. He came from Senegal, and upon hearing this bad news, he wanted to leave Zurich and return to Africa. A burning sensation coursed through my body, telling me I should go with him, and would do better to pick over rice in my hand than to continue my work.

Camisea, 19 April 1981–Easter Sunday

Walter returned yesterday. He had flown to Oventeni and from there to Satipo, where five Campas were hospitalized. The entire accident turns out to have been far more serious than we assumed at first. It is almost certain that Nico, one of the chieftains, is paralyzed from the waist down; he broke two vertebrae. A hundred and fifty more Campas were ready to be picked up, and now not one of them is willing to fly, which is understandable. They wanted to kill Nico's brother on the spot. The mood is as tense as can be. One Campa, who escaped from the wreckage of the plane, wrapped his broken arm, which was dangling limp by his side, in his *cushma* and fled into the jungle. "Stop!" the others called out to him. Despite his serious injury, the man shouted back that there was nothing wrong with him, and hurled himself into a tangle of lianas, from which they had to drag him by his hair; otherwise he would have died there. Nico was pinned under the wreckage for a long time. The pilot also sustained a spinal injury, and his face was badly banged up. It is too early to tell whether he too will be paralyzed. On the doctor's advice, Walter flew Nico to Lima and also had the pilot transported there. This was the account we received of the accident: during takeoff, a sturdy branch flew up and got stuck in the tail unit, immobilizing it. That apparently caused the plane to climb too steeply, and it would have looped completely over, plunging straight back toward the ground. The pilot kept his wits about him and shut off the engine, switching it on again quickly as the plane came down, so as to reduce the angle of impact. I recall my mother's telling me about seeing a similar accident that occurred during an air show put on by an elite unit. With a large crowd watching, the entire formation went into a backward loop at low altitude, but the unit commander had miscalculated the curve radius, and the entire squadron hurtled in perfect geometrical order straight down into a harvested field.

Has bad luck taken up residence with us? I feel a kind of aimless gratitude for every nondescript day that passes without some disaster. The sound of woodcutting echoes from far off through the jungle. The river, now quiet, is withdrawing more and more into itself.

A long conversation with Kinski about Paganini; he has brought along cassettes with Paganini violin pieces, which he wanted us to play on my porch at top volume. Over the course of forty years Paganini's son spent most of his inheritance trying to get his father buried. The violinist was not welcome anywhere. Every burial was temporary, and the dead man was sent from cemetery to cemetery. Kinski gave me his screenplay to read, all six hundred pages of it; he wants me to direct the film. One glance at the script makes it clear that Kinski's project is beyond repair. There is half a page of fucking, then half a page of fiddling–and so on, for six hundred pages. The whole thing adds up to one enormous Kinski ego trip. He will have to do this one himself.

On their underside the pieces of bark were inscribed with hieroglyphics, faithful copies of the text left behind by ants and caterpillars. Then the trees suddenly disappeared, vanished. With them vanished the insects, leaving only those trapped in amber, evidence of more plentiful times. And this, too: leaves from trees that toppled thousands of years ago are still floating around, tumbling through the void. On this land stripped of trees, only four monks are left. They hitch up their robes on an almost completely harvested turnip field and mount the unsuspecting peasant women from behind. I think this image comes from Kinski, who apparently thinks of himself and me in the plural.

I always associate Easter with my childhood in Sachrang. One time in the fall, when the stags were rutting, a bicyclist was attacked on a lonely road by a fourteen-pointer. He ran to an underpass, where empty food cans were lying around. The rattling of the cans finally scared the stag off. I also remember that on the Sturm farm a dead calf was left in the snow by the edge of the forest, where crows hacked out its eyes and seven foxes tore into it. As I approached, the foxes took off first, then the crows. The calf's face was almost completely gone. Then, when I was almost upon the cadaver, a startled fox came shooting out of the calf's abdominal cavity, lowered its haunches for a moment as if expecting to be struck, and then followed the other foxes in a long, loping stride. I ran off in the opposite direction.

Last year an Aguaruna Indian began trailing me around and finally cornered me, determined to sing me a song. It was in Spanish, about what a beautiful day Saturday was; he belonged to the Seventh-Day Adventists, for whom Saturday is apparently sacred, and was trying to convert me. The whole time he kept smiling, to make it clear to me how happy he was.

My middle finger, which I sliced open when I slipped in the Pongo, is badly swollen, oozing pus. Shooting in late afternoon in the fading light, the scene in which the Campas first board the ship: Kinski's tantrum over the still photos from yesterday's scene, when the light ran out on us. Kinski had insisted on doing them, but flew into an incomprehensible rage because he was convinced that for one of the dozens of shots the picture had been snapped at the wrong moment. After dark, we shot the rest of Scene 106 with Huerequeque and the two Indian boys, McNamara and El Comandante. All three of them handled themselves very well. Tricky Dick Nixon pulled out a clump of McNamara's hair.

Camisea, 20 April 1981

Shooting early in the morning, with hundreds of Indians. Things always look better unrehearsed. The moment I start repeating sequences, they take on a mechanical quality; the life goes out of them. Worried about my hand: the cut on my middle finger is so inflamed that it is bright red and swollen, and the infection is spreading in a red, painful line up to my wrist and beyond.

The first plane to the Pongo had already taken off with Walter, Mauch, Klausmann, and Juarez shortly before I got to Camisea, because I had stopped to grab some food and raingear from the camp; now I am waiting with Vignati at the hut, where four empty gasoline drums were left lying around in the grass. Tossed over tree stumps are two discarded airplane seats, upholstered in artificial red velvet. Flies are buzzing. From the schoolhouse we hear voices. A rooster is pecking away next to me on the raised bark platform. Down below a large sow is wallowing in the earth; otherwise everything is at a complete standstill. From very far off the sound of an ax striking a resonant tree trunk. I talked with Vignati about the Sahara. Two Germans in a 2CV Renault had gone off the road close to the border between Algeria and Niger, near Assamaka, and the car broke down with a cracked chassis. The two of them had a pretty good supply of water and provisions, and because the rainy season apparently set in, they also found water now and then. They did the recommended thing and stayed near the car, but because it was a border region, neither of the two countries made any serious effort to find them, each thinking the other was responsible. When planes flew over, they set fire to their tires to call attention to themselves, and eventually burned the whole car. After about sixty days, one of them died. After eighty-three days, when any search had long since been abandoned, the survivor was found, quite by chance. A vehicle carrying tourists, also off course, came by. They saw the burned-out wreck and took pictures. As they were driving away, one of the tourists happened to notice that two feet were sticking out from under the wreck. They stopped again and found the surviving German, who had dug himself into the sand. He still had a bit of life in him. He gradually recovered, but months later, if you asked him anything, he would stare right through you, and minutes would pass before he responded.

On the way to the airfield I took a look at the cleared swath in the jungle. Mud and groundwater are causing problems. The Caterpillar's entire rear end sank into the mud, and is now stuck. Laplace thinks it will take more than a day to shovel it out. El Tigre and several other men dug a ditch to divert the water, but that will not help much because the subsoil is saturated.

An old Machiguenga woman, who was using a forehead strap to support two heavy pieces of wood, tied together, on her back ran straight toward the plane as it was landing, followed by a galloping pig. Vignati pulled her aside. Delicate white chicken feathers are stuck to a stump, the execution block for chickens. The feathers flutter in the draft from the propeller while the plane is being refueled with the help of a plastic bucket.

We were received with questioning, annoyed looks by those who had arrived before us on the *Huallaga*. Where had we left the cameras, the tripod, and the lenses? they wanted to know. Which camera? we responded. It turned out that W. had not even unloaded the most important camera and accessories from the other speedboat in Camisea, and had instead instructed the boatman to give us the equipment, which he had not done, of course. He, the boatman, had even added a few cases of beer to our cargo, and while we were waiting for the plane had passed us several times, but had not mentioned anything. So I flew with the pilot, whose parents are from Yugoslavia, back to Camisea. As we took off from the Pongo, mud spurted in all directions. I actually welcomed this chance to have a doctor give me an injection, because my infection had rapidly moved up my arm in a red line and was looking like the early stages of blood poisoning. By now it was raining so hard in Camisea that we landed with almost zero visibility. The little plane is completely spattered with mud. Five travelers with luggage, like Peruvian domestic tourists, sat with me under the roof of the first hut, but do not know how they will get out of here. I have never seen them before; possibly they are some of our workers. I do not think we will be able to shoot today in the Pongo, because the *Huallaga* had been hauled by means of winches only half the requisite distance against the current. Besides, it was raining so hard that in any case we would not be able to take off in the next few hours.

Dr. Parraga came, filled a hypodermic with penicillin, and asked me, almost as an afterthought, whether I was allergic to it. I told him I did not know, since to my knowledge I had never been given penicillin. He was surprised to hear that in my entire life I had probably taken aspirin fewer than ten times. Just to be safe, he gave me a minimal test dose in the arm. In almost no time my arm showed a violent reaction, with round, raised, whitish welts, in addition to which my right ear felt on fire and swelled up, turning purple and blue. When welts developed all over my body, Parraga quickly gave me an injection against anaphylactic shock. He was very alarmed, sure he would have killed me if he had given me a full intravenous injection. He very carefully injected a different antibiotic in the rump, and insisted that I stretch out on the bark floor of the cabin. So, lying on my back, I studied the underside of the thatched roof. The smoke from the fireplace has darkened the ribs of the palm fronds, which have a greasy sheen. Stuck into the underside of the roof are duck feathers, presumably intended for arrows, and next to them a toothbrush and toothpaste, a ballpoint pen, a tin spoon and pliers, a wrench, and also a plastic whistle, probably for the soccer games here. A man came and brought a hundredweight of fish, which he slid off his back right next to me. Stored on the roof's crossbeams are arrows with shafts over two meters long, woven baskets, mats, a pair of patched pants. A small monkey, a *fraile*, is cavorting around. He has an amulet around his neck. He is not tethered. A duck hisses at the chickens. The rain is gradually slowing to a trickle. A dog hopped over to me on three legs and looked at me like an apostle gazing at the Lord, who has not given him a mission yet.

Upon arriving in the Pongo, I first collected two cameras already on dry land, because it was fast becoming too dark for filming. A biting chill wind is blowing through the chasm, and the water in the Pongo is fast-moving, gray, and sandy. We drank coffee and hung up our hammocks. The Swiss began to roll dice, for high stakes. The generator stopped, so we sat there in the light of two gruesomely flickering and appallingly smoky lanterns that the captain had quickly fashioned from empty tin cans that had once held peas. He drilled holes in the tops, stuffed in wicks, and filled the cans with diesel oil. The *Huallaga* keeps banging into the bluff, but it is securely tethered. Each time a groan and a long drawn-out shudder passes through the whole ship, which I feel distinctly in my hammock; when the entire ship's body moans dully and writhes and quakes, as if suffering from cramps, its agony is communicated in a painful translation to my swaying resting place. During the evening the sky cleared briefly, and through the wisps of clouds I saw two stars above the ravine. An electrical crackling came from the radio.

One of the men lit a fire in the galley; he is going to cook some chicken soup because I had told the crew to lodge the very pregnant cook in a temporary hut below the rapids. I had also brought along bread, onions, cheese, garlic, and tuna fish, which came in handy. I was overcome by massive dejection, and I called for more coffee. More! Scram, you ghosts!

Because the wind was blowing so cold, I thought long and hard about how I could get warm, but the only thing I could come up with was Kinski's coiled-up mountain-climbing rope, which I wanted to lay over my stomach as a sort of blanket. I gave up that idea, however, and instead hung up my hammock in another spot, where it was better shielded from the wind. Toward midnight there was hot chicken soup. The men in their hammocks swing lethargically until they are jolted hard at almost regular intervals when the ship bangs into the bluff.

Camisea–Pongo de Mainique, 21 April 1981
Bloody Tuesday.

Camisea, 22 April 1981
We spent a cold, unpleasant night on the *Huallaga* in the Pongo, and got to work first thing in the morning setting up the cameras. From my vantage point, the ship's pilotless trip through the rapids did not look particularly exciting, but after the ship had crashed four times into the cliffs on either side, I saw Raimund and Vignati on a promontory below me pounding each other on the back. Right near where they were standing the ship had ridden up on the cliff a bit, and I saw rocks splitting and dust rising from the friction. They must

have filmed that special moment from close up, but there were too many other dead intervals, so we all had the same feeling, and it soon became apparent that we would have to repeat the whole thing, but with the cameras on board. Five volunteers offered to go on board, and I was of the opinion that it would be good to have Kinski and Paul there, too, provided they were willing to cooperate. I promptly went to get Tomislav, the pilot, and we took off below the Pongo from a cow pasture, while those who stayed behind began to move the *Huallaga* back up through the rapids.

Kinski and Paul came along without much hesitation. Kinski took me aside, and in one of our rare moments where we revealed ourselves, he told me that if I went down with the ship he would go with me. I replied simply that he knew how the ship was built, with steel reinforcement beams inside and separate buoyancy chambers; I had no desire to drown, and had taken technical measures against such an eventuality. We hastily shook hands. I grabbed the phonograph and asked Gisela for some sewing needles, because the record player had no needle. But then our departure was delayed considerably. I had learned from the pilot, who had radioed up to the *Huallaga* from the Indians' camp, that people seriously wounded by arrows had just arrived from the upper reaches of the Camisea, and that emergency operations were already under way. I hurried to the first-aid station and saw a native man and a woman, both of whom had been struck with enormous arrows. They had been fishing for the camp three hours upstream by speedboat, and had spent the night on a sandbank. During the night they had been ambushed and shot at close range by Amehuacas. The woman had been hit by three arrows and almost bled to death. The wounds were close together. One arrow had gone all the way through her body just above her kidney, one had bounced off her hip bone, and the most life-threatening one was still sticking in her abdomen, broken off on the inner side of her pelvis. I spent several hours helping out while she was operated on, shining a powerful flashlight into her abdominal cavity and with the other hand spraying insect repellent to try to drive away the clouds of mosquitoes the blood had attracted. The man still had an arrow made of razor-sharp bamboo and almost thirty centimeters long sticking through his throat. He had broken off the two-meter-long shaft himself, and was gripping it in his hand. In his state of shock he refused to let go of it. The arrow's tip, which looked more like the point of a lance, had spliced open one of his shoulders along the collarbone and was sticking crossways through his neck, with the tip lodged in his shoulder on the other side. He seemed to be in less immediate danger and was operated on only after the woman. Here is what had happened: the man, his wife, and a younger man, all three of them Machiguengas from Shivankoreni who provide us with yucca, had gone up the Camisea to hunt. They were sleeping on a sandbank, and during the night the woman woke up because the man next to her was gasping strangely. Thinking a jaguar had got him by the throat, she grabbed a still glowing branch from the fire and jumped up. At that moment she was struck by three arrows. The younger man woke up; he had a shotgun with him and, grasping the situation, fired two shots blindly into the night, since everything was happening in pitch darkness and complete silence. None of the three saw any trace of the attacking Amehuacas; they disappeared, leaving only a few footprints in the sand. Not until the next morning toward eleven did the wounded reach us in their *peke-peke*, which the younger man, uninjured, was steering; they came just as I was about to set out with Kinski and Paul.

Since in the meantime assistants more competent than I had shown up, I did not stick around when they laid the man with the arrow through his neck on a makeshift kitchen table and administered anesthesia. I could not in good conscience leave the others on board too long in the rapids, where the water level had begun to rise crazily just as I was departing. We landed by the Pongo, with mud flying, and had zero visibility as we taxied, because the dirty water had splashed all over the windshield. Added to that, we had a slight tailwind all the way to the end of the cabbage field.

Once on board, we got everything ready: Vignati with a camera up on the bridge, strapped to the back wall, and Paul in the role of captain. The real captain was there with him, as was Walter, so that Paul could take the helm during the moments when we were shooting, something he actually knew how to handle. Next to the bridge we anchored the phonograph and nailed down a small tripod for Beatus. On the mid-deck Kinski, Mauch, and I took our places to film Fitzcarraldo stumbling onto the deck half asleep. Juarez was positioned in relative safety farther upfront with the sound equipment, and Les Blank and Maureen had joined us at the last moment. Klausmann and Raimund had set up atop a cliff in the ravine.

From the moment we set sail we picked up speed, moving on an angle, and had several good collisions with the cliffs on either side, but then the *Huallaga* turned and moved much faster, heading downstream with the current. Walter called to me from up above that we were going to hit the side on the left, and we filmed Kinski again as the cliff approached with menacing rapidity; Kinski ran past us too soon, heading for the stern, so that Mauch had to pan to follow him, with the result that we absorbed the collision facing backward. I had one arm around Mauch, and was holding him steady, while with my other hand I clung on to a window frame, but the collision was so powerful that it knocked us off our feet and sent us hurtling through the air. I saw the lens jolted off the camera and sent flying.

Somehow we spun around our axes as we ourselves went flying, and Mauch, with one hand under the camera, landed flat on the deck, with me on top of him. Mauch immediately balled up in a fetal position, screaming. I immediately thought it was his shoulder again, but it was worse; his hand had been split between the ring finger and the little finger by the crashing camera, deep into the root of his hand. He also had a gash on one side of his forehead. Kinski yelped as if he were injured, though he had only banged his elbows a bit, but when he saw Mauch he quickly forgot about himself and helped out like a good sport as we provided first aid.

Below the rapids the ship ran aground on a sandbank. The prow had curled up like the top of a sardine can, the anchor had been driven through the ship's side, and water was getting into the hull. Vignati had been buffeted around so violently in his harness that he had two cracked ribs, and when Beatus pulled his head away from his firmly fastened-down camera, he was thrown against it. He was very woozy and asked me several times whether we were going to shoot now. We decided we had to get Mauch to the doctor as fast as possible, so we set out in the speedboat as darkness was falling, since I did not want to fly with so little light. We completely forgot about the two men up on the cliff in the middle of the Pongo. Mauch and I lay down in the boat and looked up at the stars. We saw two satellites, and then fog settled over the river. Before it got completely dark we saw two condors on the bank.

Mauch was operated on by Dr. Parraga, with our extraordinarily skillful cook putting in the sutures. Since all the anesthesia had been used up during the almost eight hours it took to operate on the two people wounded by arrows, Mauch was soon in agony, and even analgesic spray did not do much good. I held his head and pressed it against me, and a silent wall of faces surrounded us.

Mauch said he could not take any more, he was going to faint, and I told him to go ahead. Then he thought he was going to shit in his pants from the pain, but he could not decide between the two options, and in the end did neither. On a hunch I sent for Carmen, one of the two prostitutes we have here because of the woodcutters and the boatmen. She pushed me aside, buried Mauch's head between her breasts, and comforted him with her lovely soft voice. She rose above her everyday existence, developing her inner Pietà, and Mauch soon fell silent. During the operation, which lasted almost two hours, she said over and over, "Thomas, *mi amor*," to him, while the patient yielded to his fate. As I stood watching, I felt a deep affection for both of them.

At night ten Campas came along to our camp to stand guard. Some of them were armed with shotguns, others with bows and arrows. They glided into the darkness of the jungle, and I did not see them again till morning, when they gathered by my cabin, talking quietly. I asked to be given the arrow that had gone into the woman's hip and also the tip of the arrow that had been shot through the man's throat. Both patients are doing relatively well; they will both live. I was able to exchange a few words with the man, who was hooked up to an intravenous drip; he could already whisper a bit. He had been incredibly lucky, because the lancelike tip had grazed his carotid artery but not severed it. I was amazed at the thickness of the extra-long arrow shafts and the sturdiness of the large feathers fastened to them.

This morning thirty men set out in the mist, almost all Campa warriors, in *peke-pekes*, all armed, to sail to the place where the attack had happened, follow the tracks and, they said, apprehend the criminals to turn them over to the authorities. May Heaven prevent that.

Almost nothing is known about the Amehuacas; they live semi-nomad-
ically along the upper reaches of the Camisea, about ten days' journey
from here, and apparently they had followed the river downstream
while the water level was so low, presumably looking for turtle eggs,
now in season. All attempts in the past by the military or missionaries
to establish contact with them failed, because the Amehuacas never
let themselves be seen, and attacked only by night. Nor could they be
located from the air, because unlike all the other tribes they do not
make clearings, *chakras*, which are cultivated for a few years before
the tribe moves on. Yet quite a bit of their language is known, because
about ten years ago a very sick Amehuaca boy came floating down on
a balsawood raft and survived in the Atalaya hospital.

I tried to prevent the sortie, but very quickly a common resolve
was reached. It was the women, by the way, who picked the warriors. So-and-so cannot go; he does not shoot well enough, they
announced, and no one protested. Half the men had shotguns. Ten
of them hunkered down in each of the large canoes. The only provisions they took along were bunches of green bananas. Their departure was quiet, almost casual. They disappeared slowly upstream
amid the mist, water, and trees, which fused into a gray, unknown
world like a vague vision.

I had a violent, absurd quarrel with Kinski about his mineral
water, with which he wants to wash himself now. Otherwise peace
and quiet. Suddenly Kinski started yelling again, but it had no connection to anything here. He was beside himself, calling Sergio Leone
and Corbucci rotten vermin, no-good so-and-sos and cyclopean ass-
holes. It took a long time for him to wear himself out. Then his yelling flared up again briefly, as he called Fellini a bungling idiot, a fat
bastard. Then in late morning I finally got some sleep.

Camisea, 23 April 1981

Last night, when I went to my cabin to lie down, I found two Campa warriors on my bed, one in the hammock, and three on the porch. I asked what they were doing there. They were my guards, they replied, and showed me their bows and arrows. Two of them, who had shotguns, seemed especially proud of serving as my bodyguards. They said they had to watch over me because my cabin was the farthest upstream and thus most at risk. Gentlemen, I told them, I feel perfectly safe with such excellent fighters guarding me, but I wondered whether they could not possibly take up their duty posts not on my bed but out in the jungle in a somewhat more forward position, where the enemy was likely to sneak up, if at all. No, they said simply, they would keep watch here, they wanted me constantly in sight. When they saw me put a pillow on the floor, they cleared off my bed and settled down on the porch, where they talked quietly among themselves all night long. Now and then one of them would make the rounds, and the swaying of the flexible bark floor communicated itself to my bed, which kept waking me. They had cigarettes but nothing to light them with, so they asked me for matches. Since I did not have any, I gave them my new lighter, assuming I would not see it again, but found it the next morning neatly placed beside me. My flashlight, which I had been missing as well, turned up in my hammock.

This morning on the ship the first encounter between Fitzcarraldo and the Indians. After they had touched him gently with their fingertips, Kinski scrubbed his hand with alcohol while we were still in the speedboat, on our way back to camp. During the shooting all the Campas got distracted and interrupted their work because from the railing one of them had shot an arrow at a fish in the water, but had missed the fish, which took cover beneath an overhang, and all of them were waiting with their bows taut for it to emerge, which, however, it did not do. The arrow dug itself into the river bottom, with a bit of the shaft sticking up above the water and swaying in a strange, extraordinarily slow, eccentric motion in the current. Walter and Vignati were at the *Huallaga* to prepare the ship for sailing out of the Pongo, the idea being that if they shifted the ballast to one side and flooded some of the watertight compartments, I could film the boat leaving the rapids at an oblique angle, but there was no need to hurry, because the *Huallaga* was jammed firmly onto the sandbank, just as we had left her. In the afternoon dynamite charges were set off, from which the Indians flee. Off camera they enjoyed the explosions and wanted me to give them some dynamite, which some of them have been using for years to make fishing easier. Several times I sank deep into the mud, barefoot, and was in a bad mood, even though the day itself did not warrant it. In the evening we all threw ourselves into the Camisea, and even Mauch groped his way into the splendid water, holding his bandaged hand high. In some places the river is only a meter deep now, so that it is hardly possible to take the speedboat to go from one camp to the other. The water is becoming clearer and clearer; now it is a transparent green, and only slightly cloudy, which lets you see to the bottom. If the water level stays this low, however, we are bound to fall behind schedule. I was in a bad mood today; even the flies got on my nerves. When we played cards, I staked everything on one card, having been winning all evening; since I had an excellent hand, and in addition drew the queen of hearts, a kind of joker, I pulled everything I had out of my pocket, but still lost to Klausmann, who was holding the bank. That assuaged him somewhat for our having forgotten to rescue him from his slippery perch on the cliff in the Pongo until three in the morning. Outside silent lightning flashed in the distance , a hopeful sign for us.

In Iquitos the chief of the secret police won half a pharmacy at cards one night, as well as a tractor and a brickworks. Because people from the tax agency are always at the table during such high-stakes games, each of the players quickly establishes a business and is thus almost completely free of tax obligations, as the Peruvian government uses tax advantages to encourage entrepreneurship in the jungle. One man won $360,000 in one night and paid only a negligible part of that in taxes, because together with his girlfriend, whom he had met that same evening, he promptly founded a company.

Today gold fever broke out in the team, sparked by Huerequeque, Paul, and Laplace, who, once the film is finished, want to pan for gold mechanically, using a floating platform on the upper Río Santiago. Now all of them are dreaming their dreams about gold. Large moths fluttering around the lightbulb are casting hasty shadows, as large as if they came from startled nocturnal birds. In my pants, when they came back from the wash, was a soggy mass of notepaper on which I had jotted down various important things, but the paper was so dissolved and stuck together that I could not decipher any of it. At night I read a Spanish comic book, printed in brownish ink in a small format. Redskins had attacked the circled wagons of settlers, and thanks to their numerical superiority succeeded in mowing them all down, including the hero of the story, a young ranger, but he was merely unconscious. He was scalped, but survived, because two trappers rescued him. Later these two, fighting by his side, were attacked with arrows in cowardly fashion from the rear, and lost their lives. The battle was necessary because the wife of the scalped hero had been captured by the Indians–they were Omaha. She always stood with her voluptuous breasts pointing at a favorable angle into the frame, and the warrior Gray Bear forced his attentions on her in his teepee. The hero, who was not completely recovered yet, managed to free her by stealth, but then he did not want to take her back, because he could not be sure that the child she was carrying was not Gray Bear's. He then set out to hunt scalps, and after he had acquired fourteen of them he was captured in an ambush. Before he was burned at the stake, he was allowed to participate in an unequal hand-to-hand match with Gray Bear, in the course of which each of them killed the other. The story ended with the chief expressing regret that two brave warriors had fallen. You cowardly dog, someone in the story said at one point to a redskin; go to hell! whereupon the white man took an arrow in the heart after doing in the Indian. *Texas 1800* was the title of this comic series. The beautiful woman always wore bras that gave her breasts a nice round shape. The scalping victim always wore a hat and suffered from terrible headaches; only in bed did he have his head bandaged. One time he outsmarted three Indian hunters with a trip wire. Among the captive women there was also a sexy blonde, but toward the end of the story she was completely forgotten.

I was told that the Campa women whose husbands went off to war had picked a plant with a black flower in the jungle; if it wilts, that will tell them the warriors are in trouble. Today an Amehuaca arrow came floating down the river, which was a cause for worry. Many boats passed today, without meaning, destination, or purpose.

Camisea, 25 April 1981
All the branches that overhang the water negate the river's movement. Likewise the bare, barkless limbs of large trees that are stuck in the bottom. Every object the river's flow takes hold of sways and swings according to the rhythm of its own strength or weakness. Some react rapidly, some languidly, some with majestic slowness, some nervously, but all in almost compulsive resistance.

A disturbing thought came to me and refused to go away: that I had failed to build a tree house for my little son.

Some of the Campas have used short strips of 35-mm film that they must have scavenged from the trash to make themselves hair bands, and today Machiguenga women from the big camp turned up with similar adornment, though made of 16-mm film, which can only come from Les Blank. Pacho, who had a thick felt-tipped pen, was pestered by the women to write their names on their forearms: Elisa, Sonia, Asunción. Today, when we were shooting on the *Narinho*, the ship drifted backward into the bend by the gravel bank and did not react when given full throttle. The ballast had been unloaded because we wanted to start pulling the ship over the mountain soon, and as a result, the screw was lifted too high out of the water and could not take hold. Then, swerving suddenly, while three boats alongside tried to prevent it, the ship turned, almost crushing the boats, which could not free themselves fast enough, while the boat drifted past the gravel bank. Branches flew across the deck, lianas were ripped down, and we floated toward a very shallow spot, where the *Narinho* would have run aground, but with all the boats pushing, we managed to nudge the ship back into the bend, from which we thought we could pull it with winches to the other bank, where the crossing of the ridge is to take place. During these maneuvers the boats with the warriors returned from their expedition, and in one boat I saw a man lying strangely curled up. I thought for a moment they had brought back a captive, but then the figure sat up, and it was one of our men, who had just been sleeping. Later, in the Indians' camp, I learned that they had not made any contact with the Amehuacas and had found no more traces of them. They reported that in one place not very far upstream they had encountered masses of *zungaros*, all well over the size of a man, but they stayed too deep in the river to be in range of their arrows. They wanted to know if we could not give them some dynamite so they could hunt the fish more easily. I told them we needed it all for the film.

Since among the warriors were the best shooters and also the best arrow catchers, I had them show me what they sometimes do for entertainment. They shoot arrows at a man, and as he leaps aside he makes a lightning-swift grab and catches the missile in midair. I had them remove the arrow tips, but the whole maneuver did not look particularly impressive. I had imagined I could use it for the film somehow, but I gave up the idea, which was good only in my imagination. A lot of *masato* was prepared, probably to celebrate the return of the warriors. Several women are chewing cooked yucca and spitting the mush into troughs. The quantity alone suggests that in the very near future we will have a lot of drunks. Now the troughs have been left to ferment. At the dinner table I listened over my walkie-talkie as Vignati, Laplace, and thirty men struggled with hawsers and winches to drag the *Narinho* to the other bank. They sound pretty desperate, because the water level is falling, and if the ship does not get to the other side soon, it will be too late.

Camisea, 26 April 1981
Last night Paul felt lousy. His blood pressure was way up, and Parraga gave him two shots. The Brazilians were throwing a party, for the purpose of which they had been nursing and feeding a fire between two mighty tree slices, which were glowing inside. *Pisco* was being passed around, and a large hunk of freshly slaughtered pork was roasting over the fire. After only a short while I was pretty drunk, and inadvertently scorched my headband, which had been drenched with sweat. Staggering a little, I left the area that Zézé had marked off with bright pennants cut out of comic books and hung up on a

string. While reading the mail I had received I fell asleep, but woke up several times because the hooting and hollering got so loud outside. I realized that my light was still on and I really should turn it off. But until two in the morning I simply could not muster the strength. This morning I woke up with a hangover and was annoyed at myself. Walter arrived yesterday, bringing word that the *Huallaga* was stuck even worse than before. Starting Monday he could fly in about another hundred Campas from a mission station, and he also brought mail that had reached Atalaya by way of Iquitos, as well as magazines and groceries. The plane was loaded almost to capacity with two hogs, which I assume were brought alive, but I did not ask for details because I did not want to have my mental image taken away: of the little Cessna with two massive hogs buckled into the passenger seats. The freight included three large turkeys, one of which keeps spreading his tail to intimidate me, gobbling, and putting on a great show of agitation. This turkey, this bird of ill omen, is a pure albino, so it is quite a sight when it fans its great white wheel, spreads its wings, whose tips trail on the ground, and puffs up its feathers. Snorting in bursts, it launched several feigned attacks on me and gazed at me with such intense stupidity emanating from its ugly face, which took on a bluish purple coloration and had tumorlike wattles, that without more ado I pulled a feather out of its spreading rear end. Now the turkey's sulking.

My shoes are rotting away under me. My underwear keeps disappearing. The *Narinho* has run aground in the bend, and its twin, the *Huallaga*, is resting by the Pongo on an island of gravel that keeps getting larger. There is one way of measuring good and bad here: high water good, low water bad. The Caterpillar needs new filters for gas and oil for its transmission to work properly. The diesel fuel that is delivered here is always diluted with water. This is not the end of our trials and tribulations. I am so directly in touch here with the fundamentals of the material world that today I was thinking I am also on very intimate terms with death. If I were to die, I would be doing nothing but dying. Huge leaves are crashing down, like planes out of the clear blue sky. The only thing left to complete the picture are a couple of pterosaurs. Yesterday I sat on the ground for a long time and cracked nuts with a machete. The green husk that surrounds them like walnuts stained my fingers brown, like those of chain smokers, and it does not wash off. Anja asked what I was doing and whether she might have some. I sat there like a Neanderthal man, cracking nuts and wiping the sand off the white edible part, and I thought to myself, I am doing exactly what I can do, no more, no less.

Not until yesterday did I receive a detailed message from Lucki, describing how risky and complicated our mother's operation had been. At first they had tried to keep me from worrying. I stared for a long time at my freshly washed socks, still damp, on which butterflies striped in black and green were carrying out some ritual. Paul had given me a wad of brownish blackish, sticky chewing tobacco, saying it would make me feel better about Mother. I stuck it in my cheek, and because it was the first chewing tobacco of my life, this moment felt important to me. From my porch I spat the tobacco juice onto the ground, and on the spot where it landed a small butterfly is sitting, white wings edged in black, which in turn are dotted in white, and the white is so white and real that it hurts, and the black as black and real as the sins of the Pope.

To distract myself, I thought back to the first detective novel in which I had guessed the identity of the murderer correctly. The story was about a Dr. Brixius who committed the murder by sending his victim's son a toy, a kind of outer-space pistol, which supposedly allowed one to see a tiny screen with a scene from a science-fiction film if one looked into its muzzle while pressing the trigger. Dr. Brixius knew that the victim's son was off at a Boy Scout camp located on a moor, and assumed correctly that the father would not be able to rein in his curiosity. Thus the victim shot himself, because Dr. Brixius had rigged the toy and built an actual loaded pistol into it. After reading just a few pages, I had Dr. Brixius pegged as the murderer, which was probably not all that difficult, given that it was a particularly sleazy detective story.

When I got to the big camp, the *masato* was almost all gone, and beneath a palm-frond roof Machiguengas and Campas were dancing to Peruvian pop tunes played on a gramophone. David, the chief, was already very drunk and spoke to me in Quechua, determined to show me that in addition to Ashininka-Campa he also spoke Quechua. Then he urged me to test his knowledge of Aymara and another Indian language, and I kept assuring him that I was very impressed. Many of the men were wearing trousers that spread at the bottom like funnels and had been in style ten years ago. One of the two little black monkeys was clinging to the neck of one of our prostitutes from Iquitos. I noticed people swarming around one of the huts, where there seemed to be some disturbance; I could hear a woman crying. Miguel Camaytieri, the young chief, was lying on one of the sleeping platforms that took up a whole length of the building, his fist grasping the blouse of a very young woman, who was likewise lying there. Apparently this woman is not his wife but someone else's. She was crying. In response to my questions about this drama, I received evasive answers, to the effect that everything would be taken care of, and I should stay out of it. The fat Dominican padre flew in for half an hour with several guests from Picha, and joined the dancing. In the forest I found a rotting tree with bizarre fungi growing on it. I questioned the Brazilian bulldozer operator, and without hesitation he told me that to clear a new swath he would need about twelve days, if he worked day and night. That sent a shock right through me. It is not raining, which worries me quite a bit. Today Kinski roasted a chicken over a smoky fire, his eyes tearing. Les fixed calamari for lunch, after a plane had brought them from the coast by way of San Ramón. I laid out test strips in the sand along the bank, with honey, urine, laundry detergent, beer, and soap, to see what attracts butterflies most effectively. They often alight in extraordinary numbers, attracted by something, and I would like to place Fitz in the middle of a swarm like that.

I had read in a two-week-old newspaper that a man in Miami failed to pay his insurance premium, and the computer, which could not handle the situation, went haywire and sent him twenty-five hundred reminders.

Camisea, 27 April 1984
It is foreseeable that our internal and external situation is going to worsen rapidly. It is getting harder and harder to say when we will be able to get back to shooting. The water level continues to sink, with the result that both boats are increasingly stranded. This morning I woke up because the three young Campa women who do the laundry for us had been constantly flushing the toilet, just for the fun of it.

In the dissonant concert that constitutes this part of the world, clouds, ore deposits, and human beings without exception did their part today to drag the nature of the creation into plain view.

Preparations for a nocturnal scene in Miguel Ángel Fuentes's hut, as if it were located on the cleared swath. All we have to do is add an identical railing to the porch. Tomislav, the pilot, arrived from Atalaya, bringing all sorts of things, but he had left behind the one really critical item, the filters for the Caterpillar. The *Narinho* is solidly and firmly aground, the *Huallaga* likewise, the bulldozer will not move, there is no rain, and the water level in the river is quietly falling toward ever new record lows. But we can still work: Fitz's cabin, Don Aquilino in the Pongo, the beginning of hauling the ship. Wearing his costume, Kinski poked around in the banana fronds outside my cabin and had Beatus take hundreds of pictures of him surrounded by the luxuriant leaves. Then the two of them moved on a few meters to the edge of the jungle, where Kinski amorously leaned his cheek against a tree trunk and then began to copulate with the tree. He thinks this is immensely erotic: the child of nature and the wild jungle. Yet to this day he has not ventured so much as ten meters into the forest; this is one of his poses. His Yves St. Laurent jungle suit is far more important to him than the jungle itself, and I snapped at him without any real reason when he expected me to happily agree that the primeval forest was erotic. To me it was not erotic at all, I spat, only obscene.

Little Michaela was riding the albino turkey today, with her mother, Gloria, holding her on, and the turkey played along good-naturedly. In a tree near me there is a spiderweb, so sturdy and close-meshed that it is filled up with heavy rotting leaves like a shopping net, and all the time I have been here it has not been torn off, even by wind and rain. In the woods I found a fleshy plant that keeps its upper leaves folded up and pointing skyward, as if praying. There is a delicate vine resembling a fern that spreads so flat over the bark of the trees up which it climbs, wafer-thin, lovely, and deadly, that I often thought it was only painted on, in dull enamel. Moss grows on lianas, and in the knobby places where the moss is thicker a leafy plant like slender hare's-ear grows out of the moss: a parasite on a parasite on a parasite.

In the rain, which does not come, our laundry always stays on the line. A river, already half-dead, had its source in the Black Forest. The sun, El Comandante told me, spends the nights lying on a stretcher. Gather, gather, gather. Gather words, my friend, but no one will ever succeed in describing fire exhaustively. From the radio all we hear are electrical whooshing sounds. Our boats are meandering about on the Camisea.

Yesterday in the speedboat one of the boatmen had left a large chunk of butter in the sun on a flat glass saucer (late-Woolworth style), and had covered it with a page torn from a porno magazine. Repulsive-looking men copulated with blowsy blondes, who strangely enough had kept their bikinis on. I saw that the butter was melting and would soon turn to liquid, so I pushed the saucer into the shade up front in the bow, but on two stops I made later the boatman had pulled the saucer back into the blazing sun. The butter is salted, and comes out of cans imported from Australia. I did not ask why the boatman was putting the covered butter in the heat that way, but with silent determination we continued the duel all day and into early evening to get the butter into the sun, then into the shade. In the last rays of the sun an enormous tree suddenly burst into bloom with blossoms of glowing yellow, as dense and as yellow as a hail of gold. It happened so fast that from one second to the next the blossoms were there, as if a light had been switched on, and just as quickly they were extinguished again.

Huerequeque found a large piece of petrified wood and gave it to me. We talked about tortoise dances, about fish dances. The notion that fish dance preoccupies me.

Camisea, 28 April 1984
While we were shooting on Miguel Ángel's porch, an Indian gave me a huge beetle with a sort of forked nasal horn. I wanted to keep it for Burro, and tried all sorts of ways to kill it, but it withstood all

attacks, and after that I respectfully left it in peace. There are cracked nuts lying around on the ground, and around them extremely fine threads and webs of fungi have formed, like cotton candy, and I saw a large ant completely enveloped in delicate white threads. Upon closer inspection I realized that the ant was not even there anymore, that this most delicate web of fungi had expunged everything and had taken on the morphology of the ant. What revealed that this was not an ant but a wad of fungus in masquerade of an ant was betrayed by this dainty, merciless murderer only because a fine stem and a tiny umbrella were growing out of the putative ant.

The day slips away from us in terrible idleness. Beyond the mountain range a storm is brewing, but it will not reach us. The sun is shining, nothing is moving, the river lies there green and still. Leaves tumbling from the trees render our condition that much more final. From the distant mountains an eagle came swooping toward us at a great altitude. An enormous blue butterfly with wings that looked as if they were carved out of jacaranda wood veneer floated past my table mechanically, as if it were being pulled jerkily on strings. I swam upriver as far as the little *quebrada* on the opposite bank, but turned back because there were too many biting insects over there. On the riverbank there I found a discolored strip of film, lying in the underbrush, brownish and sticking out of the sand. It had been uncovered as the water receded.

In a Viennese café a man orders a coffee *without* cream. They were out of cream, the waiter says; would it be all right to have a coffee without milk? In Communist East Germany a man goes into a department store and asks for a refrigerator. He had come to the wrong place, he is told; the store across the way had no refrigerators; over here there was no furniture.

In bureaucratic offices, defenseless paper comes under attack.

Camisea, 29 April 1981

Last night there was a storm in the distance, which gave us a flicker of hope that the water in the Camisea or the Urubamba might rise and let us free one or both of the ships. Then it even rained on our camp, and we got caught up in frenetic card games, in which entire weekly salaries changed hands and were won back. But today I could immediately tell from the color of the water that nothing had changed. The Camisea had risen by only twenty centimeters.

José Lewgoy was supposed to arrive here by way of Pucallpa, but somehow we lost him along the way. Apparently he made it to Pucallpa, and then flew on to Atalaya, but because the visibility between there and here was so low, the pilot refused to bring him. Lewgoy then apparently flew on to Satipo, but no one can confirm that for me.

On my porch I had some tree mushrooms that I had recently found in the jungle. This morning they were full of holes made by little brown beetles. The holes were as straight and clean as if they had been made by electric drills, and since the beetles had apparently just gone to work, their smooth, shiny brown rear ends were still sticking up out of the holes. I pulled one of these little borers out by his hindquarters, which made him very cross.

In the meantime the dreams of panning for gold have taken a new pitch: people's fantasies are circling around a single nugget, one chunk as large as a mature hog. Paul told me he would immediately construct a solid raft, after first painting the chunk black, and then he would make a run for it. We discussed whether we would find an entire petrified river out here, like petrified wood. It would be recognizable because leaves that had fallen on its surface would be frozen in place and would not move. The water would consist of diamonds, and brooks feeding into the river would have solidified into reddish brown semiprecious stone. We pictured the diamond river lying there in its grand, timeless tranquillity. Maureen was eating shrimp, and by mistake ate a red rubber canning ring, which because of its color she had failed to recognize after it fell into the dish. Once you have tasted this delicacy, I told her, you will never go back to shrimp. We also voted on whether forgotten skills such as tug-of-war, the standing broad jump, and three-legged racing should be reintroduced as Olympic sports. At one Olympiad, probably in Stockholm in 1912, pairs of runners had tied two legs together and raced as three-legged creatures.

There is a big problem involving Laplace: he took me aside and explained that Walter was constantly bickering with him, and he could not go on working under these conditions; he wanted to leave. Laplace is talking about leveling the slope to a mere 42 percent grade, but that would look like the narrow strip of land that forms an isthmus. I told him I would not allow that, because we would lose the central metaphor of the film. Metaphor for what, he asked. I said I did not know, just that it was a grand metaphor. Maybe, I said, it was just an image that is slumbering in all of us, and I happened to be the one to introduce him to a brother he had never met.

I had El Tigre and Quispe dressed in the costumes for the scene in the rubber camp. Quispe turns up at my hut almost every evening. Initially he came under all sorts of pretexts, but now he has a single, unconcealed mission: he wants to buy a fifty-horsepower speedboat motor from me, but he does not have quite enough money. I tried to make it clear to him that even if I gave him the motor as a gift he would not get any pleasure out of it, because every two weeks at the latest something goes wrong with it, and when there is lots of sand in the water, the cooling system invariably clogs, often after only one or two days, and he would certainly have a very hard time getting replacement parts; even for us, with all of our contacts, it was fairly complicated to order the right ones in Miami and get them through customs. I also tried to point out tactfully that he speaks only a little Spanish, and that in Miami they do not understand Quechua. But the motor remains Quispe's dream, and one he continues to dream boldly and persistently. To this day he has not been able to explain what he wants to accomplish, except that one time he indicated he was thinking of opening up a commercial route through the Pongo. Even if that is pointless and devoid of any compelling economic necessity, I feel embarrassed, and when we are done with our work here I will make him a gift of the motor as a symbolic payment for a week of his services.

Camisea, 30 April 1981

In the morning we shot a fairly major scene, which I had hastily jotted down last night. Lewgoy arrived after quite an odyssey, but in good spirits. He spent the last eight months performing in a Brazilian soap opera as a genial grandfather figure, and he told me that being here with me made him feel reborn. Four filters for the Caterpillar arrived with him, sent by Gustavo, but it immediately became obvious that they were the same wrong kind he had sent before. Walter hinted today that we will probably not be able to free the *Huallaga*, which is aground in the Pongo, until the next rainy season. The crew seems to have mounted a winch incorrectly, and the entire cast-iron unit cracked as a result.

I rode up the Camisea with El Tigre and twenty Campas; in a second large boat we had *pona* bark and palm roofs for building the rubber workers' camp. On the next sandbank above our camp I saw a rather large alligator, at least two and a half meters in length, and even though Mauch saw it, he did not want to believe it was an alligator and not a piece of driftwood. I had them turn the boat and head straight for the sandbank, at which the alligator slipped into the water. On the very next sandbank we saw another one, which looked even bigger. We talked about New York, where several crocodiles have been found in the sewers, brought to the city from Florida and kept in people's bathtubs as pets and when they got too large, they were flushed down the toilet. Some of the animals had grown quite big, because initially they were able to keep themselves fed on rats, and later on sewer workers, as Mauch cheerily speculated.

A story about children who want to compete in a test of courage; all six of them, brothers and sisters, lay their heads on the railroad track as a train is approaching, but with their faces turned away from the train. The winner would be the one who kept his head on the track the longest. What happened was this: not one of the children, not a single one, moved his or her head off the track, but the alert engineer managed to stop the train only meters away from the children. A story about a childhood friend of Sepp Mosmeier's in south Tyrol who climbed up a pylon and grabbed hold of the high-tension wire above a railway embankment. He was shaken for several minutes, and the current burned and charred his insides completely, but his hand remained clasped around the high-voltage wire. At last he fell off, and the most terrible part, which remained engraved on Sepp's memory forever, was the sound, the noise his friend made as he fell onto the trap rock covering the embankment. Because his bones had turned to charcoal, there was a crackling and crashing as if someone had dropped down a sack of briquettes. The story of the soccer fan who swore he would cross the Rhine at Cologne by night, balancing on the bridge railing, if his soccer team did not slip in the standings. He had made it almost all the way across when the police hauled him off the bridge and had him transported to an insane asylum, where it took him a long time to convince the doctors that he had not been trying to commit suicide.

Camisea, 1 May 1984

A day I would rather forget. Shooting without a clear sense of purpose. Standing on a pile of dirt, I quarreled with Walter. Mauch constantly squabbling with Walter; a confused message from the film lab in New York; Kinski threw a tantrum; Gloria ran away from Walter, leaving the camp early in the morning with the child, but returned in the evening. I threw away my shoes, which were falling apart anyway, and now go barefoot, like everyone who lives here for a while.

Camisea, 2 May 1984

In the morning I spoke with Lucki over the radio. The connection was clearer than ever before, probably because there was no interference caused by storms. Lucki will get here on Tuesday.

Quispe is sleeping in Don Aquilino's sedan chair, woven from lianas. Kinski is having himself photographed by Beatus, manically, for hours on end, using up roll after roll of film. The smoke from the fires over which the balls of rubber are being turned on a spit rises to the treetops. The white turkey is spreading its tail in the jungle. A man came walking through the damp leaves, placing each foot carefully. The trees bleed white. Lianas have intertwined, forming braids, and dangle thus conjoined from the crown of the sky. The jungle serves as a damper to all conversations; everything becomes quieter, calmer. A large butterfly soared like an eagle. In the jungle theater the audience was still clapping for two days after the curtain had been rung down. I put out a huge hook, not for fish this time but for alligators. Despite several tries, I did not manage to capture their growling evening serenades, their ugly mating calls, on tape. Today the jungle softened all sounds. I rolled a piece of newly poured sheet rubber into a little ball, which bounces in odd ways. My hands and the little ball smell just like smoked eel. Huerequeque brought me a type of liana known as *clavehuasca*, as thick as a man's arm. This liana has an odd structure: there are six or eight segments of dark and light wood, like wedges of cake. You can pull out the wedgelike dark pieces in a sort of strip, and the taste is delicious, the aroma unlike anything else, perhaps closest to sandalwood. They use it to flavor *pisco*, mixing in a spoonful of honey.

After work today Lewgoy was beside himself about Kinski, who was an absolute pestilence, but part of it seems to be Lewgoy's attempt to distract us from the trouble he has learning his lines. While he was sounding off, I was using a needle to dig a thorn out of my foot, and was so focused and calm that suddenly my calmness carried over to him.

Camisea, 3 May 1981
The earth lay there, a freshly plowed field. Horses gamboling in the meadow paused, their coats steaming. It was very early in the morning. In town the blackbirds in the park were bustling about. The things unspoken were patient for the time being. Nothing was caught on my hook. Rotting fruits were besieged by beautiful butterflies. A doctor was attending to a beheaded chicken. Children picked up a run-over hedgehog from the road; it was completely flattened, and dried like parchment by the sun. After days of arduous hiking

through the jungle, explorers came upon an old, worn-out automobile tire leaning against a tree. The boatman bails out the canoe with even motions, full of mechanical profundity. For a film, a white horse was led, accompanied by a torch, through the catacombs under the Villa Borghese in Rome. In ancient Greece there were stumbling gods, and they often laughed, too. One of them worked as a smith. A man sailing solo around the world grew a crop of watercress on a moldy felt blanket.

The man paused in mid-motion; his weapon clattered gingerly to the ground, his gaze was fixed on the distant mountain of his misery. Then he collapsed, struck by a bullet, while he reached for something imaginary in the void, or rather, as he seemed to try, with a reflective gesture, to hang on to his life, disappearing into an imaginary void, he hurtled into the finality of his end.

An old man, who had been the last person living on a windswept island far from the stormy coast, with the mail boat bringing him onions and flour only now and then, died one evening with the natural casualness of all things out here. Days later a very large fish was caught on the dead man's ground line, still in the water.

Camisea–Satipo–Camisea, 4 May 1981
I did not have a boat, so I quickly constructed a large wheel out of lianas, which floated well, and on which I could stand and move myself along with a pole in the water. A few other people were with me, following me on tiny rafts, crafted from three balsa trunks. When we had reached Shivankoreni, cold mist came shooting at us as if from an explosion, billowing and rolling. It was like a glacier wheezing and coughing at us. Behind it came a dull, deep rumbling

of debris and heavy pieces of rock. Then I saw a brown, muddy wall of water, about two meters high, rolling toward us. It lifted me up on my ring and swept me sideways into a *chakra*, in which corn was planted. But that was only a sort of precursor to a much higher wall of white, swirling spray, which rushed along the riverbed, as if driven by an explosion. Lifted high on our light materials, we were able to save ourselves. Once arrived in Shivankoreni, which was situated high on the riverbank but was nonetheless inundated by the flood, I saw all the people out and about, hunting for their pigs, which the water had swept away.

For the shooting we did yesterday in the Pongo, we hoisted Lewgoy onto a cliff ledge by the waterfalls. It turned out to be as difficult as hauling up a piano. Paul came with us and had us let him off with a few other men by the sandbank, so he could bury the cadaver, which was digging its way more and more into the sand. He wanted to give a decent burial to the bold swimmer, who had crossed the Pongo, after all, and conquered it.

The crew of the *Huallaga*, which is completely high and dry, told me without any attempt at gilding the situation that they were fairly sure the boat could not be floated again until November, when the next rainy season began. Before that the water was unlikely to rise significantly, unless there were torrential downpours. But there were no signs of any such thing. For days we have had cloudless skies and brilliant, starry nights. Last night Zézé wanted to record croaking frogs for the soundtrack, and went looking for a quiet spot. Eventually she set up in the little bay by my hut, and scanned with her flashlight in all directions. Very close by, the glowing eyes of a large alligator were staring at her quietly, whereupon she fled, screaming, to the other end of the camp.

The time of the white swallows has arrived. An ailing chicken is trying to make friends with our white turkey; it always sleeps on the ground, cowering in the turkey's shadow. As a child I once read a book about the ancient Germans that described how a young woman set out on a long journey on foot, for which she tied hefty pieces of beech bark to the soles of her feet as sandals. That is the only thing I remember from the whole book.

Today Mauch and I plan to fly out to Satipo to look at rushes, at least a small portion of the material we have filmed, so as not to be completely unsure of how it is coming out. The plane, which is also supposed to pick up fuel there, made a quick run down to Sepahua to fetch something else, but now it has been hours, and it is still not here. We have been waiting in the church, which has a corrugated tin roof that is heated up in the sun and is crackling and creaking. Swallows fly by, very close, without a sound. A new season has arrived, irrevocably.

In Satipo we were plunked down without warning in a strange, ugly world. The town is the last, most seedy outpost of civilization. We were taken to the revolting house of the local cinema owner, cluttered with knickknacks of the kidney-shaped table era. A dusty little keg and a set of brandy glasses were suspended from a plastic guitar, and the room also had a green plastic duck, sassy ashtrays, and even a telephone. The local phone book has about twenty entries. A repulsively fat woman, who was digging bundles of money out of a dingy old plastic bag and counting the bills on the table, demanded, without pausing in her counting, 30,000 *soles* for projecting the rushes. After much haggling she came down to 10,000. The screening was the craziest I have ever experienced: the format all wrong, so that a quarter of each frame was missing on the left, most of the sections running as a reversed image, out of focus, and the light gave out so often that it was almost impossible to make anything out. To add insult to injury, the projectionist kept trying to coax sound out of the silent footage, even though I repeatedly shouted up to his booth; but his efforts, which resulted in electrical crackling and popping that sent a shivers through one's body, would not stop. Distracted by the nonexistent soundtrack, the projectionist did not notice that an insect's wing had got stuck in the lens, presumably that of a dragonfly, whose form was most of the time superimposed on half the image. Nonetheless, with a little imagination we could draw conclusions as to how the film would look.

During the return flight Tomislav urged me to take the little plane's controls for a bit, and it felt good. Below me in the jungle I saw a deep ravine with a waterfall that surely measured more than a hundred meters from top to bottom and disappeared into a funnel of towering trees. All the rivers have shallow water, the Tambo, the Ene, the Perene, the Pangoa, the Satipo, the Picha; there is no denying that the rainy season is past. Once back over the jungle it struck me that the people in Satipo were like vomit—ugly, mean-spirited, unkempt, as if a town in the highlands had regurgitated its most degenerate elements and pushed them off into the jungle. Upon our return to Shivankoreni, which I could hardly wait for, some winged creature promptly flew into my ear, as if it had been fired at me. It felt as if its wings were made of metal, rotating like a lawnmower that wanted to bore its way into my skull. Once it had been removed and I could hear normally again, I heard the frogs outside testing the night. Night should watch out for me!

Camisea, 5 May 1984
The day began in a sleepy and depressed mood. Paul is going to fly to Iquitos to sign a contract with the oil explorers for transports on his ship. During the night, an enormous earth slide occurred on the

cleared strip where the Caterpillar had been working. No one heard anything, but it took down all the trees along the upper rim. At some point, amid the night sounds I felt something while half asleep that caused my hammock to sway slightly, and I had a sensation as if the earth were quaking and trembling slightly. In the morning the fish in the river were behaving strangely, constantly shooting to the surface. I do not really have to count Kinski's rabid tantrums. Yet when we were shooting, he was frighteningly good.

Camisea, 6 May 1981
As we were shooting at night in the chief's hut, toward the end of the scene an Indian in overalls suddenly dashed into the shot, the best take we had, but I think it happened so late in the process that it probably does not matter. He wanted to bum a cigarette off Kinski. Silent tongues of lightning licking in the distance, and we all stayed up very late, until the rain and lightning had reached us here. In the morning I woke up and knew immediately from the sound of the river that it had risen. I started up in alarm, but then saw that as soon as it was light Vignati had steered the *Narinho* to safety on the right side of the river, taking advantage of the barely sufficient rise in the water level. For a brief moment nature had shown herself well disposed toward us. The Urubamba, however, has not risen–nothing to hope for there.

Lucki arrived with Walter from Pucallpa. Upon catching sight of my brother, I was filled with brotherly feeling. They had two prostitutes from Iquitos with them, to relieve the two we have here. News and mail from our mother, and an adventure story from Burro about a river of gold in India. Otherwise, depressing news. Lucki brought a recording of *Ernani*, which he had made in an Italian opera house. I had a hard time expressing myself, and jumped from one unfinished sentence to the next, as in a brook filled with slippery rocks one keeps hoping for traction on the next one.

Camisea, 7 May 1981

All morning Huerequeque was sharpening his machete on a flat stone, saying nothing. One of the whores from Iquitos sat across from me eating her breakfast, likewise saying not a word. Last night a swarm of men had gathered hesitantly around her–the Brazilian bulldozer operators, several boatmen, and El Tigre also came by, wearing a freshly ironed shirt, the first I'd ever seen him in. He said he wanted to visit with me, but after a few pleasantries he turned to his actual goal, the woman. The river is shallow but brownish. Strange birds are shrieking on the opposite bank. An alligator drifted by, belly-up and white all over, with all four legs stretched out. The bulldozer will not start; this time several hoses in the hydraulic system are shot. In the camp numb stillness has settled in, holding everything in a tight grip. Far off in the forest chain saws are at work. A decision to move our operations to Iquitos for a while is becoming increasingly unavoidable, because here too much lengthy preparation would be necessary before we could shoot properly. The drawback is that transporting people and materials will cost us about five days, but the summer is coming down on us with swords wielded slowly and inescapably by an unknown hand. A light haze over the landscape, filled with the cries of animals.

I was startled to realize how much money we have spent already, and Walter simply did not want to believe the figures Lucki presented, because he has lost all sense of context. A shouting match today during shooting between him and Kinski after Miguel, the chief, uttered dark hints about Kinski, whom all the Campas hate.

Miguel told me I must have noticed that during Kinski's outbursts his people silently huddled together, forming groups, but I should not think they were afraid in any way of the madman's screaming; rather, they were afraid of me, because I was always completely calm in the face of his tantrums. After work I saw that some of them were using machetes and a stick with a sharpened tip to break open a large rotted tree that must have been on the ground for years. They dug out of the decaying wood fat, yellowish whitish maggots bigger than cockchafer grubs, with dark, sturdy heads. They squirmed on the men's hands before the men ate them, slurping as you slurp oysters. Suddenly they came over to me, and before I knew what was happening I had three of those writhing creatures in my hand as a gift. They gave me to understand I should try them, and stared at me intently in happy anticipation. For a moment I struggled with my civilized instincts, but then decided to eat them. They are supposed to be especially tasty when you roast them over a fire briefly, and they are also supposed to be unusually high in protein and fat.

Camisea, 8 May 1984
Last night Kinski got little sleep because on the big, swaying liana suspension bridge near his cabin a lot of most vigorous fornicating was carried out. One of the ladies from Iquitos had selected the swinging bridge as a particularly suitable spot, where she laughed and joked with her suitors before the panting and groaning began, and the bridge swayed and creaked an accompaniment. Apparently she promptly gave H.P. a social disease. Reverend Father, my fat Dominican, thou who so firmly vouched for these ladies, I would gladly do without the globs of fat in my soup and without the bread for breaking, but please restore my lack of faith! I did not see God

today. According to the statistics, 85 percent of all existing species are beetles and insects of various sorts; so where are we on the scale of God's favor?

Camisea–Pucallpa, 9 May 1981

To my great surprise, the first thing I encountered this morning was a bleating sheep with thick, dirty wool. It came toward me from the jungle, and I wondered whether it was not a dreamed sequel to a bad night, in which confusing happenings with boats torn from their moorings had kept me tossing and turning. But then I realized that Julian was sharpening his knife on a flat stone to slit open another sheep that he had just slaughtered. This other sheep had had its throat cut on the chopping block, and the one that was still alive was watching from close by, not sure whether it should stick by its comrade, to whom it seemed drawn, or should flee. So it fled a few paces, no doubt recognizing danger in the bright red blood on the ground, but then was compelled by lack of understanding and an unknown, all-powerful fate to face its own fate.

Working on the *Narinho*, which we cautiously sailed back and forth close to our camp. Then the water carried it back to the bend in the river, where it ran aground on the gravel bank on the side of the river from where we wanted to haul it over the mountain. At night some startled swallows that had strayed into the darkness under the roof over the kitchen. We played cards, and I brooded over the hero of my story, who rides into the mayor's office, smashes in a door, and gallops right into an assembly of his enemies, on whom he, as surprised as they are, lets loose a hail of bullets until both his Colts' chambers are empty. From then on he is an outlaw.

Pucallpa–Iquitos, 10 May 1981

Mist in the morning, vultures on the roof of the Hotel de Touristas, which has just been dedicated and is already heading straight toward dilapidation. Paper has blown into the swimming pool, which no one uses. The water is a slimy green, and brownish algae have taken up residence on the bottom. The rungs of the ladder have become perches for large water beetles. At the Pucallpa airport I haggled with a pushy cabdriver for a ride to the Vatican for 5,000 *soles*. In the evening, because the pilots were not taking off, I went out to eat with Mauch and Paul. We met up with Paul's friends, Marcel, the Belgian consul from Iquitos, and Felix, the German mechanic from Aschaffenburg, both of them marked by decades in the Amazon region, both the biggest crooks imaginable. Still, I cannot recall having seen anyone with as hearty a laugh as the Belgian. Paul says he was the chairman of the Iquitos tennis club, but since there are not any tennis courts in Iquitos, I am trying to translate *tennis club* into something more like *drug cartel*; at any rate, Marcel misappropriated several million and for that reason had to slip away to Pucallpa.

Iquitos, 11 May 1981

Vignati's birthday. Shooting in the foundry, then Kinski up in the church tower. Lucki, Klausmann, Beatus, and Raimund did not get here until late afternoon, coming by way of Atalaya and Pucallpa. Many things are missing, friction as a result of the move.

Iquitos, 12 May 1981

Because he could not breathe anymore within the circle, but without it was done for . . .

. . . and so as not to appear unsociable as a result of basically necessary and unavoidable murdering . . .

Iquitos, 13 May 1981

Unsociable. The children put the cat into the laundry dryer and turned it on. The cat survived. After that it was not sociable anymore.

Around my house on stilts the water is black; the banana fronds are decaying, and swarms of small, finger-length fish with thick heads gather just under the surface and fight each other for my spit. A footbridge of boards with empty snail shells and small, dark brown to reddish mussel shells lying on it now leads to my cabin. The ladder is new. I found everything just the way I had left it, but as dusty as if I had been away for years. Completely different birds and animals are around me now, also in the lake overgrown with trees and brush: *gavilánes*, a kind of eagle, herons, large falcons. They squawk strangely at each other, flap away from me into the bare branches, fish snails out of the water, and crack them open on my footbridge. The sounds during the night have stayed the same, but in the morning, when I wake up, I find myself in a different world.

When Lucki left Camisea one day after me, the *Narinho* was already completely beached, resting on the gravel bank so that one can walk around it, as if a kindly mountain had lifted it. Someone broke into the costume depot on Calle Putumayo, even though Franz and Gisela were sleeping there, and two sewing machines were stolen. The thieves drank rum, left the empty bottles lying around, and pissed on the floor. They also took some costumes. Across from our headquarters overlooking the Nanay there was a huge explosion in a boiler, fortunately after the work day in the factory there was over. The one night watchman was blown to pieces and sent flying. A smallish bloody piece of him landed with a splat on our porch. After this terrifying event the entire neighborhood sought refuge in our office, thinking Ecuador had dropped a bomb, that war had broken out again, and that we would have information and could provide some protection for the time being. An old woman had armed herself with a machete so she could defend her grandchildren. Claire, who abandoned our telex machine after the explosion and was utterly confused, handed around chewing gum and thus calmed the agitated crowd somewhat.

The old *Narinho*, which served as the model for the *Narinho* on the Camisea and the *Huallaga* in the Pongo, is up to its middle deck in water and has been dismantled by thieves from the neighborhood to such an extent that hardly anything of the superstructure and the cabins remains. We have hired a man to locate the missing parts in nearby huts and buy them back. Recently, while we were checking out a new bar in which to hire crew members, because the previous place is under water, one of the guests uttered the ultimate insult to another–*su madre*–and on Mother's Day to boot, which immediately led to a ritualized brawl, with stools being hurled through the air and other guests trying to separate the insulter and the insultee. I hired both of them as extras, after they had quickly buried the hatchet and were drinking beer together. A dwarf missing his front teeth also wanted to get into the film.

In the jungle Huerequeque had found a battered bucket seat from a helicopter that had crashed there, and took it with him as a sort of talisman. On the flight from Camisea to Pucallpa I saw in the west, toward the mountains, dramatic cloud formations such as I had never seen before. In the jungle great loops of rivers glittered like gold, and in the sky all the doomsday mythologies were playing themselves out. In a few spots it was raining, causing double rainbows to form. The sky flared up across its entire expanse, and in the clouds battles were raging, with lightning darting toward the earth like swords. The edges of the most distant clouds glowed like angry, seething ore, with black mountain ranges welling up around them, and above them red cloud banks glowed bloodily. Stormy, blazing, primeval lights passed over the forest, drawing veils of dark and orange-yellow rain with them. Everything was being transformed ceaselessly into ever-increasing ecstasy, and the horizon lit up in a pulsing madness of beauty. As night fell, it drew everything down with it. The last revolt against the darkness was fearsome and bloody and grisly; far, far off in the distance the cloud mountains writhed as if suffering cramps. The last sun poked its fingers into wounded, bleeding towers of cloud. Then, all of a sudden, everything was extinguished. In the darkness lightning flickered without pause. I had almost stopped breathing, and knew that I had seen what hardly any human being had ever witnessed.

Next the following ensued: I had crashed a single-engine plane into the jungle, but had escaped with only minor injuries. Taking a taxi into a city, which soon turned out to be New York, I called the driver's attention to a large plane flying low overhead toward the airport. From its fuselage issued a delicate streak of black smoke, which trailed through the sky above the skyscrapers, and at the moment when I realized I had crashed that day and would now experience my crash as an observer, there was a jerk, and the plane's tail broke apart, though the plane could still fly straight ahead. Large pieces of aluminum flew off, the smoke spread, as if pulled on a string and billowing darkly and malevolently, and the plane tipped slightly downward. For a brief moment I was looking down from above, probably from another plane circling in a holding pattern, and I saw the rear half of the cabin's roof shear off. I saw the passengers seated in rows, turned to pillars of salt in their fear. Behind them strips of aluminum dangled, pierced with holes, like the steering wheels of racing cars, to make them lighter. I saw the galley for the stewardesses and the rest-rooms, and two men were standing there, pressed to the wall to keep out of the gale. One of them did not have a jacket on, but was wearing a shirt and tie. For a brief, terrible moment when I saw them they were clamped fast against the wall; behind them the plane was torn off. Then I saw a young man with the raging wind rushing through his blond curls. He hastily pulled off his shoes and I saw him clamber out onto the struts and frame members poking out of the rear of the plane, which was now racing straight down into the skyscrapers. He did not want to plummet to his death sitting motionless like the other passengers. His decision was obvious from the few actions I saw. The air current struck him like a blow, hurtling him down until he was nothing but a dot in the distance, and my gaze followed him as he dis-appeared like a shot into a gorge, while the plane remained on course, though descending even more steeply. Before it plunged into the build-ings, which created a magnificent fireball that remained hanging over the city like a marsh marigold, the plane was almost entirely ripped to pieces. Just as in operas from the last century, something merely presumed to be true, a tragedy whose consequences were irreversible, like death, in other words the idea that something had happened that did not actually happen, changed an entire life once and for all. When we celebrated Lucki's and Vignati's birthdays I sat there until the last guest had left. Then I rode my motorcycle to my hut, going over the bumps and potholes so fast that my ribs hurt from the impact. In the dark, a man appeared on the road in the beam of my headlight. He was pointing with strange urgency to the ground. As I ran over the viper that was crossing in front of me and left it behind writhing, I under-stood what he had meant.

Today I encountered a religious procession that blocked my way; I assume it was taking place because of the assassination attempt on the pope, which I had learned about from a passing reference in a telex. Information on the important events in the world reaches me only in fragments consisting of simple five-word statements.

Iquitos, 14 May 1981
In the morning I can see the water glinting as I look down through the cracks in my floor; at a low angle the sun casts reflections into my room made of bamboo. At night two banana plants near my hut collapsed; one of them has fallen across my footbridge. I saw water birds as big as peacocks whose wings have entirely different colors on top and underneath, as leaves sometimes do. They have a strange way of flying, with their long legs dangling behind them. Paul commented that whether the buckshot in his gun is too fine or not is not his problem but that of the alligator. I rode to see Huerequeque to give him some reassurance about the scene we are going to shoot today, but his wife advised me to let him sleep; he was very drunk, and if we woke him, he would start drinking again.

In the evening I was the only living being in the house aside from Claire. Claire is pregnant. I am writing by the light of two skinny candles that will soon have burned down. Since this afternoon there has been no electricity. The phone calls that reach me are *long-distance* calamities, fraught from the first minute with misunderstandings and hurt feelings, interrupted by the electrical gaps that the stuttering current creates. Outside in the darkness four thousand frogs are crying for a savior. The frogs have lowly thoughts and carry on lowly research. I wish a taxi would come and take me somewhere. Yet not for anything in the world would I want to dream the others' dreams. At the candle's end, the wick curls without any reverence for the inevitable.

I miss the swallows on the Plaza de Armas. The city government decided to ignore the interests of four hundred thousand birds, and now they stay away because all the trees on the plaza were summarily cut down, leaving the birds nowhere to sleep.

Iquitos, 15 May 1981
In the middle of town, amid the throng of mopeds and motorcycles, a small, unkempt, emaciated horse came toward me; it had run away from somewhere, and no one was paying any attention to it. Ah, one horsepower, said Mauch, who was seated behind me on the motorcycle. In the burglary on Putumayo Street it was not only the sewing machines that were taken but, strangely enough, also letters that were waiting for the team to pick up. Two of them were for R., whom I tried to comfort by pointing out that at least he knew that letters addressed to him had been lost, whereas I was equally certain that there had been none there to steal that were addressed to me.

Iquitos, 16 May 1981
Arrival of Lewgoy, Grande Otelo, Rui Polanah. Nocturnal turmoil about Lewgoy, who had presumably picked up *isangos* from the grass on the airfield, as had already happened to Lucki, Walter, and Sluizer before him. He is scratching like a madman against the mites, yelling that they are from the sheets at Paul's, where we had him spend the night for the time being, since the Holiday Inn is full. When the water pressure in the entire city failed and then the electricity went

out, he apparently set out on foot in the middle of the night for the Holiday Inn, assuming that he would find both there.

We spent the afternoon in the costume depot, where Kinski also showed up, trying on a fine dark blue suit, which he liked very much. All logic and also the script speak unambiguously in its favor, but when I saw him in it, I had a hard time recognizing Fitzcarraldo; before my inner eye he has already assumed archetypal form in his white linen suit and the large straw hat. I promptly told him so and could see him working himself up to a tantrum. I told him that when I imagined myself as the audience, long after I had seen the film the figure of Fitzcarraldo had to be a fixed phenotypical concept, and the inflexible principle of a single white suit could be broken only at the end with a tuxedo—that was what my instinct dictated. Wavering between a tantrum and a glimmering of understanding that I had ignited in Kinski, he suddenly began to pay close attention, and I knew he had grasped my point. Now anyone who tried to win him over for the blue suit and pointed out the lack of logic would be chased off by Kinski in a fit of rage.

Iquitos, 17 May 1981

During the night there were powerful thunderstorms, nearby and in the distance. After that a steady rain set in. Banana stalks hurtled, rustling and slapping, into the water. There they are drifting now, with pale leaves, like corpses in the water. Water fowl with grotesquely skinny legs and even more grotesquely long toes clamber about on the rotting remains of the stalks as they drift along. More and more creatures are seeking refuge in my hut, because it is the only stable platform sticking above the water. The days are becoming more and more melancholy. The house in front of me is almost always empty, as if abandoned by refugees. We have a second young ocelot for the scene we are shooting on Monday, and a toucan. They gazed at me from their cages with such a submissive air that I was terribly moved. Water is dripping from the roof, but the rain does not refresh anything. The cat has thrown up on the porch. The chickens are standing in the rain, getting soaked. My suit is hanging from the rafters of my palm-frond roof, covered with mildew. There is mildew on my shoes and my notebook. You hang up laundry, but it does not dry. My shirts disappear without a trace. Of the five rabbits Walter wanted to use for breeding, on the supposition that they would multiply in a geometric progression to 256,000 in a year, only one is still alive, its coat pathetically matted. This morning a tarantula the size of my fist was sitting in front of me on the table, and for the first time in my life I was only half-afraid. Nonetheless, I killed it in businesslike fashion with a broom. Just as mass can undergo compression, spiders can probably also be compressed, condensed, and the result is tarantulas.

Iquitos, 18 May 1981
Today as we were working, Grande Otelo, that agile puny runt who seems to have children all over the place, and whose wife, as Lewgoy told me, killed the child they had together and then herself, suddenly appeared to me as the devil in a film unreeling before my inner eye, in which Walter Matthau would have to play God. The idea appealed to Otelo, and we agreed that in this world only one lion could remain alive, and that lion would have to be played by Rui Polanah.

Iquitos, 19 May 1981
A day of shooting yesterday that was plagued by pressure and tension, of a very uncomfortable sort. Gisela asked me toward evening to

shoot the rooster that sits on the perimeter wall and crows, prevent-
ing anyone from sleeping in the costume depot. She gave me a bow
and arrow she had brought along from Camisea. I had just drawn the
arrow on the bowstring when the whole thing flew apart around me
with a loud crack. The bowstring had snapped and struck my wrist.
By the time I had repaired the bow, the rooster was gone, and I fired
the arrow into the trunk of a banana plant, where my rage drove it in
so deep that it will probably remain stuck there forever. The arrow
will be a sort of rage cast in concrete.

A man at a stand in the market was counting fish, then counting
them again and again. Out by the Nanay a truck with a flatbed trailer
has been stuck in the river for weeks. Now that the water level has
gone down, it is on dry land. All the air has gone out of the tires,
whose wheels are rusting, and the trailer, which has no wheels at all,
is sunk into the drying, fissured mud, holding the cab from behind as
if with an iron fist. Marines are waiting for a bus that is sure not to
show up today. I saw an Indian marine who had been posted in the
blazing sun to guard the officers' quarters. He found the one patch
of shade for his head, cast on the dusty square by a transformer box
on a light pole. An hour later, when I passed by again, the soldier had
moved slightly as the shade had shifted. A woman came by wearing a
tight dress through which her breasts showed distinctly. One of her
nipples was covered by a coin she had stuck in her bra.

Iquitos, 20 May 1984
Shooting at the railroad station. I had slept for only an hour because
I was trying to get a long-distance call through. It was already getting
light outside when I lay down for a while. Piercing sun all day. I was
dripping with sweat from the heat, as if I stood in a shower. At night

looking at rushes, some of the worst I have ever seen, but I also know that can be misleading.

Iquitos, 21 May 1981
Last night a terrible thunderstorm took us by surprise. First the lights went out in the whole city while I was out on the motorcycle. I sought shelter in the Don Giovanni café. Soon there was a half meter of water in every dip in the streets. When I got to my hut at night, pillows I had left stacked up were scattered all over the porch, and in my room the mosquito netting had been ripped down. The rain had driven diagonally through the window onto my bed. Uli's cabin had its roof torn off and blown into the neighbor's yard.

The toucan we had been keeping in a cage for Don Aquilino's house and which has now been put into one of the empty rabbit hutches has been uttering hoarse cries all morning long. The cat is sneezing. Every morning when I go out on the porch I find the green, ugly skins of lizards, which the cat leaves lying around like empty sausage casings. One time I found next to the feet of a lizard a large quantity of light green eggs, like fish eggs. The lizard's four legs framed the ovaries, but otherwise hardly anything was left but a piece of ugly skin.

Iquitos, 22 May 1981
While I was sitting in Huerequeque's bar, next to me a pig kept rubbing with rapt persistence against a case of beer. Then it disappeared behind the counter. A broom is lying on the ground as if felled by an assassin. I studied a wall calendar from which the month of April had not been torn off yet: Swiss mountains with a springlike alpine meadow in the foreground. Dandelions, apple trees in bloom, spot-

less cows grazing, and behind them snowy peaks, a world wreathed in mysteries, a world that does not exist for me anymore. How often I used to study calendar pictures down to the smallest detail, trying like a detective to figure out the exact date and time when the picture was taken. Looking at a picture of the Hamburg harbor, I examined the models and years of the parked cars, figured out which ship was being loaded with what and where, found a church tower with a clock that showed the time, compared the angles of the shadows: all these pieces of information, when checked against the harbor's logbook, would make it possible to determine the day and exact time, as well as the photographer's position and the lens he had used. The picture could serve as evidence in court for a major case, evidence sufficient for a conviction.

A young woman in Huerequeque's bar had heard that I had been on a volcano that was about to explode, and I told her about La Soufrière, making a comparison with the atom bomb over Hiroshima for the sake of clarity—explaining how much more powerful the apparently inevitable catastrophe would be. Atom bomb? she asked. She did not understand. To clarify, I explained that at the end of the Second World War the Americans had dropped it over Japan. But she did not know what the World War was, either. I found that striking, and with a joke brushed aside two world wars, several continents, and a whole world whose reach does not extend to these parts.

I went through the daily reports and was devastated to see how little we have accomplished. What they call in English *crowd control* is almost impossible here; we were shooting under the utmost time pressure, with the light fading fast, but more and more curious onlookers kept crowding onto our set. One young man darted repeatedly into the frame, and as I ran toward him, I slipped on some slimy boards and took him down with me in a running tackle. Without any resentment he struggled to his feet and went on his way, muttering to himself.

Iquitos–Camisea, 23 May 1981
Back at our camp in the jungle. I found the insects I had collected in a film canister rotting, and threw them away. My mosquito net was gone, and Gloria told me she had caught the pilot's mechanic about to walk off with my small metal suitcase containing the radio and my most important possessions; he had it wrapped in a blanket and was clearly planning to steal it. He also tried to rape her, she said.

In Camisea I saw many new faces. I inspected the jungle swath we had cleared, and immediately had work stopped on the dead post, the *muerto*, which has to hold the entire weight of the ship on the slope; I wanted to film the actual work tomorrow. Laplace thinks the slope is too steep. Kinski looked at the site and announced that my plan was completely impossible, prompted by madness. He is becoming the epicenter of discouragement. On closer inspection it became clear to me that no one is on my side anymore, not a single person, none, no one, not a single one. In the midst of hundreds of Indian extras, dozens of forest workers, boatmen, kitchen personnel, the technical team, and the actors, solitude flailed at me like a huge enraged animal. But I saw something the others did not see.

I scrambled up the cleared swath again, all alone. Up above, where the Caterpillar has sliced fifteen meters into the mountain, where it was originally almost vertical, moisture is oozing out of the sidewall, and farther down bare ledge is protruding. I saw a Machiguenga leaning his face against the rock. He was catching droplets of fresh spring water in his mouth, and then, like a thirsty animal, licked the rest of the moisture off the rock. I waited until it welled up again and followed his example. I saw our dreamy boat-man lying on the floor in his hut. He was wearing faded gym shorts and playing the harmonica, while reading that same old letter over and over. Outdoors night was falling. When I stepped outside, it was lurking among the trees.

Camisea, 24 May 1981
A good day's work, but the sense of desolation in me keeps growing. When the alarm went off this morning, I could not make myself wake up for a long time, and then did not know where I was.

Camisea, 25 May 1981
Did a lot of shooting. Fitz with the phonograph, boats with Indians who board the ship. In the midst of Kinski's bellowing and raving, which brought all work to a standstill, I stood like a silent rock wall and let him crash against it. Ultimately this was the only right and productive thing to do for the sake of what will appear on the screen, because in this way the craziness inside him can be shaped into form. But no one on the set grasps this, no one in the team, and of the actors only Huerequeque has a glimmer–the man who never stood in front of a camera till now. Meanwhile I have the impression that the Indians are plotting something against Kinski. In the evening I went to Kinski's hut to confront him, and caught him naked, just coming out of the shower. To my surprise, I found him perfectly calm and understanding. He urged me again to do the Paganini film; he recognizes that he cannot keep his eye on the big picture where he himself is involved as the lead actor.

Camisea, 26 May 1981

I had ball bearings under my feet and was therefore moving very fast and very lightly without needing to take steps. At a construction site where tar was being steamrolled onto the ground they were angry with me for that. A murder had taken place, and the perpetrator was trying to cover it up by setting fire to a trolley car, but I provided the decisive evidence. It turned out that on this particular day the backs of all trolley cars had been set on fire, so that the rear half of each one was charred. In a banquet hall I participated in a game of chance, probably bingo, with people I did not know; they had taken an excursion from a rural area into the city. Usually the place received busloads of older folks, lower-middle-class types. The buffet table was set up in a huge square, and people were fighting, with unconcealed, repulsive greed, to get close to it. Kinski, who was there as a waiter, became so rude that most of the guests left. All of humanity was in a bad way, for more and more trolley cars were burning, and no one had any ideas. The thought of revenge began to take root in me; it did not matter against whom. Something attacked me at the entrance to my hut, pushed me down, and stabbed me through my shirt in front, into my shoulder. Whether it was a large spider or something else, I could not make out in my surprise, but at any rate the wound stung and immediately became infected, and I began to roll on rollers under my feet.

Working on the winches on the slope, and meanwhile we filmed the Campas hauling a pulley for the block and tackle up the hill. It weighed over five hundred kilos. The system seems to be sufficiently sturdy, but I am not sure I trust the steel cables. The physical specifications were meaningless once we started shooting the first attempt to haul the ship uphill and I saw its keel digging straight into the ground, while its hull groaned and rumbled, its whole form warped out of shape and threatening to break apart. We cheered each other up, but I am worried about Kinski, because when we are dragging the ship uphill, he will be just a kind of extra, and given his inadequate supply of human compassion and depth, he will use the only means still at his disposal to make himself the center of attention again, which is to get sick. I was betting with myself.

Today I sent Segundo, the boatman, off to fetch Kinski and Paul for a dynamite explosion we had planned for the site. But instead of Kinski, suddenly Quispe, the Quechua from the highlands, was standing before me in rubber boots, indicating with his thumb and index finger that he just wanted a brief moment to speak with me. Since I was in the middle of a debate with Mauch just then over a complicated camera movement, I told him to speak, but only if it was important. At that he came even closer and without saying anything made the distance between his thumb and index finger even smaller, as small as a kernel of rice. *Una preguntita*, he said, just a tiny question. What was it, I asked, turning in midsentence toward him. Was it true, he asked, that I needed him as an actor for the scene, or had I meant Kinski? The boatman had not been sure.

Camisea, 27 May 1984
Water is raging through the camp. It rained so hard in the morning that everything is paralyzed except the water, which is rushing in streams toward the river, becoming more and more powerful, more brown and malevolent. The curtain of rain almost completely hides the bend in the river. The forest is growing dim, opening itself up to receive the cloudburst from above in deathlike rigidity. The early part of the day will vanish like nothing. We sit and stare at the river, which refuses to rise.

Miguel Vazquez, our Mexican special-effects man, was thoroughly in his element yesterday. It seems to me he is always happiest when he is tying sticks of dynamite together with gaffer tape to form thick bundles and attaching the fuses with fine copper wire. His voice at such times takes on a jubilant resonance, and his roundish face wears an expression of cautious bliss.

I talked to Mauch about Kinski, saying we had to be prepared for him to get sick, and as if this were all part of a prearranged game, at that very moment Paul came in and told me that K. had a bad case of the flu and actually looked so wasted that he was afraid it might be something much worse. I asked whether the doctor had been to see him. Yes. Did he have a fever? No, said Paul. I told him not to worry for now, and I mustered all my patience and listening ability and went to his hut. I found Kinski on his porch, dressed, but wobbly and making a show of courageously resisting impending collapse. So I sat down, looking concerned, and listened to him for an hour as he complained that the rooster had woken him up at five in the morning; that someone had thrown away an empty beer can close to his hut, of all places; and that a light a hundred meters away had been left on all night; that all these vile tricks could not possibly be the result of mere stupidity, but had been perpetrated on purpose. He said he was going to raise holy hell, not only here but all over America. I told him I found all these skunks with their petty meanness positively uninspiring, and it cheered him up to hear that; while I was away in Iquitos, he said, they had even dumped garbage right by my hut. Kinski then invited me into his cabin, and together we pulled his bed to one side. He asked me what I thought this stuff by the head of the bed was. There was something resembling a piece of flatbread, disgustingly moldy, and I knew immediately what it was, but I had to act as though I had no idea. I knew the story of the crazy card games played during our absence, in one of which the prize for the winner was one night with the hooker, and I knew who had won and had gone looking for an unoccupied bed. When some of the others came by with flashlights to applaud the consummation of the bet, the winner had beat a hasty retreat and had probably forgotten to clean up the mess. Kinski guessed with a certain amount of perspicacity that someone had been lying in his bed and had thrown up there, and I confirmed his supposition halfheartedly and lied that I still found it hard to believe that anyone in the camp could be so debased. Maybe it was a slime mushroom from the wilds all around us, I suggested, and while Kinski lost himself in platitudes about the wildness of nature, I called for a cleaning squad, which immediately went to work. By the time I left, Kinski had forgotten that he was deathly ill.

Camisea, 28 May 1984
A confused night with contradictory instructions from Walter, Laplace, and Vignati as to where the ship should be tied up, since the river was racing, even though the level had hardly risen. Laplace had warned us against positioning the *Narinho* diagonally to the current to keep it from being forced against the gravel bank, which happened after all. In addition, the *chata*, to which no one been paying attention in all the confusion, broke loose from its anchorage and in the dark drifted unnoticed five kilometers downstream, all the way to Shivankoreni, with its tons of freight, the steel cables and parts for the enormous block-and-tackle system. In addition, Laplace is now going to leave for good. He told me Walter had chewed him out so hatefully that he could not take it anymore, and Walter had ignored Laplace's warnings that the main support post was not

anchored firmly enough. With this humidity the concrete in the hole needed twenty days to set, and besides the support should have been anchored in such a way as to prevent it from lateral shifting, which would have taken even more time. So he was washing his hands of the responsibility, because if the support came shooting out of the ground with several hundred tons tugging on it and many men were on a platform with the winch, they would be hurled into the air as if by a rocket, and there would certainly be many fatalities. Furthermore, the ship would slide backward down the slope, and that would be curtains. Nothing could persuade him to stay, not even the indisputable and unavoidable necessity of digging out the *muerto* and replacing it with a new one that would be so big and sunk so deep that it could handle a load of several thousand tons, ten times the weight of our steamboat. Laplace will be going, come what may, and he gave me to understand, with several subtle hints, that he was going because Walter was impossible to get along with, and besides, he was not sure he was really up to the task. The ship was quite a *monstruo*, a monster, with which he would be better off not getting involved. I made two decisions: no matter how long it took, I would have the deadman post replaced with an absolutely foolproof construction, and I would assume complete responsibility for hauling the ship over the mountain. The physics are known and easy to understand: the weight of the ship, the angle of the slope, the conversion of forces in the block-and-tackle system, the losses due to friction, and the remaining imponderables have to exclude the possibility that the main support might not hold, and when the ship is pulled up the ridge there must never be people on or behind it. Kinski screamed that I was a madman, and what I was trying to do was criminal, and I just told him that if the ship broke loose no one would be in danger, and all I would be doing was destroying a ship in a grand cataclysmic event. But that was not the purpose of this exercise, I said, I was here for the sake of a different vision, to which I was committed.

At noon Paul took me aside and suggested bringing the Caterpillar to the gravel bank and partially filling in the river so that the water would be dammed up and would give us a better starting point for the beginning of the traverse. On the one hand, this sounds like a good idea, but it also indicates that Paul seems to be mentally prepared for an initial attempt at something previously rejected as impossible.

We did a lot of shooting today. The young Campa boy known as El Comandante had caught himself a frog, and I asked him what he meant to do with it, and he said it was his lunch. Les Blank, who had his hair cut in a little hamlet on the Urubamba, was advised by sympathetic lighting technicians, when they saw how terribly he had been shorn, to hire a lawyer and sue the barber. In the evening I finished reading a book, and because I was feeling so alone, I buried the book on the edge of the forest with a borrowed spade.

Camisea, 29 May 1981
Laplace left today. I offered him my hand without a word, but he pulled me to him and hugged me tight, also without a word. From his expression I could tell that in his eyes I was a lost soul, done for, but he wished me luck. Yesterday he went with me to check on the steel cables, and he gave me a lengthy lecture on them: they were like rubber hoses and must not be allowed to form loops or get kinked, all things the people here know but I should know, too. He led me to an extremely taut cable and knocked on it to show me that it still sounded healthy. If the tension was increased too much, you would know from its *sick* sound that it was about to snap.

Camisea, 30 May 1981

The Campas are poking around for something in the forest. At six in the morning *** was already sitting on his porch emptying a bottle of *pisco*. I got up late, and carried my breakfast tea and two rolls from the kitchen to my hut. Today I cannot stand being around people, so I ate sitting on the wooden bench on my porch, my gaze fixed on the dumb green river.

Stagnation. Laplace is gone. Gloria is gone. Kinski's yelling pushed her over the edge. In the morning we filmed with many Indians on the afterdeck, viewed from the bridge, and all we had to do was rock the boat a bit to create the illusion on a narrow strip of the image that the background was streaming by and the ship was moving at full speed. Then a scene I had written hastily to help explain the Indians' behavior. At noon Gloria went on the radio to order some things from Iquitos, and I happened to be in my hut when I heard a horrible bellowing. Kinski, who cannot stand her voice, screamed at her like a maniac that she should shut up, and she snapped back at him, with good reason, but screeching like a fishwife: how did he expect he would have even a measly lettuce leaf on his plate tomorrow, whereupon he kicked down the entire railing of the raised eating platform, and almost fell off. Miguel Vazquez laughed at the sight, at which Kinski was even more beside himself, and Gloria thought he was going to attack her physically. Kinski was intent only on property damage, however, and came tearing over to me, bellowing and looking for something else he could turn into kindling. In the meantime Gloria had summoned Walter from the cleared swath by walkie-talkie, and he grabbed Huerequeque's shotgun, but had decided not to blast the maniac to hell because he saw him storming around my hut. I told Walter to leave me alone with him for a moment–I would get the situation under control–but he used the moment to pile his wife, child, and a few possessions into the speedboat. When I wanted to talk to him he shouted that he was already gone. Then he took off. At that sobriety returned, because despite all the friction with Walter, it was clear how important he was to the whole operation, and I was urged to take off after him. But to everyone's dismay, I first lay down for an hour in my hammock, because, knowing Walter as I did, I realized that I had to let him stew in his own juice for a while. Paul came and brought me a cup of very hot tea, saying only that I should not burn my *flute* on it, and I laughed. Then a Campa showed up who can do wonderful bird imitations by whistling into his cupped hands, and I had him do all sorts of birds for me, and he was very proud that I was so impressed. Then I played Handel's Halleluiah Chorus at top volume for Paul, who had asked me to, and all at once the Indian of the jungle whooped for joy, laughed, tried to sing along, and then accompanied the chorus with bird calls.

Reassured, I set out after Walter and Gloria and found Walter in the big camp, where he had dilly-dallied, probably on purpose, on the pretext that he had things to take care of there. I sat down with him in the sand along the river, and had a long talk with him, since in the meantime he had become quiet and levelheaded. He had realized that Gloria had not been physically attacked and if she had I would not have left her undefended for even a second. We reached an understanding, and Walter told me Gloria was still flying out because her mother in Iquitos was very ill and a break from him, Walter, would do her good; after all, he was not that easy to live with. Vignati and Miguel Vazquez, both of them men with hearts of gold, accompanied me to the airfield, and I spoke with Gloria, telling her she should at least hear what had happened after her hasty departure. While we were talking, Miguel took the baby from Gloria. The moment he had her in his arms, the little girl began laughing with him, and he made a few comments that showed his innate sensitivity and decency, and that was good. I was reminded of *Aguirre*: when everything had fallen apart and we were all perched on a raft in the depths of the jungle, hating each other. I asked for a half-hour recess, withdrew to the very edge of the raft, sat down with my back to the others, and cried. Miguel Vazquez promptly came up to me from behind, placed his hand firmly on the back of my neck, and silently sat down beside me. He stayed there quite a while, holding my neck firmly, and the only word he said was "Courage!" And gradually my courage returned, and the people on the raft who had behaved worse than animals acted halfway human for at least a day. Gloria's plane took off, and I made no attempt to keep her from leaving. Later Kinski was concil-iatory, but I canceled the shoot planned for dusk. Quispe suddenly appeared and broke into the oppressive silence between Kinski and me by breathlessly reiterating his desire for the outboard motor.

The deadpost on the slope is going to be sunk from scratch. Recently, when the Caterpillar dumped earth on everything on one side of its base, seepage on the other side welled up in a gush. Now I am going to have a drainage ditch put in, even if it means losing another two days.

Toward evening I called everyone back to work after all, because it was better that way and because we had a task that was more impor-tant than we were, and Kinski was very cooperative. I had lined up many Campas by the river, who, according to a new scene I had writ-ten, stare at the water for days after an accident. Huerequeque, how-ever, had gotten so drunk in reaction to all the turmoil that I had to carry him to his place in front of the camera, and when he missed his cue, Kinski gently stepped on his bare toes outside the frame. With this comradely support for Huerequeque Kinski was apparently try-ing to express his remorse.

Camisea, 31 May 1981

The searing realization that we are falling too far behind schedule is a slow-moving poison. Getting the anchor post installed properly is going to take days, and all the other things that have not been done yet will require technical preparations. We rode up the Camisea in the speedboat looking for a suitable spot for the blockade by Indian canoes that make it impossible for the steamboat to turn around and go back. It was important to find a place where we could fell large trees into the river from both right and left; in addition, we need a fairly long, narrow, straight stretch of river, well-bordered by jungle and with calm water, so the canoes can make good headway and not capsize. We went farther and farther upriver, and without saying anything had soon given up the idea that we were still looking for a location, because once we got a certain distance from our camp, it was clear that we would not be able to move the *chata* for the camera that far upstream against the current, and even if by some miracle we pulled it off, if we sent two hundred Indians upstream in canoes, we could not expect more than thirty or forty to arrive at the chosen location, because the rest would peel off into the bushes along the way to go hunting. We were merely indulging our curiosity, rounding one more bend, then risking a peek around the next one, and then came a narrows, which we had to get through to see what lay beyond. I am so used to plunging into the unknown that any other surroundings and form of existence strike me as exotic and unsuitable for human beings. I did not suggest turning back until we were approaching the spot where the Amehuacas had attacked.

Kinski has only one problem: that in the morning a rooster crowed again. I will have the rooster served to him as soup this evening. No sooner had the disturber of the peace been slaughtered than six more arrived from Atalaya. I had them put back into the speedboat and taken to the other camp. Wild rumors circulating in the camp here about the date of our departure; to make things worse, there are widely divergent views as to what day of the month it is; no one knows for sure.

Camisea, 1 June 1981

This first of June seems like a momentous day to me because we still have not begun to haul the ship. I keep thinking, in a panic: it is June, it is June. I wish I could hold back time. Kinski paddled clumsily and unsteadily past our camp in a dugout, without any of the gentle elegance of the Indians. He was wearing his olive-green made-to-order fatigues, had girded on a machete and a knife, and had jungle and survival rations in a small, sturdy canvas backpack. He managed to go about a hundred meters, but the illusion he creates for himself that this expedition is taking him into the heart of the inscrutable but inspiring natural wonders of the jungle apparently makes him happy. Last night we went out hunting alligators for the kitchen, with Mauch the driving force, strangely enough. For days he has been annoyed that the ammunition we had obtained for the cartridge belts in the film is too small for the Winchester and too big for the Mauser. But apparently he did not want to do any shooting himself. I borrowed Huerequeque's shotgun, and we sailed upstream, but we made the mistake of shining the flashlight too far ahead and therefore had an angle of incidence that did not match up with my sight. Nonetheless I hit the alligator on the sandbank squarely. It flicked up into the air like a trout, then threw itself into the water and dove, and even after a long search we could not locate it, so I came to my senses and called off the hunt, feeling pretty foolish.

Wisps of smoke are eddying through our camp today, and under the large, patient trees peace reigns, but it makes me uneasy because it is a peace without work. Today the sun feels gentle for the first time, without any of its usual vicious aggression. My existence is reduced to one dimension: a cleared strip leading up a steep hillside and a ship at the bottom. Farther up is a support, not fully anchored yet, on which life and the ship depend, so to speak. White, firm clumps of foam drift quietly by on the river, and they will still be doing that long after we have left these parts, and even when there are no human beings on earth, only insects. Today the jungle seemed peaceful in the mild light, self-absorbed and resting contentedly and solemnly. On the gravel bank I saw stones into which the Campas have scratched their names. I feel as if I were in a concert hall where a little-known orchestral work is being performed, and at the end no one is sure whether it is finished and one should clap. Since no one wants to appear ignorant by clapping too soon, everyone waits for a moment to see what the others are going to do: this moment of silence and irresolution in which the applause does not set in to provide release: I have been irreversibly thrust into this moment, which, however, continues for months.

The first balsa rafts for the scene with the blockade were done, tied together from freshly stripped balsa trunks, and drifted past me. Across from our camp a large balsa tree was felled into the river. The two men who had cut it down clambered onto the floating tree, whose crown stuck far up out of the water, and immediately began to work the floating trunk. Last night, a large leopard was spotted above the cleared strip, in the very spot where we have built a hut for Fitz, in which a group of Campas spend the night. Today its tracks could still be seen. My flashlight was stolen, a major loss here in the jungle. Today *** was so drunk that he fell flat on his face in the camp, and since he could not get up, Quispe kept watch over him for a long time. When he was able to walk again, he staggered into Paul's hut, where I happened to be, and asked what we had to drink. The Caterpillar got stuck in a ditch, and I did not go to look, because it seems to be embarrassing to Walter, who insists on sitting next to the operator instead of attending to his real duties, to have me as an eyewitness. Are we approaching the breaking point?

In its all-encompassing, massive misery, of which it has no knowledge and no hint of a notion, the mighty jungle stood completely still for another night, which, however, true to its innermost nature, it did not let pass unused for incredible destruction, incredible strangulation.

Camisea, 2 June 1981
Something must be said about the majestic misery of the jungle. I was awakened by a strange, cackling bird I had never heard before and was annoyed that Dagoberto had not recorded it, even though I had no way of knowing whether he might not have done so after all.

Very calmly, prepared for the worst, I began the day. Delays with the *muerto*: work was interrupted at first, even though only a little was left to be done: one of the braces for the anchor post still had to be installed, and it had to be cut at just the right moment, so it could be inserted into the hole intended for it, which opens up for just a second, but then the chain saw operator announced that his saw was out of gas. He had stood by for hours until he was needed, and every day the *motosierristas* and the boatmen are reminded to have their equipment fueled up and ready. In this case, it took so long to fetch gas, because the transport boat would not start, either, that it had begun to pour, which forced them to start the entire day's work from scratch. The world here does not seem willing to be reduced to words anymore.

Our kitchen crew slaughtered our last four ducks. While they were still alive Julian plucked their neck feathers, before chopping off their heads on the execution block. The albino turkey, that vain creature, the survivor of so many roast chickens and ducks transformed into soup, came over to inspect, gobbling and displaying, used his ugly feet to push one of the beheaded ducks, as it lay there on the ground bleeding and flapping its wings, into what he thought was a proper position, and making gurgling sounds while his bluish red wattles swelled, he mounted the dying duck and copulated with it.

Building additional rafts. I had the winch brought up from the *Huallaga*, which is completely beached below the Pongo. Hawsers for the molinettes, the Indians' turnstiles, repair of the block and tackle's main structural component, which the Caterpillar had run over by mistake. Miguel Camaytieri, the chief of the Oventeni, has been hurt. A post fell over and hit him on the head, leaving a large cut that required many stitches. I scalded my hand with boiling water.

Camisea, 4 June 1984
The camp is silent with resignation; only the turkey is making a racket. It attacked me, overestimating its own strength, and I quickly grabbed its neck, which squirmed and tried to swallow, slapped him left-right with the casual elegance of the arrogant cavaliers I had seen in French Musketeer films, who dutifully do fancy swordplay, and then let the vain albino go. His feelings hurt, he trotted away, wiggling his rump but with his wings still spread in conceited display. On a sandbank by the Pongo that the river had uncovered, a petrified turtle was found, but it must be so immensely large and heavy that it is impossible to transport. Segundo gave me a big insect, quite unusual. I heard it had been caught in Shivankoreni and nailed to a

board. It has a bulge on its head like that of a crocodile, and allegedly its bite is lethal, as Segundo reveals in a whisper. During the rubber era there were many more of them, and the only way to prevent certain death was allegedly to make love to a woman right away, but a hundred years ago, when there were so many woodsmen but hardly any women, a silent understanding developed that in such a situation a woman would be lent out by her husband, and thus quite a few men who were bitten managed to survive.

Camisea, 5 June 1984
More landslides on the cleared strip. Paul has a fever. One of his boots was chafing, and he developed an infection in his leg, which is swollen and burning hot. A new supply of antibiotics has to be brought from Satipo. Today the rain came down at midday as God's scourge strikes the impious. Kinski came to me, flickering like a candle about to go out. He gives the impression of someone moving steadily and inexorably toward the moment when he will go to pieces once and for all. Later a delegation, apparently organized by him, brought tea to my hut, where I was calmly watching the river flow by. They expressed the idea that everyone should be relaxed for a change. Very calm? I interrupted their preamble, pointing out that I was perfectly calm, much calmer than everyone else out here, so what did they want to say? They wanted to talk me out of hauling the ship over the mountain, protect me from my own insanity—they did not use that term, but their meaning was obvious. They asked whether I could not revise the script so that Fitzcarraldo did not have to pull the ship over the mountain. I said only that we had not really tried towing the ship yet, and I attempted to buck them up in their faintheartedness.

Last night Gloria came back. I had a long discussion with Beatus about a three-dimensional game of chess that I am trying to devise, but the challenges it presents are considerable and very complex. Toward evening we towed the ship about two meters, but it listed to the left somewhat, for one thing because the tree trunks we were using as skids on that side sank deeper into the mud, for another thing because the crossbeam fastened under the ship in front was attached at a slight angle to the vertical axis of the ship. I had already noticed that when I dove under the ship, and Ramon, the cable man, had tried to correct the problem by exerting more force on the beam on one side, but that did not do the trick. At nightfall they all got into their boats and announced that that was it. But I quickly instructed the lighting people to set up floodlights, and Walter and I kept the men there, though some had already ducked into the cafeteria for a beer. Ramon explained that the man who was his diver for the steel cables had left, but since I had already been under the ship once, I tied a rope around my chest, so they could pull me out in an emergency, and helped with the cable. A current took hold of me, and I tried to dive all the way under the ship's hull, but had not considered that heavy tree trunks were in the way. So I thought better of it and turned back before getting caught in the chaotic tangle of trunks. We certainly saved two hours of work that we would have had to do tomorrow, and that could prove very valuable if it rains.

There was much hammering and welding going on on the ship. Someone forced his way into the cabin where we had locked up the cameras and opened everything. We guessed it must be a member of the crew, who live in the other cabins nearby. Five hundred Swiss francs were stolen from the suitcase where Beatus keeps his cameras, as well as two $400 traveler's checks, and Mauch, who was very angry that a storage for film magazines had been opened, went through the occupied cabins with me. We looked under the mattresses, but found only cigars and tattered porno magazines. The captain had twenty wristwatches in a battered shoulder bag made of ugly fake leather, but the watches were in such poor condition that it was not likely he would be able to pawn them off on anyone here, or on the Amehuacas on the upper reaches of the Camisea. As I stepped to the railing, I saw someone walking along the gravel bank in the dark, holding a burning branch. A light rain began to fall, looking in the glow of the floodlights like falling dust.

The extent of our demoralization can be measured more and more clearly by the bad jokes that are making the rounds, especially among the camera people; today it was Jesus jokes: What was the first soccer team, etc. The weirdest one deserves to be mentioned: Why was not Jesus born in Mexico? They could not find three wise men and a virgin.

Camisea, 6 June 1984
At night I am even lonelier than during the day. I listened intently to the silence, pierced by the cries of tormented insects and tormented animals. Even the motors of our boats have something tormented about them. In the morning one of the Ashinka-Campa chiefs summoned me and gave me a little stone ax that had been found along the upper Río Tambo. At first I was utterly astonished and could not think what I might give him in return, but I noticed later that he had run out of film while taking group pictures of his people standing by the ship, so I quickly got hold of a few rolls and gave them to him.

The first attempt to tow the ship did not go well, but at least we filmed the failure. After a few meters, the ship tipped and got hung up, and I heard the mighty steel cables in the winch creak strangely and emit unhealthy sounds. Finally one cable, as thick as a man's arm, snapped, having heated up internally from the strain. It lay smoking on the ground. At the point of breakage I could see that the inner strands were glowing bright red. The ship gently slid backward, and it looked good, even if that does not help us much. The main actors in our disturbing drama, surrounded by the indifferent jungle as our audience, are no longer human beings but the steel cables, the Caterpillar, the winches, the tree trunks, the mud, the river, the rain, the landslides.

Camisea, 7 June 1984
Heavy downpours that caused the river to rise so much that it lifted the ship and the tree trunks we had slid underneath it were in danger of being washed away. Thick clumps of debris have washed up around the ship, decaying *caña brava* stalks, brush, leaves, branches. A landslide occurred between the two uppermost turnstiles on the slope. I saw no reason to get upset, went back to my hut and let the raging rage, though I knew that all it would take to break me was a few more of these gasping absurdities with which nature lashes out at me in my weakened state. But I refuse to bend as long as I am not bent. I had missed the drumming on an empty pot that summoned us to lunch, and Mauch stopped by, after he had eaten his fill, and asked me whether I thought being a martyr would stop the rain. That was not my intention at all, and I found some food still warm on the stove and the huge thighbone of a bull, still full of marrow. After that I fell asleep, worn out for no particular reason, and upon waking discovered that the malevolent weather outside had worn itself out as well. I wondered whether by sleeping I had averted a misfortune. In

the face of the obscene, explicit malice of the jungle, which lacks only dinosaurs as punctuation, I feel like a half-finished, poorly expressed sentence in a cheap novel. While hauling away a mud-smeared, unco-operative steel cable, one of the Indians farted from the effort with such force and duration that it sounded amid the roaring vulgarity of nature like the first indication of a human will to impose order. In my imagination my wishes carry me away to a place where people fly over church towers, church towers over farmland, ships over moun-tains, and continents over oceans.

Indonesia has ordered the categorical clear-cutting of entire islands.

Camisea, 8 June 1984
Shooting. Several attempts with the ship; immense effort, immense disappointments. Struggling with the terribly heavy and uncoopera-tive steel cables; placing extraordinarily heavy tree trunks under the body of the ship; iron hooks as thick as my arm bend like paper-clips. Huerequeque is having one of his cyclically recurring bouts of malaria; when I went to see him, his fever had already come down a bit. He was lying, wrapped in blankets and with a damp cloth around his head, all scrunched up in the hollow of his hammock. His eyes glowed dully from deep inside, but he told me that when we started shooting he would be there.

We inserted a fourth crossbeam under the ship, somewhat far-ther to the back, just to be safe. Because the trunks are so infernally heavy, such operations proceed only a centimeter at a time, taking all day, with steel cables and lever systems. Like our enormous deadman anchor post, these trunks are of a wood so heavy that they immediately sink like a stone in water. It is as hard and difficult to work as iron. The tree is called the *chivavaca*, or goat cow, but I suspect that is a distortion of a word in Quechua, not *vaca* but *huasca* or something of the sort. On a trunk that was cut in the forest recently, parasitic leaves continued to grow for days, perfectly fresh. The bark is dark red on the inside and can easily be pulled off the trunk in fibrous strands. The wood underneath is a whitish yellow. The captain of the *Narinho* went swimming in his pants, shirt, and hat, because the water was too cold for him, he said. Before he dove under the hull, he swam to the speedboat first and deposited his hat in it. Someone told me that Pentecost is past already.

At night in the deathly quiet camp someone was playing the flute. Finally I got up at midnight and found one of the young kitchen helpers playing on a white plastic water pipe, into which he had drilled holes. The night was so unusually quiet that I had to strain to hear anything, and got up again much later to assure myself the river was still there.

In Shivankoreni two scruffy young Americans showed up, having come through the Pongo on a small balsa raft, accompanied by a *peón*. They had placed an inflated inner tube from a truck tire around their luggage. It turned out they were actually from Israel.

Camisea, 11 June 1984
We positioned the *chata* with the platforms for the cameras farther down the river. Two boats were attached on the right and left, and in front there was another free-floating boat. In the smooth, swift-flowing water by the gravel bank the *chata* with its six-meter-high superstructures promptly drifted into the trees on the riverbank, which pulled down the rope ladder attached to the top, and for a moment it

looked as though the whole structure would collapse on the crew of about twenty. I shouted to Chirino, the daydreaming boatman, that he should untie his boat immediately, but he just stared at me in rapture. The wobbling of the structure above him thrilled him. The next moment the *chata* swiveled around its own axis and buried first one, then the other of our large boats, since they were roped together, and forced them to the bottom. Then the *chata* rolled over them, crushing the boats, and I saw Chirino and the other boatman swimming away. Bobbing on the water were the red fuel canisters, plastic oil bottles, and smaller gas drums. I leaped half-dressed into the water, followed by three or four other men, and we managed to pull the boats out from under the *chata* and turn them so they were floating keel-up. We towed them close to the bank, and there, with great effort, we were able to flip them over. Then Beatus, who had been photographing the scene, also jumped into the water and was able to capture three fuel canisters farther downstream. The boats had not been crushed but merely had a few more leaks and scrapes than before. The whole thing was so grotesque and had happened so fast that we all laughed. One of the boats had lost its battery, but the current was so fierce that we did not even try to dive and recover it.

We reached the chosen shooting location three kilometers downstream, just above Shivankoreni. There, with Vignati's help, I undertook to stretch a sturdy hemp rope across the river, but it was tugged so powerfully by the current that it was almost impossible to get it across the river and fastened. Later about eighty dugouts and small rafts hooked up on it. With Miguel Vazquez, El Tigre, and three *motosierristas* we prepared the trees that were supposed to fall into the river behind the canoes as a barrier. Miguel attached dynamite sticks to two of the largest trees because I was afraid the timing would not work out if we felled them manually. Mauch did not make the task any easier; he thought the line of canoes looked skimpy and insignificant, and he wanted us to call a halt. I had to take him around in a boat so he could see that at least sixty canoes full of Indians were tied up along the bank under overhanging branches, ready to leap into action. In the meantime Chirino kept bumping with his boat into the rope holding back the rafts, and wandered into camera range so often that I finally had to pull him off the river entirely to keep him from ruining the scene. I sent our best swimmers, among them Beatus, to organize the arrangement of the canoes. When the light was almost completely gone, I shooed all those who did not have parts in the scene back behind the cameras, and when several of the smaller raft islands had drifted into the right position, I radioed instructions to fell the first tree, which was the signal for the Campas to start rowing. All this had to be done unrehearsed. Since it took quite a while before all the canoes were moving and well distributed, I waited a long time to have the next, really large tree felled by a dynamite charge. The delay almost made the others lose their nerve. When Klausmann, standing next to me, heard the signal for the explosion, he panned with a long focal length just as the tree came crashing down, and as he followed the movement he managed to take in all the canoes spread out across the river. I had the enormous tree on the other bank felled at the very moment when I felt he had to have reached that spot with his pan.

As I had expected, Walter did not return from Lima. I had sent him there to get significantly stronger cables, reels, and hooks. Only if we have those do I think we have any realistic chance of hauling the ship up the mountain. It is not a question of available tractive power, because according to the laws of physics a child could pull the ship over the ridge with one finger, provided there was a pulley system with a conversion ratio in the thousands and enough rope.

But you'd have to pull the rope two kilometers to move the ship two centimeters up the slope.

It was already dark when I was called to the medic's station in the big camp. Up on the plateau between the two rivers, woodsmen had been felling trees, barefoot as usual, and one of them had been bitten by a snake. Snakes had never been seen anywhere near chain saws, because the noise and the exhaust fumes drive the snakes deep into the jungle, but this man had suddenly been bitten twice in the foot. He had dropped his chain saw and just caught a glimpse of the snake before it disappeared into the underbrush; it was a *chuchupe*. Usually this snake's bite causes cardiac arrest and stops breathing in less than a minute, and cases in which a person has survived a bite longer than seven or eight minutes without treatment are almost unknown. Our camp with the doctor and the antivenom serum was twenty minutes away. The man, so I was told by someone who had been working next to him, had stood motionless for a few seconds, thinking hard. Then he had picked up the chain saw, which had stalled when it hit the ground, pulled the cord to start it, the way you pull an outboard motor, and had sawn off his foot above the ankle. I saw the man—his whole body was gray. He was alive, perfectly collected, and very calm. Before they took him to the doctor, the others had tied off his leg in three places with lianas: below his crotch, below his knee, and above the stump, and had twisted the lianas with sticks to make a tight tourniquet. They had stuck a kind of moss on the stump to stop the bleeding. I had a plane readied to fly him out to Lima the next day. It is better in any case to keep him under observation overnight to make sure he does not go into shock.

Camisea, 12 June 1984

The woodsman was flown out, having stabilized during the night. An hour later the American missionary arrived from his station north-east of the Pongo and drank a good deal of *pisco* with us and his people, his flock, who had come with him; I found him very likable. He had traveled on foot through the jungle for two years before find-ing a place to settle and establish a mission station. He had appeared on American television on a game show where there was money to be won, which he needed for his mission. For him to win the big prize, his name had to appear on the front page of all local newspapers on the day the show was filmed, he had to set twenty cuckoo clocks so that they would strike simultaneously, and he had to blow out a candle from a distance of twenty feet, which had been rigged in advance and was to be broadcast as a special gag. He submitted to all these humiliations–blew out the candle with the help of an Indian from the jungle who had come along with his blowpipe, and appeared with a report on his station on all the front pages, but he failed with the cuckoo clocks, which refused to open all their little doors at once and let the cuckoos peek out. They were too many seconds apart, and all he received was a consolation prize, but people watching the show and readers of the newspaper articles spontaneously sent money.

At night I saw a satellite speeding by, eating its way through the constellations. A shy moon made the misty haze over the river, which seemed sunk in nocturnal prayer, even paler, even more ghostly. On both sides of the river, which was celebrating its nightly Mass, the jungle served as an acolyte. No animal voices, no nocturnal cries; but from a giant leaning tree an enormous leaf fell, like a pterosaur struck by an arrow. Everything outside seemed as if in prayer, unfulfilled, unredeemed. This leaves me unmoved; I am like a dry streambed being dredged. My life seems like a stranger's house to me.

Camisea, 13 June 1984

A *gavilán* hurtled down diagonally through the air, like a rock, and seized a small bird in mid-flight. Then I saw it perch on a bare branch, its booty in its talons. It paid no attention to the bird in its grasp for a long time, as if nothing were there. Don Aquilino's sedan chair has been moved under the kitchen platform for storage; it had been standing out in the jungle for a few weeks. The footrest, and only that part, is densely overgrown with grayish whitish tree sponges almost as large as a hand.

The new heavy equipment for hauling the ship will take some time to get here, because it has to be transported overland to Pucallpa, and from there up the river on a *chata*. Time pressure. Decided to move the whole operation to Iquitos because Claudia Cardinale cannot be put off any longer.

Camisea, 14 June 1984

Pressing ahead with the shooting, so as many Indians as possible can be sent home. A fiesta on the Urubamba with the Campas. Kinski's tantrums. I went back to the Camisea barefoot in the dark. From a dark hut Guillermo, the little Campa boy we call McNamara in the film, called out a greeting to me. I recognized him by his voice and said to him, *ma zonzarre*, you are a tiger, and he laughed, because I had addressed him with the name the Campas have given me, by which they usually call me. Glowing coals were revived with a branch, and from the murky darkness many eyes stared at me.

Camisea, 15 June 1984

Last day of shooting on the Camisea, for now. I cannot recall ever working under so much pressure. Usually what we completed is a program for five days. Kinski screaming hysterically, then pretending to be deathly ill, making Paul prop him up, then another tantrum. During the afternoon's shoot I happened to notice that the boatmen were moving a reel of cable weighing several tons from the *chata* to one of our freight boats by simply letting it roll from above. The boat promptly broke apart and sank like a stone. That was just one of the grotesque sideshows. When Kinski had his next outburst, the Ashininka-Campa chief and the chief of the Shivankoreni Machiguengas cautiously drew me aside and asked very calmly whether they should kill him for me. To be sure I had heard right, I said, Kill? Whom? They pointed at Kinski, and the way they spoke left no doubt that they were prepared to do the deed in the next sixty seconds. Kinski noticed that something was amiss, and quickly switched from raving mad to deathly ill.

In the evening I helped load the boats, and we set out at two-thirty in the morning to rendezvous in Sepahua with a Twin Otter we had arranged to have meet us. A big breakfast in the middle of the night with salami, ham, *landjäger* sausage, fruit salad. It was so cold that I put on all my shirts and crept under a plastic tarp. Toward evening I had sent Kinski off in a small Cessna toward Iquitos, because I could not be sure the Indians would not pull off something without my permission.

Camisea–Sepahua–Pucallpa–Iquitos, 16 June 1981
The night was very cold, and I had already had a stiff neck. By morning I could hardly move. We stopped early in the morning in Picha to see the Dominican padre because our fuel was running low; we planned to borrow some from him. He was just reading morning Mass, and we waited. Everyone was in an excellent mood, despite all the frustrations. The one in the best mood was Paul, who laughed so

loudly that all the others had to join in. Only Huerequeque was very quiet and thin, with glittering eyes. His malaria is pretty bad.

Iquitos, 17 June 1981
Preparations in the morning in House Molly. The evening before, I was at the Holiday Inn with Kinski and Claudia Cardinale. Actually I wanted to speak with her right away, but Kinski ranted and raved for two hours–it was ugly, sickening, in fact. As I always knew, the man has no resilience. He is like an overbred racehorse that can run exactly a mile and then collapses. Now it is as if the jockey has to carry the horse to the finish line.

Claudia was a good sport, as always, and the team, too, was very attentive to me just when I needed it, so I drew strength from the last reaches of my self. Shooting with Molly and her girls. Kinski's outburst, supposedly because Beatus grinned, but the reason might just as well be that he had tied his shoelaces too tight or had scratched his arm. Even so I enjoyed the work.

This morning there were pigs under my house. The yucca plants have all been ripped out of the ground, and all the banana plants around have rotted and collapsed, so there is open ground around my hut. I did not even unpack properly, just left everything where it was. The water around the cabin is gone, but the ground is still muck. Everything has changed.

Camisea, 20 June 1981
The little tigrillo is dead. We had shot our scenes with him and put him back in his enclosure, but the big tigrillo, usually so forbearing,

promptly bit him to death. Vignati has a broken rib. Working quickly on the film. For the moment Kinski is neutralized, because Sygma in Paris has sent a photographer who is taking thousands of shots of Kinski a day, so he is distracted in manic self-absorption. I observe all this with indifference. In four days we will be out of money, and what will happen then I know only too well. The pleasant things? They are all associated with individuals' names: Cardinale, Vignati, Huerequeque, Paul, the majority of the team. I began to distribute my few earthly possessions: my radio, arrows, petrified objects, my music cassettes, a *cushma*; that made me feel lighter. I saw a wall blackened by fire. In a photo of Machu Picchu I began to climb the steep rock faces. My footbridge leads for no reason to my hut, where I do not live anymore, just spend the night. We had emergency meetings to discuss the situation, as elsewhere they do emergency slaughters.

In Belén a boy was floating around in a large plastic bowl that he was using as a boat, rowing with his hands, and fetched beer from a likewise floating store. For the first time I saw one of the mighty *paiche* in a boat; it was lying bent on the floor of a dugout and had its mouth wide open, like a tunnel into a mountain. The world is spotty and hard to decipher. Photos taken with special film from planes over the Cologne–Trier area reveal the original sites of Roman structures and *castelli* in the flat fields. When cigarettes are tossed into the night, they fall into bottomless abysses, fade into the void, leaving a delicate trail of sparks as they disappear, deeper and deeper. Ah, I was thinking of a star that would be very small, from which I could push off with my foot, thus dislodging it from its orbit forever, as one pushes away a skiff in quiet waters.

Iquitos, 24 June 1984

Work in the floating House Fitz. In the evening I had a long talk with Walter on the radio; he said it had been completely dry today, and the ship had moved. If it stayed dry, he was sure it could be pulled up to the support post in only two days. He would get it positioned at the bottom of the slope, but in such a way that the quarterdeck would still be in contact with the river.

At night I got a hysterical call from a journalist in Rome, asking what was going on with Cardinale, was she still alive, would she survive the terrible accident? What accident? I asked, alarmed; I had just had dinner with her. No, the caller insisted, I was lying; she had been hit by a truck and was seriously injured.

Iquitos, 26 June 1984

Brisk work with Claudia Cardinale in Iquitos. On the 24th, the Festival of San Juan, I gave everyone the day off. Only Mauch, Vignati, and I continued working, as a kind of second unit. The whole town was out and about in a festive mood, and in the evening I put two girls from Huerequeque's bar on the back of my motorcycle and, slightly drunk, rode out to the airport, where I forced my way on the bike into the large, almost deserted departure concourse, and after making two circuits inside, pursued by a policeman, rode out again. A few birds were flying around inside the hall. I also saw a rat running away from me, which, as it took evasive action, went skidding over the polished terrazzo floor. It slid a long way in its original direction, while its legs flailed furiously, trying to brake. Outside I saw a bird with a green and brown stomach perching on a large, rusty cogwheel.

In the Italian press and now apparently also in Argentina, rumors have spread like wildfire that Claudia Cardinale has had an accident. Somehow the Italian journalist managed to reach me again, in the office. Following the promptings of inspiration, because you cannot dispel a rumor with the truth but only with an even wilder rumor, I told him the whole situation was actually far worse than had been reported; the barefoot half-caste mestizo Indian who had run over her had not only been drunk; he had promptly raped the accident victim, even though shocked bystanders gathered around. At that there was a long silence on the other end of the line, and then the receiver was hung up.

Outside the house, Doña Lina grabbed a chicken by the throat and with a quick twist tried to break its neck, but the chicken remained intact, and Doña Lina had dislocated her wrist. I took her to the hospital and went to a nearby restaurant by myself, which did me good. The waiter was pouring a glass of wine for a guest who had left long ago.

Iquitos–Camisea, 27 June 1984
Moving back to the jungle camp, with the usual complications, in a Twin Otter. Kinski flew in his own Avionetta; that was a clause in a bizarre supplemental contract he had forced me to sign and without which he would not have returned to the jungle. Yet he had always flown in a special plane anyway. Further provisions in the contract, which for some unknown reason was written in English, insisted on: a particular brand of mineral water, no male chickens in the camp–he could not think of the English word for *rooster*, and I was not about to help him–and no female voice on the radio, by which he meant Gloria, and I also told her in advance that it did not bother me if I was in charge of the radio, but I could predict that

she would be offended. I told her I was relieving her of the conflict that would ensue if Kinski had a tantrum over her; I was ordering her, as her boss, not to use the radio anymore. For the few days we still had here, I would order the supplies from Iquitos myself. I tried in vain to make it clear to her that if working with Kinski made it necessary I would even paint my clapper board green; such things did not do anything to change the one and only goal for which we were all here and that we had lost sight of, namely, to make a film.

Kinski came toward me on a speedboat on the Camisea. He was bellowing and foaming at the mouth. As he stood in the bow, he flailed with his machete at an enemy only he could see. I heard him around two bends of the river before he reached me, screaming at the boatman in French. Apparently he had seen from the plane just before landing that the ship was still at almost the same spot by the river, but he did not realize that it was already tilted uphill. He screeched like a madman that I was a traitor that he would not participate in any shooting; he would see me in court in Los Angeles. The water level in the river had gone down unbelievably, so much so that we had to climb out of the speedboat in some spots to get past shallow areas. I listened to Kinski, but as I did so was mechanically bailing out the boat with a tin plate. The forest, likewise silent, absorbed the high decibels like me with a certain ease. But Kinski is falling apart; there is nothing holding him together anymore.

Camisea, 28–30 June 1984
Brisk work for the last three days. The day before yesterday we were already shooting at five-thirty in the morning, in the fog. The most important event: the ship is moving up the slope, swiftly; tomorrow

it will reach the first *muerto*. Strangely enough, Walter gathered all the members of the Peruvian technical crew at this particular time, and they all announced that they were going on a solidarity strike unless I immediately broke the contract I had signed with Kinski that prohibited Gloria or any other woman from using the short-wave radio. Then Tercero, the bulldozer operator, delivered a bombastic, stupid lecture to the effect that he was a Peruvian and as such knew what honor was. I remarked that it was my radio, after all, and whether this impugned my honor or not, I could use it, and no one else. I also told him that I was the one who was paying him, not Walter. To judge by his surprise, that was news to him. I also asked Tercero to turn down his music at night, whether he stayed or not. Kinski's often empty, ritualized gesticulating has now found a kind of Peruvian equivalent. Later I took Walter aside and told him that if he wanted to leave, he could of course do so, and I asked him what the last three years of work, which just now was taking an extraordinary leap forward, had been all about. What of the honor of the roosters, who no longer had a home with us and had to forgo the privilege of being warmed in our pots? Walter smiled, but in order to maintain his official posture, he said the work no longer interested him. Get over to the strip, and take all your people with you, I said, otherwise you will arrive too late for hauling the ship. When we did the towing, everyone was there, even Kinski, who favored us with one of his raving tantrums.

Then further outbursts of rage by Kinski because of the new photographer from Sygma, alternating with fits of weakness, which the doctor treats with remarkable restraint, since there is nothing wrong with Kinski. Then renewed threats from Kinski that he is going to leave immediately. The problem is very simple: at the moment the ship is more important than he is. But then, because he is impressed in spite of himself, he displays flashes of contagious enthusiasm. I staged an accident in which several Campas are mowed down by a turnstile that spins backward. Fitz comes running and pulls one of the wounded away, bleeding, and Kinski shrieked with bloody hands—the blood was in a cup at the accident site, concealed from the camera—calling so believably for help that the doctor, who was aware that it was just acting, was so alarmed that he jumped between the two cameras with his first-aid kit. Out of the corner of my eye I saw this happening and managed to pull him down just in time; as they assured me later, it looked good, like a player sacking an opposing quarterback. The Campas applaud me after every day of shooting, and often after a particularly successful sequence, but this time they clapped both for Kinski and for my successful tackle. As they clapped for the ship, which toiled up the slope, groaning with resistance, without actors on board, Kinski again put on the air of one suffering from a fatal illness, and thus at least got the doctor's attention. In the evening he was full of threats: he would see to it that the film was a bust; this was not the first time; he had already done this in dozens of cases. I listened to him unmoved, although I knew what a trail of destruction he has left behind him in his life. Then he threatened to do a whole lot of other things—he did not give a fig for the laws, and for the things he had already done he should have gone to jail long ago. Then he described what he had done to his two daughters, Pola and Nastassja, probably meaning that as a threat; for that alone he would have been given a twenty-year sentence in the U.S.; I should watch my back, he was not deterred by anything.

Most of the Indians are gone, and much seems empty and useless to me. Now that they are gone, I am left behind like an accident victim at the scene. Outside the frogs are bellowing. The shadows of moths around the lamp throw crazed patterns of fear on my table. As we got into the boat, I said to the team, I, Werner, son of Dietrich and Elisabeth, will finish this film.

The ship jerked, and with a groan that almost sounded human, the cables snapped. I was on board. Moving faster and faster and finally racing like a wounded animal, the ship slid back down the slope and hit the water like a torpedo. The slide continued for miles, there was no stopping it. Parts of the railing and the superstructure broke off and were tossed in the terrible waves the ship set in motion. I saw everything as if in slow motion, especially how the superstructure was torn off. Then the ship swung around and headed backward toward a place on a beach that was full of people. I wanted to shout, but the swimmers did not hear me. The ship plunged stern-first into the crowd, drilling itself deep into the sand, burying everyone without a sound, for no one cried out. Still in slow motion I saw the ship, like a biblical plowshare, throwing an ice cream stand into the air. Spinning around itself in terrible inertia, like a leaf slowly swirled from the ground, the stand flew over the beach. Then I saw the forty-meter-high water tower in Darwin, Australia, where the hurricane had whirled a refrigerator through the air. Forty meters above the ground the enormous container displayed a rectangular dent where the refrigerator had hit it.

In the air in his single-engine plane our pilot reads comics. At the moment the airfield in Camisea is so good, he says, that he would like to land the Concorde there. I saw Japanese who had scaled Mount Everest lighting up cigarettes on the peak, at eighty-eight hundred meters above sea level.

Camisea, 1 July 1981
We got up very early, when it was still dark and foggy, talking softly. Hot tea; silent figures; very slowly, the first shimmer of light. We

had good fog, just as I had hoped. The ship on the foggy slope was like a primeval animal, asleep. While the fog lingered, I wanted to have the ship towed up to the *muerto* right away, but one of the lengthwise skids got hung up and would not move. Two hours later, when the obstacle had been worked on for a long time with chain saws, we tried it again, but with a terrible shudder one of the massive wheels in the winch broke, and the steel cable, crushed flat, became completely jammed. Because the repair can take an unspecified time, I decided to leave Vignati here with the camera as a second unit to film the ship when it reached the top. So I could send Kinski back to Iquitos in late morning.

At night on board the ship, resting at a steep angle, further work with Huerequeque, the Indian boys McNamara and El Comandante, as well as Miguel Ángel Fuentes and Paul. The people on board stood and moved vertically, but once it was dark night all around and the eye had lost any reference point, the picture was reversed: the ship was positioned horizontally, and only the people were standing on an extreme slant, as if there were something wrong with gravity. When we were back on even ground after work, gravity felt different to us, a new sensation.

Camisea–Iquitos, 2 July 1984
Up again at the crack of dawn. When the sun came out, I saw the following: a rainbow partially shrouded in fog had one end in the Camisea, right by the bend from which we wanted to tow the ship, and arched over the mountain in the direction of the Urubamba. To a man we all understood this to be an omen, looked at each other in silence and went to work with a sense of lightness. During the night the pulley block had been replaced, and so early in the day we towed

the ship eleven meters uphill in sixty seconds, almost to the first *muerto*. All the conflict and everything that had been dammed up during the long, wearing years of working together vanished, and W. and I fell into each other's arms.

In the afternoon flying to Iquitos, an orderly departure, an orderly arrival. For the first time in my life I rode a motorcycle through a movie theater. After the screening of the rushes, which I slept through, as I usually do, it was raining so hard that to shelter my motorcycle from the deluge I rode through a side entrance into the theater and past the screen, then up the middle aisle, past the rows of seats, then through the women's restroom into the lobby, which was closed off with a grille, and there I left it.

Manaus, Brazil, 3–11 July 1981
Shooting in the Manaus opera house, the Teatro Amazonas, placed in demented tropical splendor in the middle of the rain forest by rubber millionaires at a time when there was hardly any town here. Kinski in total dissolution, on the point of collapse; no one will ever know what it cost me to prop him up, fill him with substance, and give form to his hysteria. Claudia Cardinale is a great help, though, because she is such a good sport, a real trouper, and has a special radiance before the camera. In her presence K. usually acts like a gentleman and certainly has his lovable moments. Werner Schroeter handled the staging of the end of *Ernani*, because to this day I have never been in an opera house as a member of the audience. When the baritone learned that Doña Elvira was going to be played by a transvestite from France, he withdrew in a huff to his hotel room and locked himself in for two days and two nights with the phone unplugged. He was indignant. In addition, Doña Elvira does

not sing, but is merely lip-synched by Sarah Bernhardt, who has a wooden leg, while a fat singer in the orchestra pit matches her voice to her lip movements. Since we always shoot at night and during the day I am helping with the preparations, I hardly slept for almost a week; my memories are vague, as if of something very remote that I had heard rumors about.

Iquitos, 12 July 1981
No electricity, no water, everything unfamiliar, abandoned, empty. Last night I had a long conversation with Vignati on the radio. The ship is up the hill, and Walter insists that we should tow it down to the Urubamba without delay, or rather, let it slide, because that way we can save ourselves months of rental for the winch and steel cables. The only problem is that the Urubamba, usually ten or twelve meters deep, has only fifty centimeters of water at the place where the ship would have to glide in, and that would mean the ship would lie across the current until about October. It would dig itself deep into the sand, and a dramatic rise in the water level would then crush the immobilized ship. Walter also has no idea of Kinski's state of inner dissolution, and in any case Kinski is back in the U.S. now.

I sneaked back and forth over the footbridge between my hut and the office, feeling as if I no longer belonged here. Lucki is the driving force now; I have no idea what I would do without him. Huerequeque is on the mend, though he has lost weight. The caged toucan shrieked despairingly and hoarsely behind me. Tracks of snakes, tracks of hogs; dust on everything; spiderwebs.

Spent almost the entire day in complete apathy, reading and sleeping, without doing one or the other properly. Deathly silence in the town, no one out on the street because it is census time. The birds kept still as if in exhaustion, the jungle did not stir, it was like a muggy July afternoon above fields of ripe grain shimmering in the heat. A desolate day out of which all life had been drained. In my hut, which is more and more empty, the sublime and the ghostly have taken up residence like siblings who no longer speak to one another.

I had Lucki explain the financial situation to me, and it is much grimmer than I wanted to admit to myself earlier. Tidying up, doing accounts, new timelines with Lucki. I burned papers by the kilo, all of which had great value in their time and now are merely ballast.

Iquitos, 13 July 1981
In the gray of dawn, I rode out to the Nanay. The early swamp birds were screeching as if they did not want day to come, and in the first, cold light many sleepy people came toward me, heading into town on foot. In the evening a garbled radio message from Camisea reached me, from which I gathered that there were problems there.

Iquitos–Lima, 14 July 1981
News from the camp somewhat clearer. Apparently Trigozo tried to confiscate the Caterpillar and prevent the shooting. Two policemen are supposed to have turned up at the camp, but then the situation calmed down. Virginia and Sylvia were scheduled to pick me up at the airport, to get me a microphone and several rolls of raw stock for the rest of the shooting on the Camisea, but at first they were not there. When they finally turned up, they had neither the film nor the microphone, although it had all been arranged several days ago and I had been told everything was ready. Lima cold, rainy, and hateful, as always. The slick waiter in the Argentinean restaurant glanced at

my pants, etched by the jungle, and at first did not want to give me a table; allegedly everything was reserved, although the restaurant was almost empty.

Lima–San Ramón–Camisea, 15 July 1981
In the morning there was real brewed black coffee, which seemed a special delicacy after all the Nescafé, especially in Brazil. Flight in a twin-engine SASA plane over the Andes, almost brushing the snow-covered peaks. We were given thin hoses with oxygen, since the plane did not have a pressurized cabin. Tomislav was waiting for me in San Ramón, and first we hung around there for a while because his plane's engine had to wait to be inspected. We made a brief stop-over in Atalaya, and I picked up Peruvian *soles*, packed in such tight bundles that you could have killed someone with them.

When we landed in Camisea, we were received with silence at first, but gradually people thawed. On the way there Tomislav had already given me more details on what had happened. On Monday Pedro Morey had brought lunch to the *trocha*, the cleared strip, but the meat had gone bad, a scene reminiscent of the situation in *Battleship Potemkin*, where spoiled meat sparks a mutiny among the crew. Walter flew off the handle and fired Pedro on the spot, and Trigozo as well, because both of them had been increasingly neglecting their duties as administrators of the Indian camp. All the remaining Indians had worked extremely hard and hauled the ship the final distance to the top of the hill, but Trigozo treated them with complete disdain because he no longer detected the authority emanating from a fully staffed technical team. Trigozo's Peruvian honor was offended by the firing, and he tried to incite the Machiguengas in Shivankoreni. He also went to Nueva Luz and brought from there confused

Machiguengas who had never had anything to do with us. It was not easy to make out what he had told them, but at any rate he occupied the lower camp that evening, placed an armed guard outside the office, raised the Peruvian flag, and saw himself as master of the situation. The next morning the Caterpillar was surrounded by armed men, and one of them took possession of the key, without knowing that the Caterpillar could be started without it. Vignati was forbidden by these usurpers of authority to film the ship. When Walter pushed some of them aside and started up the Caterpillar, one of them fired a shot in the air. At that Gloria, who tends to exaggerate, called Satipo on the radio to request help. That same day twelve Sinchis flew in, the elite antiterrorist squad, without knowing what was going on; apparently they expected to be received by a hail of bullets, and were accordingly dressed in terrifying getups. They even had light machine guns, hand grenades, and submachine guns, but I cannot rid myself of the suspicion that they had been idle for a long time and were using this occasion as a training exercise. All of Camisea had immediately gone into hiding. When I landed, six Sinchis strolled toward me in camouflage, young figures in top condition with slow movements and alert eyes, imbued with the sense of being the best of the best. Their leader strolled, his phallus erect under his battle trousers, among his athletic fighters, all Indians, by the way. The captain, it turned out, was smart and levelheaded, and promptly called a meeting in the camp to get all the facts. He immediately sided with the people from Nueva Luz, who complained that one of our people had touched a woman's genitals. The matter was investigated right away, and it soon turned out that it was our medic, the one who had saved the woman who had gone around for eleven days with a dead fetus in her womb. The captain wanted to arrest Trigozo, who had told the Machiguengas all sorts of lies, but fortunately I was able to prevent that. The *capitán*'s profound insights into the Indians' mentality and his attentive, alert calm impressed me. He assured the Machiguengas that they could call on him for help and protection any time, and when he left Shivankoreni, it was as calm as though nothing had ever happened. Still, I can well imagine the aftermath in the press.

Camisea–San Ramón, 16 July 1981
Long discussion with Walter and Vignati. The Shell Oil Company plans to get a foothold in the area, and there is even a plan to build a pipeline. I was shocked at how fast this will happen. The Machiguengas had been asking me for my support for a long time as they tried to acquire legal title to their land between the two rivers, so they could keep out loggers, gold prospectors, and oil companies, but the problem is that there has been no survey done to establish the boundaries of their territory. We decided to bring in a geographer from Lima to make a map that can be used as the basis for their land claims. Further decisions as to how our work is to continue simultaneously at different locations. I managed to persuade Walter to haul the ship over the relatively flat terrain on top of the slope before it plunges steeply down to the Urubamba, but insisted that he not lose his head, with the destination so near, and let the ship glide into the river without cameras and without actors. During our months-long absence an indigenous family would have to live on the ship; otherwise on our return we would find everything dismantled, and another family would have to live on the *Huallaga*, below the Pongo. So we have two identical ships, one on a mountain, the other on a gravel bank, both now with firm ground under their keels. We will continue working in different locations: Walter and Vignati first

by the *Narinho*, and Lucki, with whom I spoke by radio, will fly to L.A. to see to the supplementary contract with Kinski for October or November, while I will go to N.Y. to sift through the material in the film lab, and then to L.A. myself.

Before my departure we played soccer against the Indians from Shivankoreni, and lost. In the heat of the afternoon I was immediately drenched in sweat and was panting for breath. I took a young Indio from Nueva Luz with me on the plane, someone I had never seen before. He presented himself as a student, but in the hotel later he gave his profession as missionary.

In the evening I went into San Ramón on foot, into town. Indios from the highlands. A fat, whitish moon heaved itself up the mountain slope. You could smell the fires set to clear the jungle all around. There was a smell of stale urine. Children at a table next to me in a café were doing their homework, writing clumsily in a notebook. On the Plaza de Armas I saw a procession of children carrying paper lanterns. In front was a band, and the youthful musicians marched in military formation–in Prussian goosestep. An Indio from the highlands wearing a miner's helmet slapped a shocked schoolboy hard, and–only then did I notice that he was probably insane–went looking for his next unsuspecting victim, took up a position before him, screamed at the surprised youth, and struck him with terrible, brutal rage. I watched him look for the next one, and then other people noticed what was going on and intervened, after which I left. On the ugly, two-lane bridge with iron supports stood a little girl of seven in her school uniform and silently reached out her hand with a half-eaten orange toward me. Last night around three I woke up in the camp. The moon was lighting up a pale haze over the slopes, and it suddenly became clear to me that I had to film this unrepeatable moment. I also had the feeling that Kinski was there. I leaped out of bed, naked, ran out onto the porch, and shouted, Jorge, Jorge Vignati into the night. Nothing stirred, and I called, Walter, Walter, get everybody up! And then I realized that I was standing there with my eyes open and only now really woke up. But I had seen the camp so clearly. In the uninhabited cabins lightbulbs are burning.

July–October 1984

Editing in Munich. Before I left Peru, I took two elected representatives of the Machuengas from Shivankoreni to Lima, where we had an audience with President Belaunde to talk about the legal title to their territory. Afterward the two men wanted to see the ocean, and we drove there. They cautiously tasted the water, which they knew would be salty. Then they got two empty bottles from a restaurant on the shore and waded, fully clothed, into the waves until the water came up to their chests. They filled the bottles, capped them carefully, and brought them home as proof that they had seen the ocean. The financial situation remained tense, but was not as dramatic as it had been for long stretches earlier. Another single-engine plane crashed, with serious injuries again, but all the passengers survived.

Camisea, 18 October 1984

Not until I was in the boat yesterday sailing up the Camisea did I come to my senses and realize, jerked out of the strange, unreal state I had been in, where I was and what I was doing. Before that I was in a fog. I climbed out of the small plane with such pressure in my ears that for a long time I could not hear anything and thought I was in a dream. The team's camp is going to rack and ruin. Walls are falling down. Any building material from the jungle has been reclaimed by the jungle. Dust and dry leaves in the houses, the water ran dry months ago, and the porcelain sinks and toilets have a thick layer of dirt. The Camisea is as smooth as when we left, and the Uru-bamba has just as little water. After the most terrible rainy season in sixty-five years the region now had the worst drought in human memory. The hanging bridge of lianas leading to Kinski's cabin can be used only with caution. In his washroom the floor has caved in. In Shivankoreni the beans were being harvested and dried. The women beat them out of the dry, rustling shells and separate the chaff in the wind. I was received with unusual warmth.

There seem to be more birds, and they are louder. Animals are in the camp, a little monkey with round saucer eyes; he always looks as though he were saying, "Fitzroy was here." Then a small, yellow-brown songbird, not quite ready to fly; he peeps at me, runs after me, hops onto my toes when I walk, and is constantly weaving around between my legs, so much so that I am afraid of stepping on him. He thinks I am his mother. Today he sat on my hand for a long time, chirping at me, and when I put him on the table because I had to go he was beside himself. Our parrot is still here, and introduced herself by name, Aurora. The two black monkeys, including Tricky Dick, who had roles in the film, were eaten by the Campas before they left. There are three young women in the camp who belong to the boatmen.

Quispe, who has had his shoulder-length hair cut short, fixed up my room yesterday. It was in a sorry state. The mattress was moldy and soaked through, the door half ripped off its hinges, my book-shelf half dismantled. Someone pulled a board off, and now nails are sticking out. The river seems to be waking up; there are small dots of foam on the surface, and its color has changed to a washed-out dark olive, and the water seems to be moving a bit more briskly, but that may be an illusion. Yesterday the river seemed to be standing still.

On the Urubamba I saw a little driftwood today, a sign that it is rising somewhat. It is still problematic to sail up the Camisea, even in
small boats. Right above Shivankoreni it is so shallow in one place
that it is hardly possible to get through. In the camp are: El Tigre,
the old Chinese cook, the Sanitario, Quispe, three boatmen, including the dreamer, Pedro, the machinist who got the Caterpillar started
today, and a few others. Today Tercero was supposed to arrive from
Pucallpa, but he could not be found. Walter and I wanted to go up
to the Pongo today to get a replacement for Julian on the *Huallaga*,
where he had been living, also taking upriver a speedboat motor, groceries, and fuel. We hung around in Camisea for a few hours, but
the promised plane did not show up, so we drank *masato* with the
teacher and gave up on our plan. Over the radio we got more precise
information on Tercero: he had impregnated one of the kitchen girls,
had gone underground in Tarapoto, and had appeared again only in
response to calls over the radio.

At night the camp was filled with the boatmen's male hooting
and joking. The *motorista*, who is lacking his incisors, played dances
from the highlands on a strange, thin, long harmonica. I was awakened by the noise, but then slept almost twelve hours, having gone
to bed at seven-thirty in the evening. During the day the camp now
resembles an Indian settlement; it is quiet and holidaylike, as the villages are all year long. A cautious melancholy hangs over the whole
place, like places remembered from childhood that have changed in
the meantime.

Camisea, 19 October 1984
I had photos with me for El Tigre. He had not been home in two
years, having worked for two years in a logging camp before he joined

us. He had also never taken his quarterly vacation, to which he was entitled and during which we would have continued to pay him. When he got home, he found his wife had run off with another man. He went to his mother-in-law and said, I am going to take you, then. And that he did, but he did not last more than a week with her. Then he went to Pucallpa, tracked down his wife, bought her three hundred cases of beer, took her back to his native village, and set her up in a stand that sold drinks. Chino had a similar story: when he returned to Iquitos, his wife told him, Now you have money; buy me a sewing machine. He did so. A week later his wife ran away with another man, and the sewing machine.

Large green lizards are rustling in the leaves. Fish leap out of the water as if they actually belonged to the clouds in the sky. It is only through writing that I become myself. At the other end of the camp someone is hammering a board, and the sound comes back in a hollow echo from the forest. The forest does not accept these sounds. Last night there were thousands of winged creatures hovering around the lamps, raging in wild swarms like spherical catastrophes around the lightbulbs. One could eat only with the light switched off. In the morning, by the boat landing, where a more powerful lamp has been installed, there were piles of wings on the ground, like a snowdrift. Everywhere spiders have spun their webs under the roof, near the electric light, and with such a surfeit of prey they cannot attend to every captured gift; they have taut bellies, as plump as cherries.

Camisea–Pucallpa–Iquitos, 20 October 1984
The ship, the *Narinho*, is suspended only a few meters from the edge of the slope that leads down to the Urubamba. Finally tracked down

by calls on the shortwave radio, Tercero showed up. Not only had he impregnated one of the cooks in the camp; by his own account, he had left Tarapoto for Chasuta, where he lay around drunk for three months and made all the females pregnant that, as he said, came within reach. With us, he assured us, he was fortunately safe from women.

Iquitos, 21 October 1981
Telex to Munich; for hours there was no way to get through. In the afternoon I disappeared into the abysses of sleep. I ran into Gloria, and she told me quickly that she was anemic, the little one had diarrhea, and she was pregnant again. With that she crossed herself, got up from the table, and hurried upstairs. I read the correspondence of Heloise and Abelard in an English translation. The really moving letters are Heloise's, full of boldness and tragedy.

Iquitos, 22 October 1981
The decisions have been made: we start shooting again on 1 November; otherwise Cardinale, Kinski, and Lewgoy would not be available at the same time. Dear God, let the ship be afloat by then. The movie theater in town on the Plaza 28 de Julio has a new screen, which the owner showed me with pride. Between his feet and the rows of seats and also in front on the little wooden stage fat rats scampered in large numbers. Mugginess, humidity. The photos I have on the wall have curled up from the humidity and are all mildewed, eaten away. The air hovers around bodies, dense and heavy. Above the forest a storm is gathering. The air is as fat as a pig, and lingers rigid and sweaty outside.

Lima, 24 October 1984

Costume try-ons with the conductor, Cuadros Barr, his orchestra, the singers, the chorus, for the staging of Bellini's *I Puritani* on board the ship when Fitz returns. After that I went looking for Janoud, who has moved, and whose address I did not know exactly. According to W., at one and the same time his Swiss girlfriend turned up, wanting to domesticate him into a good Swiss, and Silvia, the Dutch woman, who in that respect is more broad-minded. I forced my way through several front gardens to the windows of locked-up houses, and peeked inside, but a quick look at the furniture allowed me to cross them off the list. Finally I came to a rear house, where there was not much to be seen, except that there were Dutch coffee filters in the kitchen; the lettering on the package immediately struck me as foreign, and that told me this was where Janoud was living, and furthermore, he was with the Dutch surgical nurse. As Walter told me, Janoud had thrown both women out and told them they should be so kind as to work things out between them, but Walter did not know what the outcome had been. I left a note stuck in the door and was not surprised when Janoud turned up with Silvia in the restaurant to which I had invited Cuadros Barr. Janoud hoisted me in the air and gave a shout that turned into crazy, terrifying laughter, which shocked the dignified waiters in their tuxedos, but then they shook off their dignified air and joined the uproarious laughter. Janoud had had typhus, and felt even more like an iron rod than before, though he had regained most of his earlier weight.

Cuadros Barr told me he had been riding a horse and had seen a snake in the grass that was pursuing a fleeing rat. Rats were very fast, he said, but the snake had been even faster, faster even than his briskly trotting horse.

Iquitos, 26 October 1984

Another name for hamster is corn piglet. My bed was floating in blood, as smoothly as a skiff. On the border between Mali and Mauretania, my jeep disappeared with all my equipment, and then my money and passport were also taken from me. A frog appeared under the mosquito net and stared at me. Out on the porch I leaned against one of the posts, overcome with misery, and crushed the termites' tunnel that ran the length of it. They spilled out like water from a leaky pipe, but were not angry in the slightest. By morning they had repaired the damage to their tunnel. They had to haul material from far away, at least from the ground underneath my cabin. Which of the termites do that? On whose orders? How are such orders given for building and repairs? Or are there specialized construction squads just for that?

A zebu calf became emaciated. In Atalaya an Indian woman in the airport tavern called her daughter, about eight, Disney. Disney, bring the gentleman another beer. The boy playing the violin in the scene outside the prison is called Modus Vivendi. I was told the boy played for funerals, for a funeral parlor called Modus Vivendi, for which his father had worked before him. The city here is more than ever a city of children.

At Huerequeque's bar there was another shoot-out between drug dealers, who pursued each other on motorcycles. No police came, they do not come out to the Nanay unless people get killed. Huerequeque gave me a vivid account, leaping off an imaginary motorcycle, landing on one knee on the ground, pulling out an imaginary revolver and firing shots after the fleeing miscreants, his face distorted with rage and determination. He knows the assassin well; the man always comes to his bar to eat. Recently, in Leticia, a drug dealer was shot, but only after he had his tongue cut out–a young soccer player who is very well known around here.

Iquitos, 27 October 1984

Suddenly my room was full of light. There was a rustling in the roof. On the ground all around me, the places where stars had struck glowed and blossomed. There was white and black steam and in between tight knots of lightning. The roaches, probably sensing that they would be the only ones left to survive, ate their fill of my pink soap. In the morning I saw their tracks on the soap, as if someone had scratched it with a fine wire brush. To do something nice for me, Julian invented the news that the *Huallaga* was free, but the boat is high and dry, just as before. The rain is cowardly. At the edge of the jungle, birds were calling like mad dogs. My body is parched like a drought-stricken stretch of land. Fine cracks opened up in the ground. I rode into town on the motorcycle, taking Maria-Luisa and her little girl along. On the way back, the little girl, who was wedged between her mother and me, fell asleep. I could tell the exact moment when her little head drooped to one side and the grip of her little hands around me loosened. When I tossed a cigarette butt, still glowing, into a metal sewer grating, suddenly something like a snake shot up out of the damp, black sewer, seized the butt, dropped it again at once, and disappeared just as fast. It was a very large frog.

A man was carrying his guitar, packed in a plastic bag, over his shoulder like an ax, on the dusty road, in the blazing sun. Dogs were lying motionless in the hot sand, in the spotty shadow of several bare bushes. Since yesterday Gustavo has a little Sanyo tape recorder, like a Walkman, and I asked him where he had gotten it. He got it from customs. The customs officials stole an entire box full of them, stuck the devices into their boots, and offered one of them to Gustavo if he would remove the empty box from the customs area along with the other things he had to pick up.

Camisea, 1 November 1984, All Saints' Day
Snow had already fallen in Munich, Anja reported. A pump for the pressure tank that provided our running water had broken down, but otherwise the camp had been put back in good shape. There was a pervasive sense of déjà vu: Huerequeque swam past me, going against the current, Kinski came to me with a crazed flickering in his eyes and bellowed because Miguel Ángel had turned up his music too loud. I was tired of playing policeman, and I felt sorry for Miguel Ángel, because he tries to combat the homesickness that assails him immediately by playing his cassettes. The ship has already been moved halfway down the slope toward the Urubamba. The clearing at the very bottom by the water has to be widened and compacted today; we are still missing a smaller *muerto* and a turnstile, which the Campas will build. David is here, Miguel Camaytieri, McNamara, and El Comandante, and about a hundred Campas. A large crowd is on its way here in boats, on foot, and by plane. In two days the ship could be in the water.

Camisea, 2 November 1984
We towed the ship without any safety mechanism holding it from behind about eighty meters down the slope, calculating that it could handle the descent like a regular launching. We shot the scene from safe positions until the ship got hung up in the trees

and the tangle of lianas on one side of the cleared strip. The Urubamba was rising until noon, but then the water level sank rapidly. We concentrated on the new molinette, and while we were
filming there, to fill a break during which the cables for the ship
had to be adjusted, the Campas ran in a circle so fast that in their
haste one of them jammed his hand between the rope and the
tree trunk, which would have torn off his hand at the wrist if
Vignati had not jumped in immediately and stopped everything.
The morning was murderously hot, and since the Campas had
brought nothing along to drink, our big pot of lemon-flavored
water was empty within minutes. At noon when we went back to
the camp for lunch, we were so drained from the work and from
thirst that no one spoke.

The people of Shivankoreni had given Dr. Parraga four chickens
as a gift. They were in a little crate, where they sat with their feet
tied together and poked their bare necks through the bars. I received
an enormous bunch of green plantains, weighing about a hundred
pounds, as well as a heap of very large yucca roots. I gave them the
jerseys with the logo of the Bavarian Munich soccer team that they
had been so keen on, along with a team pennant and a new soccer
ball. Now they will beat all other teams, they are sure, especially the
one from Nueva Luz.

For days there has been a sick duck lying around by the water. At
first I thought she might be sitting on eggs, but after she was roasted
on two crossed sticks over Zézé's fire, I learned that the duck had had
the habit of climbing into the Indian laundry women's large plastic tub
when it was filled with detergent, because apparently she liked bubble
baths. But as a result she had lost the film of oil on her feathers, and
whenever she tried to swim in the river, she soaked up water and sank.

The water level rose so much that Julian detached our pressure tank and moved it to higher ground. We caught several oil drums that were floating in the river. Then, in the evening, I saw an empty dugout drift by my cabin, and as we had not sent any canoes farther upstream, I thought it had to belong to the Amehuacas. Since our boats were tied up at the time, it took a while before our people could take off after the mystery vessel. At night, since we left lights on by the dock, so many flying insects came, soft bodies with transparent wings, and in such pointlessly large swarms, that the wings they lost covered the ground there like powder snow. Our large parrot, Aurora, sat on the railing there with a heavy six-volt battery clutched in her talons and tried to eat it.

Word arrived from the Pongo that the *Huallaga* on its gravel bank now had quite a bit of water under its keel and was already shifting. If the water rose only two more feet, the boat would be free. Even though I always receive such messages with cautious skepticism, a bold image is forcing its way into my thoughts and refuses to be banished, a final, truly surreal act: that in the moment when we had finally hauled the ship over the mountain and into the water of the Urubamba, its identical twin would drift into the picture and collide with it, with the effect that these two monsters, mysteriously doubled, would suddenly sink each other.

Camisea, 3 November 1984
In the morning I took a boat over to the cleared strip. We pulled the ship in smaller and smaller stretches, until it was almost down at the Urubamba. At noon fearfully menacing clouds formed–in the morning there had already been three brief downpours–and I had taken refuge under the ship along with several Campas. But the water streamed along the lengthwise curve of the ship's hull and soaked us.

I ate some of the Campas' coarse yucca flour, which they had with them in a sack. I handed out photos I had brought along for them. One Campa borrowed a walkie-talkie from me that I was trying to keep out of the rain, and spoke into it for a long time, without being in actual contact with anyone. Then he hung two walkie-talkies cross-wise around on his chest and had Vignati take his picture.

With our goal so close, I let our heavy equipment be pushed to the limit. As the Caterpillar was tugging the ship's bow from the side, the wheels inside the pulley system snapped one after another. The pieces, boiling hot, bounced hissing into the slippery mud, yet I told the crew to keep pulling. When everything was quiet, I saw for the first time the shy cluck bird, which utters such strange sounds, sending them echoing through the treetops. Something that struck the bird as unusual must have lured it there. This bird is black and quite large, and when it calls, it rears up toward the sky and with each call shakes its wings in a courting posture. Right after lunch a powerful storm struck, and I had just time to get to my hut with a cup of hot coffee, where I lay down in my hammock to read. I fell asleep, while on both sides of me water was dripping through the roof. I was practically thrown out of my hammock by two tremen-dous thunderclaps very close by. Then word came that the Urubamba was rising like crazy, and we should get ready at once, because it was possible the ship might start moving on the slippery ground all by itself and would not be stoppable even with steel cables, or the river might rise so high that it could reach the front of the keel, which was only ten meters from the water, and drag the ship into the cur-rent. In no time I had all the men on the cleared strip. I found the Urubamba immensely swollen, full of tree trunks and dirt, and the gravel bank on the opposite side had almost completely disappeared. To the left of the cleared strip the Caterpillar had sunk deep into the mud while trying to position another *muerto*. It took one and a half hours before we could loop a cable around a tree higher up so the bulldozer could winch itself out. Because we had too few people to help move the cables, I pitched in, together with almost the whole technical team; it was killing work. So much time passed while we were trying to get the Caterpillar unstuck that all we had was a quarter of an hour before the light was gone, so everyone supported my decision to give up our plan of shooting today. I am willing to bet that if we just straighten out the ship slightly, it will start sliding down the compacted path on its own. The water, grumpy and dirty, swept past us, its level going down somewhat.

In the light of the crescent moon, the Campas began to sing and drink, and in no time the cleared strip looked like a battlefield sown with beer bottles.

Camisea, 4 November 1984
We had chosen two camera positions: Mauch with a handheld on the *chata*, whose floor was as slick as soft soap from oil and mud, so much so that he could find a firm base only by sitting on an aluminum suitcase; Klausmann very close to the ship, squeezed into a corner of a little spit of land, from which, however, the only escape route was straight into the water. But his position remained risky, because once the ship really started to move it could conceivably tear down the earth berm and plow him under. We conferred about this for a long time. Raimund, the lighting technician, and several Campas posted themselves above his perch, ready to pull him up and out of the danger zone. For myself I tried to find a somewhat higher lookout, from which I could see both cameras, as well as the position of the bulldozer. I had visual contact with both Walter

and Tercero. In case something unforeseen happened, I could warn the cameraman below me in time. In fact the ship did initially veer toward the earthen berm by the camera, and I saw Raimund leap to the other side of the camera to get it out of the way, moving it toward the water, while the Campas held themselves in readiness to rescue Klausmann. But Tercero managed to get the ship swung back in the other direction. Once half the ship was in the water, it keeled over so breathtakingly to the side, against the current, that it seemed inevitable that the boat would capsize and sink. Tossing and turning in a confused, chaotic fever dream, the ship heaved from one side to the other. I lost sight of the Caterpillar, which had bravely jammed itself under the tipping boat, so I ran around the ship, out of range of the camera. As I did so, my bare feet came down on the razor-sharp shards of a broken beer bottle, which the Indians had left lying in the mud after their nocturnal fiesta. I noticed that I was bleeding profusely, and that there were lots of other shards lying around. Rushing on, I was paying more attention to the broken glass than to the ship, which I assumed was a goner. By the time I had reached the other side of the ship, the Caterpillar had already stuck its blade with brute strength under the ship's hull, with the result that the railing, which was almost scraping the ground, was crushed with a terrible crunching sound, but the ship, by now almost entirely in the water, righted itself.

I did not even feel my bleeding foot. The ship meant nothing to me—it held no more value than some broken old beer bottle in the mud, than any steel cable whipping around itself on the ground. There was no pain, no joy, no excitement, no relief, no happiness, no sound, not even a deep breath. All I grasped was a profound use-lessness, or, to be more precise, I had merely penetrated deeper into its mysterious realm. I saw the ship, returned to its element, right itself with a weary sigh. Today, on Wednesday, the 4th of November 1984, shortly after twelve noon, we got the ship from the Río Camisea over a mountain into the Río Urubamba. All that is to be reported is this: I took part.

EPILOGUE

Even then my trials were not at an end. We still had shooting to do in Iquitos, for which we needed at least one of the two boats, but on the way downstream both of them ran aground several times, which kept adding to the delays. At the last moment, when Claudia Cardinale had to fly home for another film, the Huallaga *arrived in Iquitos. When I saw the ship pulling into the spot where we were planning to film, a ten-meter-high pier, I was so overjoyed that I dove headfirst into the water. That dive could have cost me my life—what I did not know was that just a meter under the murky brown water's surface enormous beams were bolted parallel to one another. I grazed one of them with my shoulder.*

For several days we had also been having problems with one member of the team. It was becoming more and more noticeable that he was acting frantic, distracted, incoherent, to the point that I suspected him of being on drugs. What I did not know was that he had gone temporarily insane. He arrived emaciated, altered, confused. I finally decided, in order to keep an eye on him, to have him join us at our headquarters on the Nanay. I gave him my hut on stilts and moved for the time being into the house up front. The first night, just before dawn, my hut went up in flames. He had set it on fire, and, wearing only a loincloth, had jumped onto a motorcycle and raced into town, a large machete clamped between his teeth. He had also painted his face black, so as to be invisible like the Indians in the film. In town he seized two young travel-agency employees as hostages, but fortunately released them before the police opened fire. Weeks went by before we had managed to pay enough bribes to get all the charges against him dropped and could send him home, escorted by a doctor and a paramedic. Fortunately this turned out to be a passing episode. To this day, he is someone for whom I feel undying friendship.

Twenty years later I returned to Camisea, on the trail of my collaboration with Kinski. I had taken a boat through the Pongo de Mainique and stopped over in Shivankoreni. There I found two of the Machiguengas who had offered to kill Kinski for me. The village has hardly changed at all. The same huts, the same landing. Only the soccer goals have been dismantled, because many of the young people have left. One hut is new, roofed with corrugated tin. It is the medical station, the pharmacy, remarkably well stocked. The oil company put it up; otherwise the territory of the Machiguengas between the two rivers, to which they now have legal title, remains untouched. Directly on the other side of the Camisea the oil company has a large installation, hidden away in the hills of the primeval forest. One of the world's largest deposits of natural gas, if not the largest, was discovered there. The Amehuacas, I was assured, had been contacted long since and had been tamed into good Peruvians. I found not a trace of either of our camps, even after a careful search—not a nail, not a post, not even a hole where a post had been. The strip we had cleared was completely overgrown, as if we had never been there. Only the forest was a lighter green there, if you knew where we had dragged the ship over the mountain. But the vegetation had grown up to its previous height. It was midday and very still. I looked around, because everything was so motionless. I recognized the jungle as something familiar, something I had inside me, and I knew that I loved it: yet against my better judgment. Then words came back to me that had been circling, swirling inside me through all those years: Hearken, heifer, hoarfrost. Denizens of the crag, will-o'-the-wisp, hogwash. Uncouth, flotsam, fiend. Only now did it seem as though I could escape from the vortex of words.

Something struck me, a change that actually was no change at all. I had simply not noticed it when I was working here. There had been an odd tension hovering over the huts, a brooding hostility. The native families hardly had any contact with each other, as if a feud reigned among them. But I had always overlooked that somehow, or denied it. Only the children had played together. Now, as I made my way past the huts and asked for directions, it was hardly possible to get one family to acknowledge another. The seething hatred was undeniable, as if something like a climate of vengeance prevailed, from hut to hut, from family to family, from clan to clan.

I looked around, and there was the jungle, manifesting the same seething hatred, wrathful and steaming, while the river flowed by in majestic indifference and scornful condescension, ignoring everything: the plight of man, the burden of dreams, and the torments of time.

PERSONS AND PLACES

Mario Adorf	German-Italian actor. Played the role of the captain until the first phase of shooting was broken off.
Gustavo Cerff Arbulù	Peruvian production assistant. Worked previously on *Aguirre*.
Belém	Belém do Para, Brazilian provincial capital at the mouth of the Amazon. Not to be confused with Belén!
Belén	A floating quarter of Iquitos, located on rafts and pilings.
Uli Bergfelder	Expert on old Provençal poetry, film designer, set decorator. Longtime Herzog collaborator.
Les Blank	American director. Numerous documentaries, including *Spend It All*, *Chula Vista*. Made the film *Burden of Dreams* about the creation of *Fitzcarraldo*.

Franz Blumauer	Fashion and costume designer from Vienna. Later did costumes for opera productions, among others *Tannhäuser*.
Camisea	Indian name: Shivankoreni. Machiguenga village at the confluence of the Río Camisea and the Río Urubamba.
Claudia Cardinale	Italian film star. Played the role of Molly in the film.
Dr. Claude Chiarini	French Foreign Legionnaire, doctor and neurologist. On staff of a mental hospital near Paris. Collaborated with Herzog on earlier films as a photographer.
Francis Ford Coppola	Producer and director of films such as *Apocalypse Now* and *The Godfather*.
Zézé D'Alice	Brazilian sound assistant.
Carlos Diegues	Brazilian director of films such as *Os Heredeiros* and *Bye Bye Brazil*.
Lotte Eisner	Film historian, studied archeology, fled in 1933 on the day of Hitler's seizure of power. Mentor to the New German Cinema. Publications such as *The Haunted Screen* and monographs on Murnau and Fritz Lang.
Miguel Ángel Fuentes	Mexican actor. Played Cholo.
Abel Gance	French film pioneer, made *Napoleon* and other films.
Henning von Gierke	Painter, set designer, opera director. Longtime Herzog collaborator.
Maureen Gosling	Longtime collaborator of Les Blank. Cutter, director of *Blossoms of Fire* and other films.
Rui Guerra	Brazilian director of *Os Fuzis, Erendira*. Acted in *Aguirre*.

Jerry Hall	American model, married to Mick Jagger at the time.
Rudolph Herzog	Son of Werner Herzog, known in childhood as Burro. Professional magician. Director and producer of films such as *Cat and Mouse*.
Tilbert Herzog	Till, Werner Herzog's older brother, helped with the financing of *Aguirre*.
Paul Hittscher	German captain and shipowner in Iquitos, Peru, restaurant owner. Played the captain.
Huerequeque	Huerequeque Enrique Bohorquez, owner of a bar on the Río Nanay. Played Huerequeque.
Mick Jagger	British rock star. Played Wilbur until the filming was broken off. The role was later cut out of the script.
Werner Janoud	Worked as a miner. Fled at eighteen from the German Democratic Republic, spent three years biking from Canada to Peru. Photographer. Longtime personal friend.
Dagoberto Juarez	Brazilian sound engineer.
Edmund Erwin Kemper	Mass murderer, serving eight consecutive lifetime sentences in Vacaville, California.
Klaus Kinski	Played Fitzcarraldo. His filmography includes more than two hundred films. Earlier a stage actor and reciter of poetry. Directed his own film, *Kinski Paganini*.
Raines Klausmann	Swiss cameraman (second camera). Later collaborated several more times with Herzog, for instance on *Scream of Stone*.
Joe Koechlin von Stein	Peruvian businessman, ecologist. Helped with the financing of *Aguirre*. The first impulse for *Fitzcarraldo* came from him.

José Lewgoy	Brazilian actor, usually in soap operas. Played the rubber baron Don Aquilino.
Tom Luddy	U.S. amateur golf champion, political activist. Director of the Pacific Film Archive in Berkeley. Collaborator of Coppola. Founder and director of the Telluride Film Festival.
Laplace Martin	Brazilian engineer, expert for heavy loads, resigned during the filming.
Thomas Mauch	Cameraman from the very beginning of Herzog's career, worked on *Signs of Life*, *Even Dwarfs Started Small*, *Aguirre*. Also cameraman for Edgar Reitz and Alexander Kluge; later director and producer of his own films.
Errol Morris	American director of *Vernon/Florida*, *Fast, Cheap, and Out of Control*, *Fog of War*, among others.
Sepp Mosmeier	Pastry chef, opera fan. Founder and president of the Munich Black-and-Yellow soccer club.
Grande Otelo	Brazilian actor, played the forgotten stationmaster.
Dr. Parraga	Peruvian doctor. Established the medical outposts in both jungle camps.
Rui Polanah	Brazilian actor, originally from Mozambique. Played the role of a rubber baron.
Pongo de Mainique	Rapids in the upper reaches of the Río Urubamba.
Pongo de Manseriche	Rapids on the Río Marañón.
Beat Presser	Photographer from Basel. Numerous exhibitions and publications, among them *Alpentraum* and *Kinski*. Director of video productions. Longtime Herzog collaborator.
Resortes	Mexican actor.

Jason Robards	American actor. Played Fitzcarraldo until he withdrew on account of illness, which led to Herzog's breaking off the first attempt at making the film.
Glauber Rocha	Brazilian director of *Antonio das Mortes*, *Terra em transe*, and other works.
Gloria Saxer	Peruvian wife of Walter Saxer. Provided catering for *Fitzcarraldo* and other films.
Walter Saxer	Line producer from St. Gallen (Switzerland), Herzog collaborator from the early films on. Director of a sound studio, producer, screenwriter for *Scream of Stone*.
Volker Schlöndorff	German director. His films include *Young Törless*, *The Tin Drum*, *Homo Faber*.
Anja Schmidt-Zähringer	Responsible for continuity. Longtime Herzog collaborator for organization.
Werner Schroeter	Director of film, theater, and opera; credits include *The Death of Maria Malibran* and *Day of the Idiots*. Staged the excerpt from *Ernani* for Fitzcarraldo in the Teatro Amazonas in Manaus.
Larisa Shepitko	Ukrainian director in the former USSR of films such as *The Ascent* and *Wings*. Gymnast and basketball player on the national team.
George Sluizer	Dutch director of *Utz* and other films. Producer. Director of production for the Brazilian part of the shooting.
Walter Steiner	Sculptor in wood, two-time world champion in ski flying, from Wildhaus (Switzerland). Lead actor in *The Great Ecstasy of Woodcarver Steiner*.

Lucki Stipetic   Herzog's younger brother and closest collaborator, starting with *Aguirre*. Producer, director of film production and worldwide distribution. Previously independent businessman.

Gisela Storch   Costume designer. Longtime collaborator.

Hans-Jürgen Syberberg   German director of *Ludwig—Requiem for a Virgin King* and *Hitler*.

Miguel Vazquez   Special effects, Mexico.

Jorge Vignati   Peruvian cameraman, director of documentaries, assistant director for *Fitzcarraldo*. Longtime collaborator on *Aguirre* and *The Dark Glow of the Mountains*, among others.

César Vivanco   Peruvian from Cuzco. Directed the construction of the camp on the Río Marañón and the Río Camisea. Previously collaborator on *Aguirre*.

Raimund Wirner   German gaffer.

Kitty Witwer   Former Playboy Bunny, sheriff, warden of a San Francisco prison.